Threshold

Threshold

A MEMOIR OF CROSSING THROUGH THE TERRAIN OF LOSS

DEBORAH CUMMINS

SWP

SHE WRITES PRESS

Published in 2026 by
She Writes Press, an imprint of The Stable Book Group

32 Court Street, Suite 2109
Brooklyn, NY 11201
https://shewritespress.com
Library of Congress Control Number has been applied for.
ISBN: 979-8-89636-062-9
eISBN: 979-8-89636-063-6

Interior Designer: Kiran Spees

Printed in the United States
Names and identifying characteristics have been changed to protect the privacy of certain individuals.

Deborah Cummins (1949–2023)

This memoir reflects the love, caring, and devotion that Deborah bestowed on her loved ones. My Barnie's unique strength of character and unselfishness radiates throughout this beautiful narration of a heartbreaking journey.

—Robert Cummins

Give sorrow words; the grief
that does not speak, whispers the
o'er-fraught heart, and bids it break.

—William Shakespeare

Contents

(EN)DURING

GONE

PREFACE

On a sunny July morning, half a continent away from where I lived, my brother's obituary was being written.

Joseph Anton Bolda Jr. Born February 25, 1962. Died July 9, 2007.

Dates. The easy bits. And the matter-of-fact inclusion of his survivors, of which I was one, as were my parents, my sister, Joe's wife, his two young children.

Education also merited a mention: Shadow Mountain High School and Northern Arizona University. Though not requisite but so noted were a few high marks of a career "in the wine business," the pursued interests in skiing, hiking, and biking, and a love of the outdoors, mountains, and the Arizona desert.

None of which tells the whole story of a son, brother, husband, father. A life compressed into a newspaper's single paragraph.

Death is an everyday occurrence . . . until, of course, it happens to someone you love.

It is a day that separates itself off like an errant cell breaking away, up to no good. A day forevermore attached to the irrevocable. Naturally, memory-worthy dates preface it: dates of first symptoms, early exams and scans, and a doctor's initial warnings preceding a diagnosis of liver failure. Dates followed later by attempts to fill in the blanks, of countless, it seems, beginnings and endings.

A death is a survivor's beginning, though she may not recognize it yet. With a death she so yearns to refuse, she must begin again and again to recognize grief is universal, and hers, though intensely individual, is not more extreme, unusual, or special. She must remember there is no going back to a day or date, wondering how, if the smallest thing had been changed, as though it were as simple as mapping in the mind a left rather than a right turn, the ending could've been different.

The day my brother's life ended, my journey began. As a survivor. And as a maker with words, a reluctant examiner.

I

THE LAST OF THE BEFORE

The Last of the Before

Rather than beginning at the end or going back to the beginning, let me start here.

Rome. A warm Sunday morning in late April 2007. A woman, a solo traveler, sits at an outdoor table at the Bar Marzio. She's snagged a ringside seat on the Piazza di Santa Maria de Trastevere. At her fingertips, a drained cappuccino, the flaky remains of a cornetto in its waxy paper sleeve, the *Herald Tribune* she's not yet opened.

She looks up from her spiral notebook just as the campanile bells of Santa Maria toll out the commencement of Sunday Mass. Opposite her, beyond the scallop-rimmed fountain splashing its water into a deep basin, a man in a suit trots up the wide stone steps, yanks open the cathedral doors, a toddler tucked under one arm. Over the cobbles, a pair of vendors bump their carts and wheeled suitcases laden with scarves and made-in-China jewelry of "authentic" Etruscan design they'll soon hawk on a bridge crossing the Tiber. A middle-aged Italian woman, a fashionably dressed *bella figura* precariously perched on stilettos, hurries past, pushing a stroller in which her bambino gums a fat wedge of pizza. Two teenage girls, shrugging off their backpacks, slump onto the fountain steps and pass a cigarette between them. Across the piazza, the green shutters of a top-floor window bang open. A bare-chested man leans out, hoists his hands in what can seem like a bottomless reservoir of insulting Italian gestures, and shouts down to the soccer-playing boys using his double wooden door as their goal. They laugh and give the ball a last kick, a loud resounding thud.

All of this is duly noted and recorded as the woman at Bar Marzio, pencil in hand, again bends over her notebook.

I am that woman. Or, rather, was.

The present tense is tempting, as though time had not yet been cemented into the hard-and-fast past. An attempt, perhaps, to distance, remove, and maybe even absolve myself.

So let me be clear: I was that woman. Having an unusually commitment-free spring, I'd come to Rome to stay in an apartment my husband, Bob, and I had rented previously. I was solo for a couple of weeks before he arrived and we'd head to Umbria.

As a solitary woman traveler of late middle age, I'd already learned I was largely invisible except—but only slightly—to the waiter who plunked down a fresh cappuccino with his customary brusqueness and a mere "*Signora*" acknowledgment . . . after he had heard my "*Ancora*" as I tapped my finger against my empty cup. If not invisible, I could have been anyone. Even, possibly, a woman open to reinvention.

Beside me, chairs scraped back as a young American couple in athletic shoes and baseball caps took the last available table.

"It's such a beautiful day. I say we do the Palatine Hill and maybe the Colosseum. We can save the museum for a rainy afternoon."

"So does that mean you're wishing for rain, my dear?" the woman said, as she removed her hat and shook her long hair loose. Reaching up to scrape it back into a fresh ponytail, she looked my way but quickly turned back to the menu card. However, not before I saw in her expression a look of, what, sympathy? As though I was not alone by choice?

Hunkered over a map spread atop their small table, they went about planning their day's itinerary. I already knew where I was heading, my decision having no impact, being of no consequence to anyone else. I'd leave Bar Marzio, cross Ponte Sisto, and see where my footsteps led. Perhaps I'd turn onto Via Giulia and pass beneath Michelangelo's arch dripping with wisteria. Eschewing the map I carried in my tote, I'd follow the advice of writer Anthony Doerr—"You find your way through a place by getting lost in it."—and surrender myself to the warren of narrow streets winding through the *centro storico* near Piazza Navona, small *vicoli* that defied the inner GPS instincts of a woman reared on her native Chicago's gridded street logic.

But I cannot say with any factual certainty where my footsteps led that afternoon. As has been too often the case, my journal as an aid to that time period's reconstruction is of little help. Where I wound up, I can no longer recall. I'm pretty certain it wasn't at the Roman Forum, which had become familiar ground for me, and where, if given the choice and having the gift of time, I knew not to head with a busy weekend's heaving press of people snaking up the Via Sacra toward the Colosseum. Throngs of antenna-toting tour guides and folks hoisting cameras, seeming not so much to situate themselves in the continuum of time but outside the flow of it, took photos against memorable backdrops, perhaps for a Facebook post that announced, "I am here." Or on some future day would proclaim to a viewer, "I was here." The proof, even if downloaded, copied, and saved, would likely not, given our digitalized age, make it into any tattered family albums and would become lost, like ashes carried away by wind and current.

In Rome, I'd already learned that the past seems ever-present. It's just outside the door, within easy reach. It resides in the temple fragments and columns, dwells at the bottom of the ruts on Via Sacra, exhales from the holes of the Colosseum's walls where white marble slabs once hung, crouches in the dark gaps between the ancient stones of the streets I was headed for. A historical past that is known, interpreted, passed on . . . a past capable of being vividly imagined but not open to being amended or altered.

At Bar Marzio, on that morning I'd chosen to start, in a willed effort, to savor the present, I had picked up my notebook to record what I observed in the piazza. It's likely, too, that in contemplating time as Rome insisted I do, bits of the past rose up like flotsam riding a current. But mostly, and my notebook attests to it, I mused about the future. Almost recklessly foolish, I indulged in speculating how, by being alone voluntarily, I was somehow practicing for the future, for a possible future without Bob, which, given our fifteen-year age difference, a seemingly helpful insurance agent referring to actuarial tables had recently encouraged me to consider. But to entertain that by sitting alone, contemplating time, I could somehow prepare for such loss, or worse, *practice* for it? As if such a thing were possible, like breaking in a new pair of shoes or trying on a jacket to check the fit?

As I bent over my notebook, the American couple folded up their maps, having agreed to head to the Spanish Steps. Within the quiet of an inner dialogue in which I might raise the question *So where shall we go today?* the silent absence of a response resounded. So perhaps it was then I projected, *So maybe this is how it might be or maybe even will be?* Perhaps to the couple, particularly the woman, who seemed unable to stop fiddling with her hair, I appeared as a late-middle-aged woman, comfortable and confident, having no need for a map, who requested her check—"*Il conto, per favore*"—with accomplished pronunciation and inflection; who had no mistakes she had to cop to and no need to examine her past; and who offered no clue she was precariously balanced between the exhilaration of being without obligation to anyone else in her day's decisions and terrified by such absence.

All easy to pull off with the knowledge that Bob would join me in a few days.

I started with a Sunday morning at Bar Marzio because I had been so foolishly naive to think, even if momentarily, that I can rehearse and experience loss preemptively, as if there's such a thing as anticipatory grief.

I had yet to fully recognize that the kind of loss I was contemplating was not something merely bumped into in the dark and then I could go back to sleep. It was the real deal to wake up to again and again.

And when it comes, grief is never what it's imagined to be.

A Day in May

My suitcase was still parked by the front door. I'd yet to shuffle through the mail piled on the kitchen counter. But I was already on the phone with, surprisingly, my brother's sister-in-law, Jenna.

I could barely summon a picture of her—long brown hair and a little pudgy? Vaguely, I remembered her from my brother's wedding in Phoenix nearly fourteen years before, her smile almost permanently affixed. She was the kind of person who, I imagined, hitched a conga line of exclamation points to nearly every sentence of an email. How did she get my number? Did anyone on my family's distant Arizona home turf know she planned to call?

Jenna launched right in. "I'm worried about Joe. I think you need to call him. Maybe he'll listen to you."

"What's going on?"

"He's bad. Really bad. He's lost more weight."

"But he seemed to be doing better when I talked to him before my trip," I said, as if Jenna, a near stranger, would know I'd been away. "And he looked good in February when I was out there."

That was indisputable, wasn't it? Someone with a serious liver problem would surely have looked worse.

"Oh, that. It was all a show for you. Trust me. The haircut. The fact that he'd shaved. I don't think he's gotten his hair cut since. He looks terrible. It's like he doesn't care anymore."

Holding the phone to my ear, I moved into the living room. Sunlight streamed through our large front window. Just outside, azaleas were almost punishingly bright with bloom.

"What do the doctors say?"

"I'm not sure he's even following up with them. He refused to go to the last appointment with the specialist."

So it had come to this. I was getting new, important information from a woman I barely knew. "Jenna, where is Joe now?"

For months my brother had been shuttling back and forth between his house in Phoenix and my parents' in the Prescott foothills where, over the winter, even my father had finally acknowledged that Joe's illness had become more serious. I'd also learned then that my brother's marriage was in trouble.

Jenna said, "He's back at home, with my sister and the kids. But I don't think that's working out so well. You know how my sister can be."

Actually, I didn't. Not really. Over the years, by mutual design, my sister-in-law Carol and I had seemed to ensure our paths seldom crossed.

"Honestly, being at home may not be the best thing for him right now. I really think it would help if he got away for a while. Maybe you can get him to come up to Chicago for a visit. I know you've offered."

In the past few months, I'd extended many invitations to my brother. Now that he was no longer able to work, I'd even sent him a check for an airplane ticket and made inquiry at a small residential hotel just a few blocks away.

"That way, you can have some privacy but still be in walking distance of us, the movie theater, the park, and the lakefront. The studios are small but they have kitchenettes."

If he accepted, this would be the first time in decades we'd be together for any measurable time. It seemed like a chance for him to rest, get stronger, and, far from Phoenix, gain a different perspective. Somehow, here, on my turf, doing ordinary things—Had we ever as adults just gone to a movie together?—there'd be greater clarity, better answers. And, yes, I, the Fixer, could make a difference.

Instead, since my last trip to Arizona in early February, there'd been phone conversations . . . long calls to my parents' house in Prescott where he'd lived for several weeks, whether voluntarily or forced to depended on who was doing the telling. When Joe was asked the question, he said, "Oh, it's like a roller coaster. One day she loves me, the next day she wants me out."

On these phone calls, I was never sure who the "real" Joe was. Was he the clear and alert one, almost cheerful and hopeful, as he'd been in February, admitting that he was getting better and now it was a matter of seeing the docs, taking his meds, sticking to a low-fat diet, watching his intake of protein, and not drinking? Or was he the muted voice I struggled to hear, the rambling sentences and the unfinished thoughts, which, I later learned, meant his ammonia levels had probably spiked?

From my seat at the window, I looked up. Bob had entered the living room, car keys in hand.

About to leave for the grocery store, he asked, "Everything okay?"

Nodding, I motioned for him to go on ahead. I'd fill him in later on what wasn't okay, like Jenna now saying, "Deb, this is different. Joe is getting weaker. It's like . . . I don't know . . . he's giving up. I don't think he's listening to any of us, not even the doctors." She sounded like she was choking back tears. "I'm afraid. I'm really afraid for him."

My suitcases were still at the door, on the threshold, just sitting there, unattended, looking unclaimed. Coming upon them, it would be unclear if someone was on her way in or out, leaving or returning, a journey ended or about to begin. But Jenna's phone call was making it clear that a beginning point for serious concerns was well past, and I had yet to play catch-up.

Secure in my carry-on was my journal I'd written in while away—penciled musings about permanence and impermanence, the beginning of an essay about the many ways Rome messed with my notions of time, and copious notes pertaining to place—essential, I'd thought, for work I'd recently started and was envisioning as my next book. I'd even gone into elaborate detail describing how, in a restaurant one hot afternoon, I'd observed another solo diner at lunch, a sixty-something Italian man who, in spite of the temperature and without a bead of sweat, wore a wool tweed jacket and silk tie while meticulously peeling and eating a banana with a fork and knife. But within all those pages, among so many words, there was scant mention of Joe.

The indictment was clear. The evidence rested with my note-taking, my recollected musings. While away in Italy, I hadn't thought much about him.

Joe was only nine when my parents, surprising everyone, hauled him and my sister, Chris, cross-country in their sudden move to Arizona. Newly out of college, with my first job and a shared apartment in the city and lacking any desire to uproot to the distant Southwest desert, I stayed behind.

In the years that followed, Joe and I pursued separate paths, the distances between us increasingly untraversed. Until the past few months, we'd seldom spoken at such great length on the phone. Our estrangement was a kind of mutual, self-inflicted indifference.

But even without frequent and direct communication or correspondence—Carol signed all holiday and birthday cards and tried to make Joe's signature look different from hers, as if anyone would be fooled—I knew that he, my little brother Joey, was in the world. I needed to know he was here, on the same planet, of this life, even if separate and apart, a physical presence with clamor in his head, blood pumping in his veins, all brain synapses firing.

And I must've believed—Why not?—that some future possibility was still out there, some circumstance or event in which we might be propelled to seek common ground, to find some crossing points, to bridge distances created by time, geography, and neglect, by years of indifference and our radically different views, particularly in politics and faith. It hadn't helped that Carol and I shared a mutual disregard, even with only minimal exposure, that seemed to intensify over the years. It did little to explain and clear away the evidence.

I'd offered my sick brother a place to stay and opened my wallet. But just as easily I'd flown to Rome and left behind my good intentions, as though they rested at the bottom of a packed bag I'd forgotten to take along. Worse, I'd swerved from a newly attempted attentiveness to near disregard. Walking those streets in Rome, I was the selfish, globe-trotting sister.

Had the trip occurred at some later date in whatever time I had no need yet to identify as "after," what words would have filled my journal's pages? Surely, I wouldn't have needed the ruins of an ancient city to trigger thoughts about transience or redefine *fragility* and *ephemeral.* Perhaps instead of just hoisting my camera and taking photographs of Rome, I'd have carried some photos with me.

Like the one of Joe on the back porch swing at my parents' house in Prescott, a photo I was told later was taken in January 2007, less than two months before Joe's forty-fifth birthday. Unposed and seemingly oblivious of the camera pointed at him, he'd been captured in silhouette, looking out to the scrub-covered hills that extended beyond my parents' yard, his cheekbones angular, pronounced, the skin across them taut, his cheeks hollowed out, much of his hair gone gray. He was an aged and aging man, with the face of someone living with and within pain, whose body had likely been lobbing warning signs for a lot longer than he'd let on. Who, in this photograph, revealed the barest hint of resignation, not the defiance he showed later, inexplicably refusing to see the specialist in spite of our urging, a resistance that was perhaps his last act of independence, of ambition and intention.

That I didn't come to possess this photograph until months after my Italian trip didn't let me off the hook. I could've slipped into my suitcase the photograph I took in early February when I'd asked my parents and Joe to pose together at the entrance of the Hermosa Inn where, on the initial afternoon of my visit to Arizona, we'd all met for lunch. It was the first time I'd seen my brother in nearly a year. And, having only heard about his illness, having his appearance described to me but without any verifying images, I had no idea what to expect.

Slowly, as though attempting to camouflage any pain or discomfort, he unfolded himself from his little Mazda as my parents and I waited. How relieved I felt, seeing, mostly, the brother I knew—thinner certainly, but his skin more tan-looking than jaundiced yellow, his cheeks fleshed out a bit, his hair looking newly trimmed and freshly washed. He wore jeans and a black, zip-neck shirt he'd obviously taken some care in choosing.

"Hey, Sis." He cracked a big smile as I stepped forward and stood on tiptoes to embrace him. He responded with one of his quick, hard hugs in which it had always felt that, without much effort, he was about to lift me off my feet. But none of that now.

Briefly, beneath my encircling hands, I felt his shoulder bones jutting from his back. Staggered by how vulnerable and unprotected he seemed, I took a step away. My hands now clasped his upper arms. Reluctant to let him go, I wanted to anchor him in place, to try to cement in my mind's eye a glimpse of the fit young man he'd been not so long ago—the marathon runner, skier, hiker of mountain and desert still surfacing in spite of his wedding band dangling from a silver chain around his neck. Though symbolic of his troubled marriage, it was mostly the slipping-off-the-finger result of significant weight loss.

"Let me get a picture," I said, urging Joe and my parents to pose.

"Now? Here?" my father asked.

"Yes, now. Right now. Over by the entrance."

A photograph that had to be taken that instant, as though time itself were unstoppered, running out, with opportunities draining away. And yet, of the photograph that resulted with the three of them backdropped against a blossoming prickly pear and a tangle of bright-pink bougainvillea spilling over an adobe-like wall, my brother posed between my parents, all three of them grinning, it looked as if this were any occasion, as if in the months ahead, there'd be plenty of time for more memorializing of the picture-taking kind. Not once did I think, *This is the last time we will do this.* It never entered my mind.

Perhaps my sudden, urgent need to hoist my camera had also been a wish to record the evidence and bolster my relief. Here was proof Joe had turned a corner, was on the right track. And, not so incidentally, proof that I, the picture-taker, had traveled to Arizona specifically to see him. The good sister checking things out . . . before skipping off to Rome.

Listening to Jenna, I'd taken a seat overlooking our small front yard with its thick sprawl of ground cover, unclipped boxwoods and viburnum, an outlier in a neighborhood of well-tended lawns. A sparrow repeatedly poked around in the euonymus and then flew up to a branch of our large black walnut, up and down, again and again, as though attempting to retrieve something lost.

Periodically, Jenna paused, waiting for an interjection, trying to make this more of a dialogue. I felt my face growing hot.

"So, can you call him?" Jenna asked.

"Yes, of course. I can. I will."

I'd turned my back on the suitcases in the foyer, but the verdict was in.

For all those weeks away, about my brother, I did not remember to remember.

The Facts, Please

After a diagnosis, any of us can go online and gather articles, study statistics, obtain the correct medical terminology, stockpile proper acronyms, view images of our damaged selves, and find the proof that our human bodies are not a total mystery.

A sister half a continent away from her ill brother had secondhand information and whose brother didn't offer up medical terms or even a specific liver disease diagnosis because . . . why? He didn't have one? He was in denial? He'd come to rely on his wife or in-laws who accompanied him to appointments and gathered the facts? She could look things up and learn the following . . .

The human liver weighs three pounds. A large, meaty, reddish-brown organ on the right side of the belly, protected by the rib cage, it consists of two large sections: the right and left lobes. The liver's main jobs are breaking down harmful substances, filtering and removing waste products from the blood, and storing nutrients and vitamins. It also metabolizes drugs, secretes bile, and makes proteins that are important for many functions, including blood clotting. Working with the gallbladder, pancreas, and intestines, the liver helps digest, absorb, and process food. Just as our heart beats, our brain's synapses fire and snap, and our pupils dilate, all without any need for our willful say-so, the human liver filters, detoxifies, and makes protein. Or, like Joe's, it doesn't.

A liver can be damaged in a variety of ways. It can become inflamed, usually due to hepatitis but also by way of allergic reactions, obesity, and heavy drinking. Cirrhosis of the liver, a type of long-term damage, causes permanent scarring. A cirrhotic liver cannot function properly and usually leads to liver failure.

Generally, it's not known if a liver is damaged until problems get serious. Early symptoms of fatigue, vomiting, diarrhea, and abdominal pain are easily overlooked or point to other causes. Not so easy to ignore or confuse are the later symptoms: jaundice, itching, easy bruising, mental confusion, malnutrition, the abnormal accumulation of fluid in the abdominal cavity known as ascites, and, when indicated by liver panel tests, elevated levels of bilirubin and ammonia in the blood.

Yet these facts didn't answer all of my questions. They didn't explain how this happened. They didn't make clear where to assign blame.

Later, in the report of the medical examiner, there will be other facts.

"The body is of a normally developed, slightly jaundiced, 5'11", 150-lb., light-skinned man whose appearance is consistent with the reported age of forty-five years." It will not include the fact that, at 150 pounds, this man had lost nearly forty pounds, nor will it conclude that his "gray-and-brown scalp hair at 2.5 inches long" suggested he may have needed a haircut.

I will learn that his "natural teeth are present and in good condition," that his "abdomen is protuberant." I will read, "The chest is unremarkable." But I will refuse and I refuse still to think that what beat inside that chest, Joe's heart, individual and singular, was anything but remarkable.

Of that heart I will learn that "the aorta has slight atherosclerosis," a condition that, unchecked and possibly worsening, could have contributed to his eventual death had he lived a normal lifespan of another thirty years.

I will read of what is revealed through "serial sections of the cerebrum" and "transverse section of the brainstem" after the skull was sawed open, the brain exposed, lifted out, and sliced in a bright room with instruments clattering against a cold, unforgiving metal table. My brother's brain, after being hoisted to a hanging scale by a pair of cupped hands, weighed 1,625 grams.

These were facts I never thought I needed to know.

Perhaps I don't need to know. Maybe too many facts are just that: too many.

And yet these facts are necessary for what was simply laid out in a handy, recognizable Roman-numeral outline. The pathological diagnoses were jaundice, ascites, gallbladder disease, and a collapsed left lung due to fluid with bacterial culture positive for pneumonia. I will learn after consulting a medical dictionary of bacteria from the gut when the liver is no longer filtering properly and prescribed amounts of lactulose no longer help the body absorb toxins.

More simply stated, the cause of death was end-stage cirrhosis due to chronic alcoholism.

The fact I want to refuse. Alcoholism.

Alcohol abuse versus what had surfaced in one of his doctor's assessment reports: "chronic alcohol use from two decades in the wine and spirits industry."

Abuse versus *use*. Words and their meanings that, in the stance I feel I must take, are not separated by too fine a distinction.

Alcoholism. A fact that didn't square with other facts. How, for example, Joe was not a falling-down drunk. He'd held a series of good jobs, supported his family, ran marathons, and possessed numerous friends.

Small solace resided in the fact that "high-functioning alcoholics" abound. In our workplaces, pews, sports clubs, and families, we rub shoulders with them all the time. Drinkers who deflect, camouflage, and fly under the radar. Who, if not unmasked, seem to do remarkably well for many years, unless, of course, their livers give out.

But at forty-five? Didn't it take decades to destroy a liver? Wouldn't there have been more warning signs?

My mother was certain she had the right facts. She knew where to assign blame.

Not armed with the smallest bit of Internet-sourced information or by way of a question posed to a doctor, she declared, "Rh negative. Bilirubin. All that jaundice. It messed up his liver."

We'd heard the story for years with its rudimentary elements: my mother Rh negative; Joe, her youngest child, born premature at just four-and-a-half pounds; and the mix-up in the test of blood drawn from the umbilical cord. My mother was Rh positive, not Joe. His tiny body turned bright yellow with jaundice before anyone noted the mistake, his bilirubin levels spiking off the charts, his red blood cells dying, his liver enlarged. What should've been a diagnosis of Rh incompatibility was missed. And, once detected, the decision, based on evidence long ago lost, that an exchange blood transfusion would be too risky. Thus, with the modest measures then available, the wait-and-see approach was used.

A tiny preemie grew over the years into a robust man who climbed, skied, biked, and ran.

No reason to give the liver a second look.

No reason to think that a mother, decades later, might be onto something more than wishful thinking.

For how many years, and having no idea what it meant, did I love the word *bilirubin* simply for the sound of it? This word had played a key role in my mother's telling the story of my brother's birth. This word gave the story and its teller an unmistakable authority. It was a sort of benign-sounding but somewhat exotic word that, using it and having heard it often, somehow stamped our family history and my brother's survival with something special.

I'd elevated bilirubin beyond its decidedly mundane, if essential, definition as a waste product of the normal breakdown of red blood cells that passed through the liver and was eliminated from the body, high levels of which cause jaundice and almost always point to an improperly working liver. Never did I dream that one day I'd need to know this or that its levels would need to be watched so closely. Nor did I realize that reaching beyond the elements of a family's near mythical story, I'd search for new facts. I needed to know that Rh disease is a serious condition but less common today due to advanced screening of an Rh-negative mother and her unborn child, minimizing danger. But if Rh disease did occur and a mother's blood antibodies waged battle against her unborn son's positive red blood cells, he would still try to compensate by releasing immature red blood cells, which could cause the liver to enlarge, resulting in potential liver damage.

Potential liver damage, to which I insert potential *long-term* liver damage.

Sometimes a belief transforms into fact. When, for example, I, like my mother and, increasingly, my father and sister, needed to believe and found it easier and more implication-free to become convinced that rather than possible booze abuse, it was a failure of detection and treatment at Joe's birth that jump-started my brother's eventual decline, the ticking time bomb he carried into his strapping adulthood.

Accepted: A compromised liver. A liver predisposed. Rejected: the predisposal toward alcohol abuse within our family history.

Clearly, any undetected at-birth liver damage could not undo or change the ending. But it allowed for predisposition and the possibility of a seemingly sudden onset and its inexplicably rapid trajectory in which recovery options were so quickly and cruelly diminished. A compromised reasoning that saved us—me—from having to accept what I could not. I somewhat ironically adopted an alcoholic's power of deflection, of shifting the focus away and toward something less painful—yes, my brother drank, but the cards were stacked against him. The kind of relief, perhaps, that comes to the family of a long-time alcohol abuser when, after a medical examiner slices open the stiff body, it's discovered the cause of death was in fact hypertension.

All deaths must have an official cause by what, forevermore, we're known to have died from. The dead can do nothing to change it—in some cases, a stamp of guilt or rippling shame.

If only I could strike chronic alcoholism from cause of death. And strike what else I wish I didn't know: "The body is received in a zippered body pouch secured by evidence seal number 246933."

It was as if Joe had been an anonymous homicide victim bagged and tagged on the street and not a brother, a son, who'd collapsed at home, died in the shower, his body discovered by his father, the shower still running, the water cold.

A Last Good Time

Driving back to Prescott from Flagstaff one winter afternoon three years before Joe's death, he and I had come down out of the mountains and foothills on a long flat stretch of highway crossing a scrubby, open semi-desert landscape that did little to hold my attention. I better appreciated the expansive sky, the way, in a stiffening wind, the massing clouds swiftly passed overhead, although it seemed as if the sun were in passage, ducking in and out of the clouds, alternately plunging the road ahead from bright light into deep shadow.

Up in Flagstaff, our father was being treated for a staph infection in his spine, likely the result of an open hand wound that had not been cleaned properly after he'd worked in the yard. Not until he could barely walk or move his neck had he sought treatment, soliciting a neighbor to drive him to the emergency room. From there, his condition so severe, he was airlifted to a Flagstaff hospital for immediate surgery. Meanwhile, my mother, less than two years after her life-altering stroke, was recovering at home from a cracked pelvis. She'd fallen when one of the legs of her metal walker got tangled in a throw rug that she insisted on keeping at the kitchen sink. I was between teaching gigs and able to fly out, unlike my sister, Chris, who'd just started a new job where she lived in Wisconsin and had a young son at home. Each day, I drove up to Flagstaff to see Dad, consult with doctors, and then headed back to Prescott to care for my mother. One afternoon, Joe came up from Phoenix to join me.

He was sitting in the passenger seat, his near six-foot frame accommodated by my small rental car only if the seat was fully pushed back. He wore a black, puffy down vest over a red flannel shirt. When he'd arrived at my parents' house, I'd been surprised by his weight gain. His face was uncharacteristically round and full. He had a gut. His running days, I'd long ago surmised, were over. Also abandoned was the vegetarian diet he and Carol had pursued for many years with the fervor of converts.

I'd already been filled in, if somewhat vaguely, about his recent embrace of a church, its denomination unknown to me, but clearly of some fundamentalist or evangelical stripe.

"What's up with that?" I'd asked my father in prior phone calls.

"It's some church that Carol got involved with."

No surprise there. As with their previous dietary habits and exercise regimens, my sister-in-law's fingerprints were all over this.

"It has a private Christian school and that's where Matt is going. Or I guess you'd call it that, if junior kindergarten means you're in school. It's sure expensive, though."

"Is Joe actually going to church, too?"

"Yep. And whenever he comes up, he brings some pamphlets for me to read."

This was a first. Joe, best I knew, had never gone to church services, not even back in Illinois. By the time he came along, our devoutly raised Catholic father had long before abandoned his churchgoing, and my mother, with just a glancing exposure to Presbyterianism at an early age, didn't press it. Unlike my sister and me, Joe hadn't been subjected to meatless Fridays, confessional Saturdays, long hours of catechism class, drills, and rote memorizations requisite to marching down the aisle of St. Jude the Apostle for First Holy Communion.

But now, surprisingly, here he was: a believer, a tither.

Bad enough that so much evangelicalism had inserted itself front and center in recent national politics, with many of its followers swearing to be ardent upholders of the US Constitution while ignoring those pesky parts about the separation of church and state. Or that for some time Joe had obtained his staunchly held political views via his in-laws, who were as seemingly devout to Fox News as any religion. All this was quite removed from our blue-collar, solidly Democratic roots in Chicago where, for years, during Richard Daley's reign, our grandfather had been a precinct captain. And where, even without campaign signs hammered into our lawn, no one ever had to ask my parents who they voted for, nor our family's electricians, carpenters, and millworkers.

At least on our afternoon drive, I didn't feel the need to wonder how Joe felt about the proliferation of climate change deniers. For all his newfound faith in a sinner's redemptive promise of a hereafter, it was hard to imagine he'd sanctioned the neglect of this world, an absence of stewardship that seemed to suggest it was okay to use up all the trees or allow the ice cap to melt before being whisked up to a better world elsewhere.

But I did wonder what he now newly believed and how it had happened.

For several minutes following our shared impressions about Dad's progress and what the doctors had reported to us, and after our somewhat aimless conversational drift, we'd fallen into an uncomfortable silence.

"So," I ventured at last, "I understand Matt's going to a new school."

After Joe extolled its many virtues, I asked, "And you're going to church?"

As my brother began describing and explaining, but, other than the repeated inclusion of the word *Christian*, failing to provide me with something on which I might hang a label, I recognized I was in foreign territory. How did a man who'd never struck me as someone with an "examined life" get to this place? How did someone like Joe achieve conversion? What had to be embraced; what, perhaps from the front of the church, hands raised, had to be pledged? What had to be copped to in order to become—my brother's term—a "true Christian"? Were there stepped programs or a ranking of virtues or sins, like a Catholic's distinguishing between venial and mortal?

In my brother's church, what was forbidden? Could the kids still dance? Was Harry Potter banned from the school library? Had Elmo been excluded from its video offerings? Did his church adhere to the belief that homosexuality was nothing more than "sexual deviance"? I didn't wonder at the time about what such questions said about me, my lack of understanding, and intolerance. Among his fellow churchgoers, there surely were productive citizens and good parents, folks who, like my brother and like me, pushed carts down grocery aisles, cheered sons and daughters from the sidelines, and erupted into smiles at a stranger's kindness. And who, not so incidentally, cheated on their spouses. Or gambled. Or drank.

As though reading my mind, Joe said, "My pastor knows about my job." At the time, his job was as a top-producing wine salesman. "And he's okay with it."

Meaning what? I didn't, but maybe should've, asked.

As we sped along, closing in on Prescott, the odometer was toting up the miles. But time felt stalled, like the sun behind mountains when you're waiting for sunrise.

"I'm on our church's landscape committee," my brother said. "We have a lot of work to do. The building's new, and there's not much planted around it."

I imagined a gravelly patch, a newly striped parking lot, a small church with bright light and rows of pews, stacks of hymnals, and the walls unadorned except for a crucifix.

"So who put you on to this place?" I asked. "Carol? Her parents?"

His in-laws, Joe conceded, were still devout Catholics. "But," he added, "they're happy for us. They understand our beliefs." And yes, it was Carol's idea to check out this church after she'd learned about it from a gym friend who, like her, was upset over public school policies and had begun to explore opportunities other than homeschool.

Making it clear that he'd not been coerced, but his upper body seeming to tense up as though bracing for a fight, Joe declared, "I know I've come to the right place, Deb." And he added, "I pray every day."

It could've stopped there. It had become clear that interrogations were not welcome, no matter how polite and well-intentioned, which, perhaps, mine were not.

"Do you read the Bible?" I asked.

"Of course."

I confess: I don't know my Bible.

Still, I asked, "And you think everything in it is fact? What about its conflicting messages?"

I glanced over. He'd bowed his head, his attention seemingly riveted on his black vest's zipper. Was this when I noted, or am I just remembering now, how his leg had been jittering nearly the whole ride back, like that of a fidgety kid who has to use the toilet or a man eager to reach for something he needed badly?

"What are you asking me, Deb?"

What was I asking? What did I want from this conversation? Was I trying to make it into an argument, a debate I felt confident I could win? If so, to what end? Couldn't I have tried being happy for him and left it at that?

I'd long before this stopped noting the landscape we were passing through. I now stared straight ahead. Joe, too, was keeping his eyes on the road, as though vigilant, my driving no longer to be trusted.

"You've mentioned salvation several times," I said.

"Yes. I do believe I'll be saved."

"I don't really know what that means. Saved from what?"

He offered no explanation. I took the plunge. "You can't mean . . . What I mean is, if the end, the whatever you call it"—I stumbled over the words—"the rapture? End time? If that occurred, you'd be saved, and I would not?"

"Yeah."

"Like right at this minute, in this car?"

"Probably."

"Oh."

Up ahead, a long, straight stretch of road bisected the desert, and though the terrain on either side had looked nearly identical with its scrubby shrubs and yucca, it suddenly seemed as if some kind of before-and-after demarcation had taken place. As Joe and I sat in silence, I had flashes of the pavement suddenly buckling, splitting open, my car being swallowed up, sucked into a pit of flames. Or would there be a bright flash, a bolt from overhead, smoldering ash floating down, flames and destruction all around, and, next to me, just a few shredded pieces of my brother's vest, perhaps his singed Nikes, all that remained after he'd been whisked skyward?

My brother? A possible end-timer? Or, in the more common

political parlance I was familiar with, one of those kooks or nuts? He'd been going to this church less than a year. How had this happened?

While our common interests, few as they'd often seemed in recent years, usually intersected over talk of wine and good restaurants, I'd long believed Joe and I still shared an appreciation of the natural world and the wild things that resided there. My brother, who studied forestry at NAU in Flagstaff before dropping out his sophomore year and who, had he continued, might've pursued a path to help nurture and restore the wild. Best I knew, he still cared about such things. Maybe one day, besides agreeing on a good vintage of California pinot noir, he and I would take a long walk together, open ourselves to some part of the world no human hand had made, feel sunlight press its warmth on our backs, and admire a sunset that required no sermon or choir. Our only certainty would be that a creative power was at the heart of things. Our shared prayer would possibly be three lines from Navajo poet Luci Tapahonso: "Bless me hills / this clear golden morning / for I am passing through again."

Instead, driving the road that did not buckle, beneath a sky that in its bright blue and billowing nimbus suggested no malice, we were traveling where I no longer wished to go. I kept my mouth shut. It was my brother who got in the last word.

"Deb, I hope you'll respect my belief."

In the years that followed, Joe and I never made reference to that afternoon, not even during our many long-distance phone conversations in his last months, when I'm sure that, though he believed in an afterlife, he'd not lost hope of living in this life. I didn't ask him if he was still a member of the same church. He never allowed, at least not to me, that his illness was a part of "God's plan." I'm not sure how

I'd have responded if he had. Though his pronouncements may have been fewer and more toned down, faith, I believe, was still a comfort to him.

Still, our exchange on that afternoon drive years before Joe's diagnosis was something I'd not been able to forget. For me, it had become a sort of fulcrum, a pivot point in our relationship. Perhaps too conveniently, I made of it a wedge, a way to justify our growing estrangement I did little to change. I allowed the differences between us, as exemplified by our exchange in the car, to somehow absolve me of my failure to attempt bridging the gap between us.

Perhaps our conversation—particularly the "end-time" moment—belongs to the category of memories, and their stories we choose not to excavate, preferring to leave them belowground, untended, and out of sight, the way in Rome certain excavations are sometimes not undertaken for fear of damage to existing structures, to the seemingly functional surface of things. But then, unexpectedly, a relic may be unearthed, like a significant first-century mosaic tile that halts progress on Rome's decades-long project to extend an underground Metro line. Or, much more mundanely, a family's relic surfaces, like the old, empty cigar box collaged with clipped magazine photos, one of the little family gifts I made one Christmas decades ago when I was a broke college student. A relic that somehow on the last night of my visit to Arizona in February wound up at the center of the kitchen table. An object I had forgotten about, had no idea still existed, was even embarrassed that it had been kept and significance still attached to such a crude and amateurish effort. Yet there it was, inexplicably hauled into the light the last time I was with Joe, though I did not know that then.

My parents, Joe, Chris, and I were sitting at the kitchen table after dinner. A clutter of empty take-out Chinese food boxes littered the counters. We'd come inside to eat after a couple of lazy hours lounging on the patio. Present all afternoon had been the unspoken and unrecognized—my brother's illness, his and Carol's estrangement, and the shaky ground beneath both. Also in attendance was resentment and recrimination, including mine toward Carol and in spite of my not knowing what she may have been through, the probable frustrations with my notoriously passive brother, though his passivity had surely for many years served as a welcome yin to her yang.

As dusk approached, someone switched on the overhead light fixture shaped like a wooden wagon wheel. Somewhere—on a placemat, a calendar, a wall plaque—an emblem of a bright-red apple gleamed. Conversation was winding down as the inevitable goodbyes of my last night waited in the wings. Then somehow the cigar box was introduced, and, as though they were somehow tethered, it prompted us to retreat to the safest of memories . . . those couple of summer weeks we had spent at my uncle's cottage in Michigan during much of my childhood, the only vacations our family ever took.

Suddenly, we pivoted to shared stories. First, how my somewhat dark and exotic, half-Italian "bad boy" cousins, Bobby and Timmy, brothers who were forever losing or breaking something, managed to disengage a stalling outboard on their father's new boat only to watch it sink out of sight. In another, Dad reminded us how he and his fishing buddies had been caught in a skiff by a sudden storm on Lake Michigan far from the Saugatuck breakwater.

We invoked the strenuous hikes up Mount Baldy in ankle-deep sand, the seemingly obligatory visit to Dutch Village in nearby Holland, Michigan, where, ignoring the sad kitschiness of it, we wiggled our feet into clunky wooden shoes to be photographed in front of a windmill, as though it were the Eighth Wonder of the World.

We relived the stomach-lurching dune buggy rides and the

summer's first taste of fried lake perch. Ordinary times that with summoned choruses of "Do you remember . . . ?" and "Who could forget . . . ?" transformed them into the extraordinary.

The heavy, laden air snapped and crackled with energy. We thumbed our noses at whatever lurked in the corners. We unshackled our hands from the yoke of time to brush a thin layer of mythmaking veneer onto the commonplace. Spanning gulfs of time and distance and divergent paths, we reminded ourselves, "Yes, we were once a happy family. Here is proof."

We retreated to a shared past when Joey hadn't been born yet or was a mere toddler. We had to fill in some of the blanks for him, in stories that were now his to pass on, although, unbeknownst to us, for too short a time. Sitting at the table where the cigar box, like a repository, reigned, Joe listened, his face bright with his signature crooked smile. A new animation lit up his eyes, an eagerness for another story, for what was yet to come.

Recognizing something I did not want to end, I found myself growing more forcefully exuberant. I willfully extended each remembering or tried to summon a new one with, "Don't you remember, Dad, how you . . . ?" Or "Joe, listen to this. You'll love this . . ." It was as if I was playing my intended role, how for this alone I'd flown halfway across the country to orchestrate. And that this had all been preplanned, our retreat to a time in our shared past when our family's youngest couldn't remember such details but seemed hungry to know them: "Who was Pat? Where was that river? Who drove the boat back, Dad?"

In such telling, we didn't have to be reminded of, didn't have to face the unknowable and possibly grim future. We left the future behind. For a couple of hours, we hauled the past into the radiant present. Everything still treatable. Still reparable.

Reading the Sky

In late May 2007, I was a little past midway into what had become an annual journey from Chicago to the Maine island cottage where, for almost a decade, I'd been spending most summers—a nearly 1,300-mile drive that I typically completed solo in just two days. Usually, my driving trips were merely fraught with road construction delays or a serious thunderstorm's driving rain, neither of which was hampering me as I sped along the New York State Thruway.

Sipping my coffee, fumbling with the radio dials, and eyeing my speedometer, I'd found myself musing on an essay I'd begun the previous month. In it, I'd asked, "When do you know you're at the beginning of something? Or that something has come to an end?"

I'd gone on to observe that, were I an ancient Roman seeking answers to such questions, I could've looked to augury—the divination of omens interpreted by augurs who studied the flights of birds. To them, a flock's sudden swerve either left or right held meaning. Certain cackles and caws helped signify the will of the gods, as did the pecking patterns of sacred chickens—the fowl that, ancient Roman writer Pliny declared, may have once held "the supreme empire over the empire of the world."

In ceremonies known as "taking the auspices," augurs didn't predict the future but interpreted signs that might foretell the fate of some specific action. A flock of birds turning one way signaled the time to prepare for battle. A turn in the other direction advised postponement, portents that any leader ignored at his peril.

I'm no augur, but I do watch birds.

In Maine, I'd become a devoted observer of crows. At first, I had no choice.

Crows are hard to ignore. They have no respect for property lines or clocks, and they're loud, especially at dawn. Many mornings, especially in the weeks just after my seasonal arrival in late May, I'm again convinced the island's entire crow population has convened outside our bedroom windows. I'm not especially convivial before light has fully entered the sky, and I could do with fewer wake-up calls from my feathered friends. I've also long wondered just what on earth do crows have to converse about, and so raucously, at such an hour? Still, I'm an admirer. Crows delight and puzzle me as they swagger across our yard, looking like avian sheriffs with holsters buckled to their hip, or from a nearby tree they seem to study my every move in the garden, emitting low, guttural rasps of approval or a clacking-beak reprimand when it appears I'm about to do something stupid.

But absent any augury skills and despite my close observations of crows, I did not know—I couldn't know—that midway into my drive east, my mother had begun to play a larger role in the unfolding narrative of family illness in far-off Arizona, especially since nothing had hinted at it in February as she sat across from me at a table beneath a wagon wheel light. There had been little reason to suspect that my brother was not the only one with imminent trouble on the horizon. Confident that things were now moving ahead in a positive way, he had shifted his focus to visiting me in Maine instead.

But as an incoming call to my cell phone broke into the peaceful confines of my car, along a route that had become so familiar to me I've often claimed I could drive it in my sleep, the focus again shifted.

"Aw, Deb," my father said, "it's your mom."

"What do you mean? Is she okay?" I eased my foot off the gas pedal and slipped into the right lane. Two 18-wheelers barreled past.

"She's at the hospital. They're doing more tests."

"Why? What happened?"

"All day yesterday she kept complaining about her stomach. She said she had pains and couldn't get comfortable. It got worse last night. I finally called an ambulance."

How many times had I told my parents to dial 911 at the first sign of trouble? Years before, when my mother had her stroke, she'd apparently been exhibiting symptoms—slurring her words and having trouble raising a spoon of ice cream to her mouth. She went to bed early and she and my father only understood how serious things were at 1:00 a.m. when she woke, tried to get up to pee, and fell to the floor, unable to move her right side.

"They think it's her heart. Something wrong with a valve."

"That doesn't sound good."

"Yeah, I know."

But he didn't know. Though I peppered him with a barrage of questions—"A valve problem, Dad? But what does that mean? Can it be fixed? Will she have to have surgery?"—he had few answers. He had never been the most reliable purveyor of accurate information. Even if he thought he was listening carefully, he was really waiting for the results . . . the plan . . . the action of what-comes-next. What, in their wisdom, the doctors would do next. And how, when it came to issues with Mom, he would fit in. As though he were a walking GPS, he fixated on the route he'd take to the hospital or clinic, the best times of day to travel it, the busy intersections he'd avoid if he could. Other specifics like the medical terminology of a diagnosis or even the names of drugs had never been his strong suit. After a stent procedure in his leg for pulmonary arterial disease, he'd told me the doctor had prescribed Novocain.

"Why on earth would he give you that?"

"Okay, so maybe not Novocain, but it sounds something like that."

Another time, he'd told me about visiting his neighbor Dick, who'd just returned home from an angiogram—or at least that's what I inferred from Dad's description.

"You know, one of those Roto-Rooter things they do to your heart."

"Is Joe there?" I asked, as I pulled into a rest stop. Clearly, this was not the conversation to be having while humming along at 70 mph on the thruway.

"He's out. He said he was taking a drive up in the hills."

"Oh, does he do that often?"

"Pretty often. I think he stops somewhere. He says he goes for long walks."

That made sense. I could see him out there. Walking. Being in a landscape that spoke to him was as familiar as a Maine island's shores and wooded trails had become to me. Maybe there was a lake up that way where he and Dad had fished on weekends. Some place of retreat. Or maybe he hiked among the Granite Dells, a place I'd driven through once and had to concede with my jaundiced view of the Arizona landscape that it was indeed quite beautiful. But little of where my brother might go held any specificity for me—places that, in their unfamiliarity, were not merely strange to me, but unknown. Places where he might be drawn, but which I knew nothing about. And the man walking them alone, his collar turned up against the chill of a higher elevation, possibly in need of a shave and a haircut—about him I knew woefully too little.

"So, when Joe gets back, have him call me, okay? Maybe by then, you'll both know more from the doctor."

Ironically, just two days before, my phone conversation with Joe had not focused on him. After talking briefly about his most recent doctor appointment and new prescribed diet, he said, "Geez, Deb, you ought to see what Mom eats. It can't be good for her. Her idea of a salad is some kind of creamy dressing with a few leaves of iceberg lettuce. Yeah, she cooks, but I swear, I think she'd be just as happy with bread and butter. No, make that butter with bread."

Of course, it's easy to sling rocks at someone else's habits or addictions when they're the very ones we've abandoned or kicked. Was there a more righteous crusader for no smoking than the former smoker? From what I'd gathered, Joe's surprising shift over the years from stringent vegetarianism had carried him all the way to the opposite spectrum, to the red meats and fatty foods that may have contributed to his current health problems. A symptom of general indifference or neglect? The by-product, perhaps, of a busy job, a working spouse, and two kids that tempted him toward the convenience of burgers or even, he'd once sheepishly confessed, Taco Bell. Or the result, perhaps, of his many years in the beverage and hospitality industry, the increasing work-related focus that revolved around food, wine, and dinners out, when reaching for and hoisting a glass of wine took precedence over whatever else, perhaps mindlessly, went into his mouth.

But there had been something else in that phone conversation with Joe. An underlying, unspoken current, revealed, possibly, in a photograph only unearthed much later. Taken by my father, the photo appeared to chronicle life at home back when Joe, becoming more alarmingly ill, lived with them . . . Dad's idea of a semblance of normalcy. It was a snapshot proof that his youngest child was recovering in the warm embrace of his parents' kitchen. In it, Joe was at the sink washing lettuce. Mom, propped against her walker, was at the stove. She was making dinner, wearing her bathrobe . . . evidence of what Joe had claimed.

"Mom doesn't leave the house much. She takes a lot of naps. Many days, she just stays in her robe, or in, you know, one of those things she calls housedresses."

Evidence of my mother's tilt toward probable depression that over the past few years she'd refused to acknowledge or do anything about. Evidence of what Dad ignored or had become blind to, although maybe we'd all been complicit in a willful ignorance.

If I'm to be honest with myself, I didn't just fail to see the signs sitting at a table beneath a wagon wheel light—I looked away. Away from the puffiness in her face, her overall weight gain, the goblet in front of her brimming with red wine. I didn't question when her chosen form of self-medication had started up again.

Our mother, so good at giving advice, so free to criticize what Dad ate and cite every instance of a diabetic no-no, who thought her annual wellness checks were a "waste of time," who, after taking prescribed antidepressants for a mere handful of days, tossed them out, saying they did no good and that what she really needed was something for anxiety. Who'd more recently dispensed to Joe some Ambien when he couldn't sleep, certain that there were no issues of further liver damage, no concerns of toxic interaction with his prescribed meds. All of which, upon learning about this, prompted me to drop any guise of tolerance, and spout, "So, Mom, I must've missed it growing up. Whenever it was you got your medical degree."

But before all this, as if he were an augur, my brother, who fretted over her health, sounding peeved and even angry at times or with deeply heaved sighs, resigned, had read the signs. Maybe it was a matter of his understanding her better than either my sister or I did. Or that he more quickly forgave her any shortcoming. Our mother, with her sorrows, her increasingly protracted life, and negative outlook of recent years, was a burden that pressed down hardest on him, her youngest child. Joe, who, after my parents moved to Arizona when he was only nine, had grown up in a place, a house, a family dynamic so different than mine. And who, clearly, was more linked to his mother in genetic and hereditary ways . . . her youngest child, the preemie, the child she almost lost.

And now, his mother's emergency in a time of his own scary illness, when he'd have to prop up Dad, too. It was a heavy lift. Possibly even a tipping point?

Though augury had long gone the way of chariots, I had learned that birds gathering in the skies above the Eternal City still attracted attention with their flight patterns. One early evening, I'd almost concluded a familiar route back to my rented apartment. I'd climbed a series of old stone staircases and walls to stand atop a large, semicircular parapet high on the Janiculum Hill. As usual, my attention was riveted on the view of Rome's historic center, of myriad rooftops, church domes, bell towers, the remains of the Forum and Colosseum, a view extending to the distant hills studded with umbrella pines black against brittle blue. This time, however, a great massing of starlings high overhead was part of the mix. Joining other observers with their faces tipped skyward, I was mesmerized by how hundreds of starlings coiled, funneled, tumbled, and banked. A true spectacle emerged as they unwound like trailing scarves, and then, suddenly, often with sharp, rapid turns, snapped back together, plunged toward earth, before swerving away, gathered and rising. All synchronous, in admirable, even breathtaking, precision. An aerial ballet choreographed, but by what? How to explain this phenomenon of what, I later read, can top ten thousand birds stretching into quarter-mile bands?

I've also since learned that starlings most often mass together at dusk. They do so, it's theorized, to protect themselves against predators likely to take to the skies at the same time. As individual birds, they seek protection in large groups, but each bird belongs to a smaller, immediate family unit that soon, come nightfall, joins up to roost together. Not so dissimilar, in my mind's imaginative eye, to a family in Phoenix gathered beneath lamplight around a table to which the excavated relic of an old, collaged cigar box has been introduced, evoking stories and recollections but offering no signs to an augur, evoking no divination of gods. Just as nothing that night in a mother's face portended of something about to begin. Or end.

I sped along the bland thruway, the miles on my odometer measuring the increasing distance, my drive carrying me away from my native Chicago and even farther from the Arizona landscapes my family claimed as home but which never were and never would be home for me. I headed east into Massachusetts, New Hampshire, and finally, Maine. Though this annual early summer journey was of somewhat recent origin, it made me feel as though this had always been the direction I was headed in—farther away.

Joe, however, was being drawn closer, as if the umbilical cord that held my mother's and his mixed blood had never been cut.

By the time I crossed the bridge onto the island after a long day of driving, I learned that while undergoing tests in the Prescott hospital near my parents' home, my mother had suffered a heart attack. She'd have to be transported to Phoenix for surgery. Later that night, I was told she required a triple bypass and a heart valve repair.

But what I would never know firsthand, I can only imagine. First, the call my brother answered at my parents' house delivering the news of my mother's heart attack and the actions that followed. I can only invent the scene of a late May afternoon when Joe, at the same time I'm driving on the opposite side of the country, gets into his car and drives to the local golf club where Dad, bored with retirement, had taken a part-time job. Not bothering, as was his custom, to search out a scrap of shade in which to park, Joe struggles to get out of his car, and hurries to find Dad, who's at the pool, getting it ready to open for the season and, for what probably seems like the umpteenth time, is tinkering with the skimmers.

Joe calls out, clutching his side, "Dad, we've got to go. The hospital called. Mom's had a heart attack."

I will never know nor can I justifiably imagine what other baggage and fears Joe carries with him to deliver this burdensome news and the level of awareness of this sudden shift, its new urgency. How deep are the shadows cast by the rising specter of serious consequences, even death? Of what is this an omen? What does it portend for him?

I must also imagine the scene that unspools later that evening before my brother and father head to Phoenix for my mother's surgery, a scene based on skimpy evidence and which has perhaps wrought unjust accusations from Carol. Joe and Dad are sitting at the small table on the back deck of my parents' house. The sun has nearly set behind the hills. Darkness hovers, though no lights have been switched on in the house behind them. Just the amber-tinted porch light sheds its feeble glow in which a few moths flutter. My father cracks open a can of cold beer. It sits on the table within easy reach.

He perhaps thinks, *What harm can be done by just one?*

He slides it toward his son. Or doesn't object when his son reaches for it. All but forgotten in that moment: Who is the one seriously ill?

But even without the benefit of augury, I can do the math: Now there were two.

II
ARRIVAL

Arrival

Back in 1995, I arrived at a place I'd never been. Deer Isle: a 12x7-mile island that on a map appears as no more than an inconsequential speck at the northeastern corner of the North American continent. I arrived to eleven-foot tides, a rented cottage on a cove, and a clam flat's high-stepping birds I couldn't yet name.

In the summers that followed, I arrived with a clutch of expectations, an Audubon field guide, an in-progress life list, and the newly obtained knowledge that a spring tide's definition had nothing to do with the season. Words like *hackmatack* and *sculpin* felt less foreign on my tongue.

Approaching the island in 2002, I again crossed a 2,500-foot-long vehicular suspension bridge with a main span of more than 1,000 feet and a drive deck arcing 100 feet above Eggemoggin Reach. I again crossed the causeway. This time, however, I turned down a still unfamiliar mile-and-a-half dead-end road and followed a narrow lane through spruce trees and ferns into a small clearing of a house, a yard, an old, wide-armed sheltering oak, a bordering garden, and a wind-scoured bluff. I arrived at an edge of an edge of an island, a parcel of land and a house that a newly signed deed declared was Bob's and mine.

An arrival to things that we didn't yet know we needed to know:

the seven-gallon-per-minute recovery rate of our well and the recommended frequency in having a septic tank pumped out. An arrival to a house with a kitchen and bath badly in need of renovation and, even sooner, an immediate fix of a horrifying color palette of blue, yellow, and lime-green more Palm Beach than Penobscot Bay. An arrival to a house whose contemporary style snuffed out my long-held dream of owning a snug, New England cape or a classic cedar-shingled camp but offered a nearly unbounded prospect of sea and sky. An arrival to a house where I was confident that, over time, I would coax from its interior the havens I needed to sleep, eat, laugh, welcome family and friends, heal illness, and lick wounds.

"A house is not simply a building," Wendell Berry reminds us in *The Long-Legged House*. "It is an enactment. To ever arrive at what one would call home even for a few days, a decent, thoughtful approach must be made, a clarity, an opening." The mere fact of a house must be somehow turned into meaning. Necessity, he claimed, must be made a little ceremonious.

So, even before hauling in my first load from the car, I went from room to room, assessing. I reintroduced myself. I raised the blinds, screwed on lampshades, rehung art, cleared a spot among the photographs on the refrigerator door for this season's tidal chart, and fingered the striped "wishing stones" heaped in a wooden trencher. By opening, sweeping, cleaning, and clearing, it's as if I had earned the right to be back here. Necessities met, order restored, and as Berry notes, so, too, the old recognitions.

Beneath my hand, the feel of the linen closet handle was unmistakable. Were I to wrap my fingers around a similar one anywhere else, I'd be transported here the way a chair's struts hitting me in a particular spot on my back returns me to long-ago Thanksgiving dinners at my grandmother's dining room table in her tidy brick bungalow on Chicago's South Side. In rituals that inscribe another chapter in what I've hoped will be a long history here, I opened more windows and made the beds.

Other women came to such seasonal places carting more family history. They made their annual pilgrimages to cottages and camps where previous generations learned to swim, sail, fish, had first kisses, received marriage proposals, conceived babies, and planted gardens once tilled by ancestral hands. They mourned deaths, healed illnesses, overcame fears. The first summer I returned to this house, stood before a closet and pulled bedsheets from shelves, I tried to imagine that for decades my family's hands preceded mine in this same gesture. In doing so, I was struck anew by the unlikeliness of my traveling here, many miles and years from my childhood realization that the privilege of owning or renting a seasonal place belonged to other families.

No matter how ample I see my childhood now, with its simple and utterly essential pleasures of a public library, a backyard tree house, and a comfortable bed beneath a snug roof where it was safe to lay my head, I recall how my early lessons in class distinction were only further reinforced in college when classmates "summered" (Who knew there was such a verb?) on the shore or within a swath of pristine woods bordering a glimmering lake. I have yet to cease marveling at my journey to this island house, at all the riches that, through a mysterious confluence of chance, opportunity, and work my life contains, include the freedom and means by which I'm able to be in such a place.

A small island in the northeast Atlantic might seem a surprising choice for a lifelong Midwesterner who didn't swim very well and was transformed into a welter of thumbs aboard a boat . . . whose family never traveled to this part of the country . . . who had no claims to it, no connections or ties. But in 1995, well into middle age, as if I'd been meant to cross the bridge, the needles of my inner compass pointed me in this direction. I might have first traveled to this particular part of Maine by way of chance and contingency, and though I was merely seeking a two-week change in perspective, I seemed also to be scratching an old itch, as though following through on an unaccountable urge where I felt pulled here, the way a migratory bird blown off course might.

Each year's arrival to the island since has marked a beginning, a new season's turning with anticipated, recognizable harbingers. Like the high-pitched *kew, kew, kew* of the nearby Heart Island ospreys signaling their return, their journey complete—a four-thousand-mile migration, much of it over open water and with hurdles all along the way—it made my first day's island-bound and otherwise impressive seven-hundred-mile interstate drive in a car rigged with cooler air, music, and audiobooks a somewhat puny accomplishment. Our resident ospreys that, were they not to return, would be a loss hard to accept.

But that was before the summer of 2007 when I was still measuring loss by an absence of ospreys and the recent death of a beloved dog.

Compromised

"You know, she came to us compromised," said one of the doctors in the Phoenix hospital where my mother, following her heart surgery, was now in ICU.

It was another phone call of news and updates in a series that had already stretched across my first few days back in Maine and with a frequency and intensity that at times made whatever enables telephone connection between a small island on the northeastern seaboard and the desert Southwest seem as untenable as a childhood experiment with paper cups and string.

"Multiple underlying conditions are impacting her recovery. High blood pressure, high cholesterol, worrisome blood sugar levels. She has COPD. And, of course, there are the physical limitations from her previous cerebral vascular accident."

"The stroke?"

"Look, she's still weak but we're going to try to get her up today. We're always worried about the lungs, keeping them clear. I've ordered physical and occupational therapy for this afternoon. We'll see how that goes."

"The nurse said something about her kidneys?"

"We don't like her creatinine numbers. They're not where they should be, so we're carefully monitoring that."

"Do we need to be worried?" I asked.

"Not yet."

Compromised. Another meaning for a word I'd long thought familiar but now with a growing list of definitions. Did those pertaining to my mother and her health fall under "to impair by disease or injury"? Or "to damage, weaken, or lower"?

In recent weeks, we'd all been compromised or had compromised. Differences may not have been settled, but concessions had been made. In Phoenix, my brother returned home on what appeared to be a more permanent basis when he and Carol reached some kind of agreement in their roller-coaster relationship. And for the first time since Joe's illness, she and I had begun to speak a little by phone.

"Joe," she conceded, "is not doing well." And when she told me she'd gotten him an appointment at the Mayo Clinic in Scottsdale to begin a process for treatment and a possible liver transplant evaluation, I had to give her credit. This was a more hands-on involvement than I'd anticipated or been led to believe she cared to make.

But now with such news—a possible liver transplant?—I had to recognize that the somewhat vague talk about my brother's "liver problems" previously coming by way of uninformed parents, a passive brother in probable denial, and the filter of a sister-in-law whose version of things, given old history, I could neither completely trust, confirm, nor—given HIPAA and spousal privilege restrictions—circumvent had compromised my understanding of what was clearly a more serious diagnosis. It also added another new meaning to *compromised.* This one was under the category of "to concede to something detrimental or pejorative."

At my computer, I googled Mayo Clinic's liver transplant

program to learn more about the somewhat lengthy procedure in becoming a candidate. I read again about acute liver failure. Scrolling past hepatitis, fatty liver disease, and liver cancer, all previously ruled out, I bumped up against cirrhosis, gradual liver-scarring damage that typically can't be undone. Reading further, I hit the wall at end-stage liver disease. At the top of its "causes" page was chronic alcohol abuse.

And just what compromise existed for my further denial? For repudiation of the fact that my brother was a drinker? But didn't my family and I already know that? During Joe's two decades–plus in the wine and beverage industry, he had the requisite consumption that went with the territory of his positions as sommelier, wine cellar master, and winemaker's rep. He'd already admitted to doctors that he'd been drinking four to six glasses of wine nearly daily for the past several years, although, as I was to learn, a medical professional's rule of thumb was that if a patient's consumption seemed problematic, double the quantity of whatever the patient confessed. And Joe's consumption had become unquestionably problematic. He'd been more than compromised. Someone didn't just get accepted for evaluation by the Mayo Clinic transplant program without solid, probable cause and a medical record's cold, black-and-white facts.

Simply saying Joe was a drinker was a little like saying he had "liver problems." A failure to consider that my brother was an alcoholic, a failure—another definition, "to make a dishonorable or shameful concession"—meant we were all compromised.

Still, even if Joe was an alcoholic (even now I still stumble, finding it so tempting to say if he had a drinking problem), he was only forty-five, and all heavy drinkers, including those decades older, didn't get cirrhosis. Nor was he pathetic or depraved, one of those miserable losers, the Jack Lemmon, *Days of Wine and Roses* types portrayed in movies. Or the bums swigging from brown-bagged bottles that the older kids chased from beneath the glass-sharded viaducts in the Chicago neighborhood where I was born. The *real* drunks were drunks that let booze define and destroy them. Who couldn't hold onto a job. Who didn't have family or friends. Who were crazy and unpredictable and sometimes made households scary, like, perhaps, the one my mother grew up in, where, as a young girl under the same roof as an alcoholic father, she learned early that one meaning of compromised was "to weaken by accepting standards lower than desirable." Of having to accept to survive.

That girl grew into a mother who had recently offered her own definition of a son's compromised liver. A mother's diagnosis borne out by my further googling and learning that what contributes to those who do get cirrhosis, whose alcohol use goes from normal to necessary regardless of how much is consumed, were factors of diet, lifestyle, and mental health. Of inherited genes and family history—and why not insert a newborn's missed diagnosis? All these factors influence the development and slow but relentless progression of the disease. Of—no compromise here—*end*-stage liver disease.

My previously singular focus on Joe had been diverted by my mother's hospitalization and increasingly worrisome recovery. It compromised my attention and dispersed my concerns and worry across two fronts. Some days I resented it.

Attempting to get some updates, frustrated by parents who never became computer-literate, my father still fumbling with a cell phone, my sick and now unemployable brother eschewing email and no longer possessing a cell phone, his home phone unanswered because its voice mailbox was full, I erupted to my sister.

“This family is a bunch of idiots!” Hanging up from a call to ICU to get the latest status reports on my mother, I found myself irrationally shouting, fortunately into an empty house, “Why now? Why did this have to happen now?” before calling my father, who was relying on me to obtain the facts, who, without much aptitude for it, was being stretched in two directions. Obviously struggling, he’d been compromised further by the hospital’s location in Phoenix, the heat-shimmering valley he left years before, some ninety miles from his foothills home.

Some days, I felt as though I had to choose, pick a priority. Who got what first? What about whom did I wait for before buying airline tickets and embarking on a long journey from a small island along the northeastern seaboard to the distant, desert Southwest? I was still worried about the weight of my mother’s illness pressing hard on Joe. The hospital, the medical machines in her room, her precarious condition, all signaling what might lie ahead for him. Could it produce, possibly, an “I need a drink” kind of stress, the lure of that remedy and relief?

I still feel guilty admitting that though it was my mother in ICU, my thoughts usually went first to my brother. Truthfully, the relationship between my mother and me had for some time been compromised. Not by one specific event, but a gradual accretion. A slow but progressive scarring.

In February at the kitchen table in Arizona, we sat across from each other beneath the wagon wheel lamp, within arm’s reach. Yet that night, it was as if a great divide yawned between us, a gulf vaster than the physical, continent-wide expanse that would soon separate us again. That night, there was no attempt to reach across and grope our way back to whenever it had not been like this—a wordless recognition of distance and difference, of possibly indifference. Maybe, even defiance. My mother at one point stared at me as though daring me to say something, a full goblet of red wine at her fingertips, the alcohol that for the past several years she'd turned away from but apparently no longer saw the need or lacked the desire or will to do so. Her look declaring, "I'm not my drunk father. I can do this."

Meaning, "I can and I will."

Beside her, Joe was possibly—probably—dying of alcohol abuse. A fact that, it's fair to say, we all turned away from. How, despite the seeming improvement back then of Joe's fragile scaffolding that held him upright, vertical, functionally drinking for years, it still enclosed that dark place, the empty room within, home to his possible, unacknowledged addiction.

"It's hard to believe, isn't it?" I'd whispered to Bob in Assisi, Italy, less than two months before my mother's hospital admission.

We were craning our heads to survey the soaring ceilings of the thirteenth-century Basilica of St. Francis of Assisi. High overhead, little evidence remained that a series of earthquakes in 1997 had sent tens of thousands of fresco fragments crashing to the floor where we stood. Many pieces had been minute, some nearly rendered into dust. Thought lost in the heaped rubble was Giotto's masterpiece of St. Jerome and Cimabue's major work of St. Matthew. But with an impressive feat of restoration spanning eight years, fragments were digitally photographed, a computer system matched most of the rough-edged fragments, and an army of hired experts and volunteers restored St. Francis to the archway. Up in the rib vault, St. Jerome assumed his place at his desk.

Unfortunately, St. Matthew above the high altar had not fared as well. According to the photographs and numerous information boards posted at the basilica's entry, this fresco had been less stable, its pre-earthquake condition already questionable. Added to the challenges of reconstruction was its faded, somewhat murky monochrome of tan and gray. Only 20 percent of it had been preserved.

"Can you make out his face?" I'd asked Bob, whose eyesight had always been superior to mine. But seventy feet above us, whatever was saved appeared as no more than a faint shadow. Whatever had been Cimabue's intent at conception was lost. St. Matthew now looked to be in the act of receding, disappearing.

Weeks later, sitting at my desk on a small island in Maine, taking a break from the phone, I realized I'd barely looked at my Italy photographs, much less begun to edit them. Nor had I sorted through my many notes. The essay I'd begun in Rome that I'd felt held much promise sat untouched, like a nearly forgotten relic of another time.

Things happened. Unexpectedly. Earthquakes, illness, a diagnosis we least expected. Suddenly, pieces of what used to be rained down on us, piled like rubble at our feet. What choice was there but to stoop down, retrieve the pieces, and put things back together again. Or try.

I'm no restoration expert. I've never been a historian or archivist.

As I tried to piece together the ruptured fragments of my family's recent past, I discovered many gaps. All the pieces couldn't be retrieved. Reconstruction might never be completed, St. Matthew always to some degree fading.

Over the years, I'd kept journals and notebooks, preserved numerous photographs. Even so, conversations went unrecorded, events undocumented. I trusted memory. Attempting reassembly, I had no assist of Assisi's computer programs. I couldn't refer to placards, like those in Rome's Capitoline Museum that identified excavated sculpture fragments and ceramic shards by place and time. I had no map with a legend like the one in the museum portico overlooking the Roman Forum, without which I'd have had no idea that eight immense columns were all that remained of what was the Temple of Saturn.

At my desk, I dug into my journals, notebooks, and photo albums, but I was compromised by what wasn't there and by what I did not know, what I had turned away from, ignored. Obviously, the reconstruction of my family's past was of much less importance than Rome's. No aspect of civilization hinged upon what happened to us, our small story, a minute fragment, so easily lost in the sweeping currents of time.

And even if I were to strap on a headlamp, ready to dig with a pick and trowel to uncover fragments, hadn't I already proven myself to be a careless sifter?

Between more calls and updates, I was also trying to get ready for an upcoming writers' conference. As a faculty member, I'd lead a workshop, give a talk, do a reading. A commitment I'd made months before and had to try to keep, life in the Northeast trumping for the moment any departure for Arizona.

But my focus was compromised, my attention dispersed among multiple fronts. I moved from choosing workshop exercises and jotting down notes for my talk to surfing the Internet for connections between depression and alcoholism, for facts to better understand creatinine levels and the need for dialysis. And there was still the necessary gathering of facts from Arizona in case decisions about my mother had to be made and my father sought my advice. What if the doctors did indeed prescribe dialysis for my mother "to get her over the hump"? I imagined one saying the same words used when a friend's mother struggling with pneumonia was put on a ventilator that was never removed until she died a few weeks later. And though I'd surely not be asked for advice by my sister-in-law—Why be granted an important role now?—I worried about what would happen next after Joe's evaluation at Mayo was completed, after the tests of his compromised liver, the scarring damage that could not be undone. Without a transplant, could future damage be limited? Or, hardest of all to contemplate, could he survive?

Some days, it felt as if I were trying to find my way in a Roman catacomb with only a sputtering votive, until, occasionally, memory served up some free-floating snippet, as though on a dark stone wall, seep and salt threatening to destroy it. An image of Joe, jittery, on edge, unable to sit still in my parents' living room on a bright Arizona afternoon. An image without date or time stamp. Was it the '80s, that decade of excess, of social factors supporting elaborate wine lists, when it was so utterly normal that everyone drank? Or the early '90s, the sharp if brief downward turn, a cultural shift toward abstemiousness, when Joe turned in his sommelier's silver tastevin and late restaurant nights to be home with his children?

Whatever the time stamp, most clear to me still was the way he had crossed and uncrossed his legs, shaken his sneakered foot, stood up, paced, sat down, and again, the foot, the leg. Impossible, however, was the retrieval from a seeping wall, the emergence of what he had said. If I had to guess or invent, it would, as usual, be something laced with humor, his customary camouflage that foretold nothing.

Instead, it's my father blurting, "Can't you sit still? What's the matter with you? Got ants in your pants?" Asked of his son, a seemingly healthy and sociable young man who still exercised, had a good job, a new house in Phoenix, was loved by his wife and two young children, but who, perhaps, though perched on a chair out in the open, was hiding, had already on that bright afternoon begun to stumble in the dark, to be ambushed by alcohol's progressive hold sneaking up on him.

Though this rememberer had never been around to see him drunk, to note a stagger, the heavy lids or the too-loud voice, a more attentive person might have suspected a body screaming out for a drink, that secret still tucked away, hidden in a dark corner. Resistant to the feeble light's probe of the careless sifter who, at the time, recorded none of that afternoon in her journal.

Meanwhile, on the island, the glittery promise of summer had unscrolled, but not being fully present, I'd allowed so much easy slippage into things becoming unremarkable. I paid scant notice to the osprey hovering over the bay. I barely noted the absence of fox kits occasionally tumbling about on our lawn that likely meant the den in the adjacent bluff was empty for the first time in years. I spent little time musing over the mysterious disappearance of lupines emerging in the nearby meadow or wondering which of my friends had arrived for the season. Though I'd duly checked for damage a long winter had wrought upon my garden, I had yet to cross back over the bridge and make a beeline to the peninsula's garden center.

I may have occasionally lamented such things just as I yearned for those moments when the world around me—the sky, the trees, the sounds of birds nattering at the feeders—dwindled, almost disappeared. When I was accompanied instead by words on the page. When I forgot about being discouraged by all the books already written by people more talented than I or the many writers with busy agents and publication contracts. When I clawed my way through sentences, a paragraph, and, lo, a page. Then reshaped, revised, trying, perhaps, to capture traces and footprints, the flashes on seeping stone walls. Trying not to compromise what made it onto the page, compromise the language as it surely was in, "Oh, that was the booze talking," or

"She was just trying to drown her sorrows." Going deeper, inching into the darkness with a candle stub's quivering flame.

And then, regardless of what triggers it and whether I'm ready for it, being plunged back into light, the world's stark reality. The uncompromised truth: My brother had end-stage liver disease. My mother's kidneys were failing.

Oakdale Avenue

Home is where you start from.
—T. S. Eliot

A redbrick ranch on Oakdale Avenue. The house that inhabits me. The house that when I close my eyes and return to it, I so easily wander its rooms, negotiate each turn, instinctively reach for the doorknob and closet latch, the floor plan imprinted upon my body memory.

The house and a neighborhood that for years, in my adolescent yearnings, and later, in my still amorphous but keen young adult ambitions, I wanted to escape, knew I would leave behind. The house where so much happened, where so much, in memory, happens still. The house my mother truly loved. And though my father, grandfather, and uncles hammered and mortared it into physical existence, to my seven-year-old eyes, in our departure from a cramped South Side Chicago two-flat apartment to a redbrick ranch on an elm-shaded corner lot, it was the house that, with clipped magazine photos and sketches drawn at a kitchen table, my mother dreamed into being. Decades later, it remains the place where I can most clearly situate her.

WHO

Leona Helen Borst, the middle child of seven. Daughter of an alcoholic father who, after years of inflicting misery on his family, accidentally shot himself while cleaning his rifle. In the hospital, he was forced to dry out.

"Go ahead. Fix him up, but don't send him home if he's going to drink," my grandmother had instructed. A man who became the angular, sinewy, withdrawn, and unaffectionate man I would come to know. A father and grandfather who didn't offer us a hug or kiss.

Leona Helen Borst, born into a family whose men worked in the trades—carpenters, brick masons, construction laborers, welders. Men who drove trucks, came home in dirt-and-oil-encrusted clothes. Who cashed their paychecks on Friday nights, celebrated another week's end at the corner tavern, and, still refusing the weekly security of a punched time clock in the belch and stench of Acme or Bethlehem Steel, spoke little of the weeks in Chicago's long, cold winters when, like my cement mason father, they'd be out of work, unable to surprise their wives and kids with greasy take-out baskets from The Perch Shack.

Leona Helen Borst—Lee—born on Chicago's far South Side, a resident of neighborhoods with two-flats and tiny homes, with viaducts, churches, train tracks, and freight yards. Of mostly Poles, Czechs, Italians, "Bohunks," all Catholic and identified by their competing parishes. Neighborhoods that collectively, until the '70s, held back the encroachment of Black people, thanks to Mayor Richard Daley's strategic planning of bifurcating expressways and ghettoizing high-rise housing projects.

The daughter who, at eighteen, in the spring of 1948, barely a year out of high school, in a ceremony without gown or veil, reception or honeymoon, married Joseph Anton Bolda, her high school sweetheart. A bride who lived the first months of married life in her mother-in-law's squat, brick bungalow until her firstborn, a son, born nearly three months premature, lived only three days. After, a retreat to a rented room several blocks away and then to the apartment on Prairie Avenue where, in early November 1949, just two months after she turned nineteen, I was born and carried home. Home to the first floor of a two-flat, in the hulking shadow of St. Anthony of Padua Cathedral, with its school, rectory, and convent, its nuns who, about any misery, advised we "offer it up." Around the corner from Pat and Matt's, a smoky tavern lit only by revolving Hamm's beer signs and an Italian bakery with stacks of torpedo-shaped bread and glass jars of seeded, anise cookies. Adjacent to a weedy vacant lot struggling to be prairie, where Mrs. Alekna kept a garden of strange greens and one spring, tethered a bleating lamb whose connection to Easter dinner young Lee and her husband had yet to make.

WHEN

In 1956, the redbrick ranch on Oakdale Avenue in a suburb at the edge of Chicago's southern industrial base was the newest house in a neighborhood of straight, curbed streets, of small postwar brick bungalows with tidy front yards and severely clipped shrubs. Kids of mostly young parents spilled into the streets safe enough to ride bikes, trading cards popping in the spokes, or to play boisterous rounds of Red Rover and Kick the Can until dark drove them home. A modest neighborhood rich in its simple declaration: We were not Chicago two-flats or cramped apartments. We were a neighborhood bordered by a highway and freight tracks bisecting the narrow cornfield of a small farm soon to be swallowed by an "I-Like-Ike," optimism-fueled suburban sprawl. But we were also bordered by a swath of woods and a murky river, an offshoot of the Calumet that, miles to the east and well out of smelling distance, wound past steel mills, paint factories, forsaken grain elevators, and warehouses, past slag heaps and industrial smokestacks occasionally belching orange sulfurous flames, before it narrowed, grew sluggish, and by the time it reached us, offered up sun-basking snappers on its cat-tailed banks, an occasional river rat or duck, which, somewhat miraculously for a city kid, lay just a short trek from our back door.

A neighborhood of houses built on concrete slabs that answered postwar demand but also reflected the narrow cookie-cutter vision of a builder whose idea of choice was to line one side of the street with nearly identical frame houses, the other with brick bungalows and concrete stoops. Here, the building of a house such as ours became a neighborhood event. A modest redbrick ranch but with a basement—"Lucky you!"—and a glass block bathroom window—"How modern!"—and, just as amazing, a laundry chute to drop our dirty clothes directly into that wondrous basement within easy reach of the washing machine. For a time, our house, the mere construction of it, made us special.

Before it was finished, our house became a magnet for the neighborhood kids, with its piles of excavated dirt, the possibility of climbing among the raw-cut joists and studs, our feet pounding the bare floorboards as walls sprang up around us. Better yet were the days my father showed us he knew his way around Ready-Mix concrete trucks with their large, revolving mixer-drum bodies and their long chutes where the churned concrete poured out, Dad directing the flow as though he were a cowboy herding cattle into a pen.

It remains a fixture of my childhood: the smell of wet concrete, the *whoosh* as it first hurtled into the chute, the almost magical transformation of some thick, heavy, stone-embedded soup into a foundation, the buried walls against which the weight of the earth leaned and a house of light and dreams stood.

On his hands and knees, as effortlessly, it looked to me, as my mother lifting a spatula of frosting above a cake, he troweled into existence our porch and steps, our smooth sidewalk and patio.

Those days, as the sun lowered behind the nearby bordering trees, my mother silently wandered among our house's fragrant lumber frame, measuring, dreaming, planning, looking almost serene, still so steadfast and certain, as though the newly nailed studs and joists were gaining strength from her presence alone and would withstand whatever happened beneath its roof.

WHAT

But let us, at long last, step inside. Through the aluminum storm door with its curlicue wrought iron design. Behind us, it slowly wheezes shut with a hiss. Our heels click on the tiled entry. We've come in the front way, as though we are guests, travelers returning from a long distance and after many years away.

Room by room, the redbrick ranch reveals itself:

Living room: Here, the two large picture windows take advantage of our corner location, maximizing the light. Here, too, a working fireplace with raised fieldstone hearth, bookended by a pair of high-backed wing chairs long coveted and finally obtained via monthly installments and, over the years, endlessly, it seemed, reupholstered—paisley-patterned, a nubby tweed, but here in the original blue brocade. My young mother, seated, poses for a photograph. It's 1956, her first Christmas in her new house. She's wearing a plaid skirt and a red cardigan, her hair, except for a fringe of bangs, pulled back, secured by a pair of slender, rhinestone-embedded barrettes. In the background, hanging from the mantel, are the felt Christmas stockings she embroidered. Here, surely, over the years, there'll be more stockings. She'll pose again with all her children and her children's children because why would she ever want to leave? From the turntable of the corner high-fidelity console, Perry Como croons "Silent Night," the holiday 78s sandwiched between the "Best Hits" classics, sleeved record sets offering a tasting menu of Beethoven, Dvořák, Rimsky-Korsakov, about which, she once declared, "I may not know much about this kind of music, but you kids should." Nowhere in this room is there the merest hint of wallpaper, no reminders of our two-flat apartment and some former inhabitant's inexplicable choice of a pale-green, palm-frond wallpaper pattern, especially inappropriate one Christmas Eve when my father's bachelor uncle tramped through the rarely used front door into that room with its palm-bedecked walls, carrying the bitter cold on his heavy woolen coat. In this new living room, on her first Christmas in her new house, a young woman claims her place. Her open and youthful face with its contented smile suggests her longings and yearnings have been met. Her life brims.

Dining room: Adjacent to the living room, just big enough for the buffet and hutch with its early, still-sparse collection of flow blue glass and blue-and-white Willow Ware, and for the thick-legged maple table with its burnished top, blemished in one corner with a deep crack, an imperfection my mother claimed "adds character," and not so coincidentally, contributed to her getting a good price at Gatelys Peoples Store, our South Side blue-collar version of Marshall Field's. The table where, some afternoons, she lays out yard goods, plucks straight pins from her puckered mouth, affixes tissue paper Simplicity patterns, and, hauling out her Singer, makes her daughters' clothes. And where on Sunday afternoons, she spreads a tablecloth, attempts squabble-free pot roast dinners.

Kitchen: Just a few steps away, passing the rotary phone, Edison 3-5058 etched into my memory's Rolodex, the kitchen is a modest space of maple cabinetry and an L-shaped counter. Where my mother assembles her lunchtime favorite: peanut butter and banana sandwiches—"Hey, Mom, just like Elvis!"—or, on some Thursday nights, a signal that things are tight, she flips a batch of dinner pancakes. Here's the back door through which we explode after school, shrieking and holding our noses if she was cooking any of the dishes my father grew up with, all of which seemed to involve simmering cabbage. And against the wall, the drop leaf table increasingly nicked and scarred with shared functions: coloring Easter eggs, cutting out construction paper Valentines, hatching clever Halloween costumes. Here she rolls out egg noodles like her mother's, makes her signature—"The best, Lee!"—date crumble bars. Here, too, she sits over coffee, puffs on cigarettes with neighbors Ruth and Marilyn, a circle that, when my adolescent summers sputtered into late August's insufferable boredom, I tried to squeeze in on, hoping to learn "I know not what" but certain that whatever news got reported here, I'd be the first kid to know.

Hallway: Let's pause in the short narrow hallway, home solely to a small wooden bookcase. Shelved here, the sturdy leather volumes of *Encyclopedia Britannica* bought on time and old copies of *National Geographic* with their bright-yellow covers passed along to us, though from whom I no longer remember, but which, by their very presence, like the console's "Best Hits" classics and our weekly trips to the library, promise an Elsewhere.

Bedroom: Finally, the last stop on this abbreviated tour, the bedroom I share with my sister—a pair of twin beds with matching, white-wicker headboards, a room subject to my mother's decorating whims that are as much a product of budget constraints as her still youthful energy to strip, paint, and stitch. My favorite reincarnation: peach-colored walls, avocado bedspreads, tie-back curtains trimmed with pom-poms. Here my sister has to endure my unrelenting, dramatic readings of Kahlil Gibran's *The Prophet* but where, later, over and over, she subjects me to the soundtrack of *Born Free*. Here I retreat after the breakup with my first real boyfriend, and my still young mother sits on the edge of my bed and tells me my world will not end. But when I nurse my wounds here after not being invited to a popular girl's graduation party, I tell her nothing, as though to confess this latest rejection might suggest she'd done something wrong.

And here, in 1968, my second summer home from college, is where I hide, but not cleverly enough, my birth control pills. A discovery made by my mother, who demands one evening, "What are those pills in your drawer?" even though she knows what they are and are for, but may well have declared, daughter to mother, "I am no longer yours." Her demand made as soon as I'd come through the door from my summer job in the city, that summer of newfound freedom, of riding the sooty Illinois Central railcars, their splintery seats ruining countless pairs of hose. Of climbing the steps to the IC's wooden platform above Art's Roller Rink to catch the train that screeched to a stop, the platform vibrating, and then just as loudly departed. As if it, too, was eager to escape the cadence of the rails as it picked up speed chanting, *Away, away, away,* as it passed industrial lots, a paint refinery, freight yards, and factory stacks before the glittering Chicago skyline with all its promise proving more than a mirage. A ride during which I started to read the newspaper, expertly folding it into quarters like the businessmen in suits.

WHERE

Oakdale Avenue: A street name suggesting something bigger but that was just a single block in length. On which the redbrick ranch anchored one corner.

A block in a neighborhood where lives were measured mostly by ordinary triumphs: well-mowed yards, well-tended flower beds of peonies, lilies, and gladioli, of well-shoveled walks, well-washed cars and trucks, any tinkering under the hoods done in back cinder alleys. Of men whose work pants dried on backyard clotheslines. Of women who took on waitressing jobs to make ends meet. Where your kids going to college was not the norm. A suburban neighborhood at just enough of a remove from Chicago that there was little need to fear a repeat of white flight from the city's South Side.

A neighborhood unscrutinized by the larger world, its secrets and betrayals largely kept behind closed doors, though, of course, news of the saddest sort seeped out: a lost job, a leg lost to a train in the freight yard. Of depression, alleged abuse, and, most unthinkable of all, a popular neighbor's suicide in his garage as his family sat down to dinner.

Behind the doors of our redbrick ranch, anxiety often bubbled with the usual resentments, unresolved conflicts, all characterized by loud outbursts and slamming doors, and once, my father speeding off into the dark. I was not one of those children who only heard her parents fight by way of muffled voices behind a closed bedroom door. But I knew that, after, the rolling boil would be dialed back to a slow simmer in which silence and deeply heaved sighs prevailed.

All of which was the run-up to the day in 1972 when my mother and father, with my siblings in tow, walked out the back door of our redbrick ranch for the last time, their sights set on the distant West.

WHY

"What do you mean, you're *leaving*?" I found myself demanding of my mother on the phone as I sat at my desk in a small office cubicle, employed in a much more menial position at an advertising agency than what, previously, at my parents' kitchen table, I'd pumped it up to be. More important than my recently obtained bachelor's degree were the facts of a weekly paycheck and a lease to a city apartment shared with a couple of my pals.

As the first college graduate in a family whose members didn't all possess high school diplomas, I blazed what for a lot of folks was a customary trail. Venturing forth into what was foreign territory for my parents, it was as if I were an early pioneer setting out to cross the unmapped plains. A journey that soon became less about what I was moving toward, as more urgently, what I was leaving behind. My path now pointed toward advancement and potential achievements and away from what Oakdale Avenue, my neighborhood, the work examples of my father and mother, my uncles and neighbors predicted for me. *Away, away, away . . .*

What I hadn't bargained for was not being able to return.

Suddenly, as my mother laid out plans to pull up stakes, leave Oakdale Avenue, and move to Phoenix, Arizona, it was as if all my parents' arguments had been leading to this singular decision, a point on which they finally agreed. An embrace of some unknown opportunity. A decision that couldn't have been easy. Especially for her.

But away from my father's botched business partnership with her brother, away from her well-intentioned but meddlesome sister, Hazel, and now, with her mother dead and her estranged father long gone to Florida, better things might await, be hers to take. Perhaps she was tempted by what she envisioned in that desert landscape of spaces wide and open enough to accommodate big dreams. There, perhaps anger and resentments and an unhappiness that had to include blame would dry up, trickle away in the sand. There, in her faraway Elsewhere.

With one sweeping decision, she became the true pioneer, exchanging relative certainty for who-knew-what, trading in shading elm trees and green, pliant lawns for prickly saguaros and yuccas in a distant desert landscape where I couldn't imagine her beloved maple hutch and ladder-back chairs ever fitting in.

Before leaving, she purged. She brutally scoured the basement and closet shelves. I rode the train down on weekends to discover rooms stripped to their bones, mere vessels of what they'd once been, all increasingly stacked with boxes. On walls where shelves and paintings were removed and paint had faded, it was as if ghostly writings had appeared, already the encrypted messages of former inhabitants. I couldn't understand why so much was being jettisoned—the baby food jars of nuts and bolts so carefully assembled on my father's workbench, the last and best of my horse figurine collection, the stamped, tin-covered light fixture that had long shed its golden light over our dining room table as if it alone could make of our Sunday afternoon dinners a Norman Rockwellian composition. Grim-faced and with a brusqueness that became more and more customary, my mother said, "We don't need it." As if she was pitching possessions from a Conestoga wagon hub-deep in the mud.

Only much later would I wonder, *Was her ruthlessness a response to regret over a decision set into motion? Was she bracing against a potentially overwhelming loss by shucking so many possible reminders of a former life? In what boxes did she pack her secrets? Her dreams and longings?*

On a midwinter morning in 1972, my father sat impatient at the wheel of his car parked at the curb. His garage workbench, the pegged board where he'd hung his tools, the basement rec room that he'd paneled with knotty pine, all seemingly nothing to him now. In the back seat, about to leave the only home they'd ever known, to embark on a leave-taking they could neither influence nor change, my sister tried hard to absent herself from the reality of being uprooted from high school in her junior year, and my brother, looking dazed and confused, picked his fingernails until the cuticles bled.

My young brother whose first nine years, which had been lived in this house, were, I'd yet to learn, the years in which I knew him best. So few years, a sad, lamentable pittance, but I know now, a precious gift. On that winter day, he was driven away from the redbrick ranch on Oakdale Avenue, a house and neighborhood that became lost to both of us. Long before he became lost to me. The only place where I can, with personal knowledge and specificity, easily situate him playing hockey at the vacant lot flooded each winter by a friend's dad. Joey, a fearless four-year-old goalie among boys twice his age, as equally defiant on summer afternoons when, with countless Golden Books, my chore was to read him into naps but the only eyelids that drooped were mine.

My family left. They took that short walk from the back door, past the flower bed where my mother's tiger lilies flourished each summer and armies of ants marched among her peonies' pale petals, past the small plot where my father and brother staked beefsteak tomatoes. Past that place in the sidewalk where, many years before, we'd pressed our palms into wet concrete, beneath which my mother scratched our names with a stick.

At our corner, you could, by turning your head left, see the entire length of Oakdale Avenue. Was that where my mother was looking just before she lowered herself into the car? Before that, had she passed one last time through the empty, echoing rooms to say her goodbyes to the redbrick ranch? Did she cry? Have regrets? Want to change her mind? How many miles did they have to drive before the only things rising up into her view were not those empty rooms?

It's said that what hurts, what's lost, slips into the flux of time. The loss of her firstborn. The loss of her first house. I left Oakdale Avenue as I long planned. My mother left it, too. But how much more did it cost her?

HOW

The various houses in Arizona where my parents lived have largely remained for me a series of nearly featureless places on streets I can no longer name, in neighborhoods I do not know.

More than anything, the familiar objects they boxed and moved with them each time made those houses recognizable to me. Houses, each house with a kitchen window—the one, small thing my mother wanted—and which, on my visits, I checked for and was soothed that she got. Houses in a far-off state that never felt like home to my sister, who in her early twenties returned to Chicago, but that certainly became home to my brother. In that far-off place to which I felt no connection, he grew into a man and father with dreams and fears largely unknown to me, the product of otherness, distance, neglect. In a journey that began the long-ago morning they pulled away from the curb.

In 1996, surprising me again with another move, my parents left Phoenix and headed north to Prescott, traded desert valley for nearby mountains, and saguaros and mesquite for deciduous sycamore and locust trees. This time, I could actually identify perennials in my mother's raised garden beds. Again, my parents uprooted, this time not as pioneers heading into the American West but as transplants forsaking desert heat and valley traffic after my father's retirement.

Their Prescott house with its yellow siding, carport, and covered front and back porches backed up to foothills and federal grazing land. Quail bobbed their way down to the yard. Occasionally, javelinas squeezed beneath the back porch or tromped onto it, raiding the covered bin of birdseed. At night, coyotes yipped and howled. Up in the higher, cooler elevation that my father sought and my mother initially resisted, her irises thrived. Before moving in, my parents refinished the kitchen cabinets, stripped the living room wallpaper, retiled and painted the master bath a pale green. Once again, my father was asked to sleep amidst white wicker in another pink-and-white-floral bedroom.

In the first photos they sent, I knew this house was theirs. I recognized their signature touches, but I did not know this house. I could not claim it. No map of its floor plan would I ever carry in my tissues. It was not the redbrick ranch on Oakdale Avenue. Which made me wonder then as I wonder still: *Did my mother ever love a house as much as that one? Was it the place that, when she closed her eyes, she returned to?*

Decades later, I cannot say if she embraced the move west with its promised change, or if, reluctantly, weighing potential benefits against the toll of severing ties, she gathered it to her like the shards of something cherished that's been broken, but may, when put back together into something new, still possess a resemblance to what was lost.

It took grit for my parents to pull up stakes and move so far from their roots. Deciding to leave may have been compelled at first by my father's signature impulsiveness, but was leavened, I believe, by my mother's desire for the possibility of a brighter future with fewer setbacks and disappointments, of feeling less pinched. Unlike my gradual middle-age move from the Midwest to Maine, the result of choice and chance, my mother's abrupt move to the distant Southwest was, I believe, compelled by necessity.

Hers a brave decision I've come to appreciate, even admire. I wonder if I ever told her that.

The past is both a time—back then—and a place—back there. It is a body of space not effaced by time. Not generic or vague, but a specific house, a block, a neighborhood. The province of personal history. For too long, I didn't understand: Oakdale Avenue could be the place I came from *and* the place I wanted to leave.

My parents' first February in their Prescott house, it snowed. I'm not sure they were prepared for it. My mother especially didn't welcome it.

"Can you believe it?" she sputtered on the phone.

Still, after claiming so many houses in the Phoenician desert for almost twenty-five years, it was as if they were, almost, by way of snow and distinctive seasons, by a garden not characterized solely by cacti or succulents, moving closer to what they'd left behind on Oakdale Avenue.

Worthy of Untangle

Life is what happens to you while you're busy
making other plans.
—John Lennon

I

"Here are the plans," Peter, our contractor, said, pushing up the bill of his cap and wiping his brow, as though he'd just jogged to our house midday rather than parked his pickup in the drive on a cool morning in early June.

Knowing I might be leaving soon for Arizona, he added, "You may not have much time to look at these now, but I wanted you to have them before you go. And once you're back, maybe we should look at the shingle samples for the roof. A wicked price hike is coming."

I unrolled the drawings and specs on the dining room table, our plans to make our Maine house year-round. After having notched several summers into our homeowners' belts, following years of renting summer cottages spanning the island, Bob and I wanted the freedom to stay later into fall, maybe fly back at Christmas, return earlier in spring. For some reason, as if it were the pint-sized equivalent of the wildebeest migration on the Serengeti Plains, I was eager to witness at least once the annual salamander migration in late April. I wanted the chance to be here for whatever wet and warm spring night abruptly aroused yellow-spotted salamanders from their subterranean slumber to begin their big night—an urgent but slow, often death-defying trek across highways and roads to reach a breeding spot such as the vernal pond we have on our property.

Before coming here, I had no idea that vernal pools were also where migrating warblers pause to sip, where caddis flies swim and wood frogs quack like ducks, and where spring peepers, like ambassadors from another world, seem to pour their bodies into song. A clamoring, chiming chorus, one of the purest signs that on the heels of another long and brutal winter, a new, much-welcomed season was about to arrive. Another sign that the cosmos still clicked along according to cycles that long predated me.

These plans, Peter explained, reflected what had already been accomplished: the central heating system installed the previous year, the myriad, already completed renovation projects stretching back across the seasons since this became the house I returned to each summer. But now, the last, most complicated and expensive phase awaited—new windows, roof, exterior siding, and extensive insulation throughout. It was a big step with big implications.

Implicit within these plans was my faith in the future. A belief in ongoingness. Here, the place for my tomorrows, on this bluff of the island-studded bay with its expanse of sea and sky, elements that influenced my day, assured me they'd be there in the days ahead.

Make plans. It's what we humans do, no? Make plans, forgetting—perhaps needing to—that so much in life depends on a few moments we didn't see coming. Humans and their plans so unlike the ospreys that return to nearby Heart Island each spring or the loons to the bay from the lakes in late September, or the salamanders in their springtime migrations. Theirs is a deeply embedded drive. Primal and instinctual. And, best I know, unplanned. Even using satellites and computer programming, can we humans ever know why a particular day, perhaps in its slant of light or dip in temperature, tells the ospreys *now*? Some pre-migratory planning may be suggested by goldfinches stocking up at my feeders at a feverish pitch in September, small eating machines that send me out with buckets of sunflower seeds again and again. But what follows is largely instinctual, fueled by a hunger to survive.

We have it, too. The instinctual drive—and the conscious will—to survive. And so we plan.

"Let's plan on it," I'd told my brother on the phone just before I left Chicago, certain the need—his? mine?—for visiting me in Maine was great enough to overcome the obstacles of distance and his weakened condition.

It had been easy to imagine it.

How, his first night, we'd cook together while listening to his favorites by Neil Young, then kick back on the deck watching seabirds on the water, a prelude to sunset over the bay. I imagined him saying something like, "I love knowing places like this exist. I'm glad you found it, Deb." Our pre-dinner walk to the end of our road would not have materialized—walking longer distances still too tiring for him—but the lure of the shore the following morning would be too great to resist. And so we'd grab a couple of walking sticks and, rather than pick our way over the slippery rocks where tidal pools beckoned, we'd take the safer route along the wrack line, something easier for exploring difficult terrain. I'd continue trying to see things through his eyes, including what for me was not just a familiar stretch of the shore but, I'd long thought, a shifting tidal zone of transformation and change.

"Geez, you're right about the tides. Look at that. How far the water's out," Joe would've noticed, perhaps as he lowered himself onto a boulder to rest.

Before leaving the house, we'd have studied the tidal chart and timed our walk to coincide with the lowest point of a full-moon ebb so I could show him the sun-bleached sand dollars, the desiccated remains of slipper shells, whorled whelks and sea urchins, the kind of specimens I'd collected among the rocks and under the bladder wrack over many summers and had assembled on a shelf, like a deconstructed curio box.

"Matt and Abby would love these," he'd say.

Were he able to scramble over the rocks to the water's edge and bend down to poke and pry among the tidal pools, he'd find his own specimens. Instead, I offered, "We'll pack some up so you can bring them home."

Here was where it was easy to imagine us walking and talking about many things. We had so much between us to rediscover, uncover. No longer could I deny that my brother had, perhaps for years, been drinking too much. But had he really evolved into the kind of drinker to stash a bottle behind the toilet, at the back of a closet, in the trunk of the car? Who occasionally had to steal away from the table in a restaurant or the house to sneak a few swigs in the bathroom or garage? The previous night, over dinner, neither of us commenting on the absence of the customary wineglasses on the table, I may have come close to asking, "So, Joe, do you think you're an alcoholic?"

And if not then, maybe I'd ask on the shore where I knew to tread carefully myself, avoiding the slippery rocks. But if I did not follow through with my plan to ask him, did such failure say more about me than Joe? That I still found his possible answer too scary? Or was it shame, how his answer would reflect on me?

It was almost easy to imagine myself inching in the direction of the as-yet-unasked question there on the shore, but instead, seeing his fatigue, I may have asked instead, "How are you doing, Joe? Want to walk any farther?"

"No, I'm good. I just wish . . ." He heaved a sigh while stabbing his walking stick into a pile of stones near his feet.

"Yes?" I crouched down beside him.

"I just wish I'd gotten here sooner."

"Oh, me, too. Me, too."

So here's the deal with plans. Too often they're botched, aren't launched, don't come to fruition, in spite of the best intentions.

Joe didn't come to the island. We took no walk on the shore. I didn't ask him what I felt needed to be asked. In what I'd imagined, he looked much like he had in February when I saw him last, in what by all accounts then was an improved condition. And that's how I was still seeing him, even though all the more recent calls and reports about his decline declared this no longer possible.

"Let's plan on it," I'd said to him on the phone, but that was weeks before . . . before obstacles more than just distance had made any walk on the shore, where questions more easily, naturally, might've been asked, also impossible.

Joe's trip east didn't happen. Even so, I continued to imagine it because, no matter how detailed, well thought out, and laced with the best intentions were my plans, imagining what might've been was all I could do.

And Joe? Surely he did not *plan* to start drinking again. He knew what was at stake. According to Carol, the team of doctors that evaluated him at the Mayo Clinic's liver transplant program was unequivocal. At the end of their initial evaluation appointment, they ordered various tests. Based on those results, they'd determine how to treat Joe's liver disease while he waited to become eligible for the donor wait list.

"But," they made clear, "you cannot drink. You must be alcohol-free for six months to qualify. One drink and you lose your spot. Understood?"

But even before the testing began, Carol discovered unfamiliar charges on her credit card. Without a job and too sick to get one, without easy access to cash, my brother had been using her cards. Looking into the charges, Carol learned they were for six-packs of beer. And then another.

"Or, who knows," she somewhat wildly speculated on the phone, "maybe it was vodka. You can't smell vodka."

"But those purchases were made *before* Joe's evaluation and the doctors' warnings, right?" I asked, pushing back, perhaps reflexively, on what had long been her penchant for overdramatizing.

"I don't care. Even the doctors said he wasn't supposed to drink. Period."

Of course she was right. All other options were long off the table.

"He betrayed a promise to me. Worse, he lied."

And he'd added doubt to the assumption that the only reasons for his increasing confusion, tremors, and rambling conversations were his liver disease and the lack of an appropriate treatment plan yet to be put in place.

"He's jeopardized everything," Carol said. "I can no longer trust him." To Joe, she delivered her ultimatum. Demanding his car keys and driver's license, she told him, "If you're going to stay in this house, then I have no choice. You've lost your right to privacy." With the help of her father, she took the door to Joe's study off its hinges.

Among the many aspects of a suddenly even more grim and uncertain future, I had to abandon any thinking that if, as planned, he'd come to the island for a solo, unfiltered, and unmediated visit, the right questions would've been asked and some new terrain explored. He'd have felt no need to fasten on the dopey grin of our family's funny kid.

No longer was there any point in my wishful thinking that if, as planned, he'd gotten away from Arizona, come to the island where we walked a shoreline as familiar as Oakdale Avenue was once to both of us, I might've made a difference.

Instead, the terrain had dangerously shifted, and it was becoming increasingly clear that I didn't know where to step or what questions needed now to be asked.

"Good news," Peter, our contractor, had declared long before dropping off the final plans. The idea of a major house renovation had barely germinated when we'd followed him into the cellar. "See here, your foundation is solid and dry. The carrying beams are adequate." He demonstrated by attempting to poke his pocketknife blade into some worrisome-looking timber. The knife sunk no farther than its tip. "See, the posts show no rot." He told us, if we did go ahead and remove the fireplace, "I think we'll only need to put in one brace to support that span."

Removing the fireplace. To think that, at one time, such a plan seemed so radical.

Peter had sounded so confident with reassurances easily offered. Having some solid carrying beams meant fewer reinforcing joists. A solid foundation and a dry basement meant we could retrofit with radiant heat. More recently, he'd described the project's timeline.

"Once you leave in September, we'll put up some scaffolding and tent the water-facing side of the house with tarp. The northeast wind will blow up wicked come January, but with protection, we can work right through the winter. Unless we uncover some unforeseen problem along the way that could throw off our timing, I'm figuring we can be finished in spring. It'll be tight but we should be able to get her done."

As I'd listened to him, a mental checklist took shape. A chart, an orderly progression.

Now, on an early summer morning at the cusp of a new season on the island, Peter drove off, leaving me not just with plans but reassurances as well as options. Just as Joe's were falling away.

Only the day before, Dad had informed me that the insurance company through which Carol obtained insurance at work, and under which Joe was now covered, had denied him coverage for the liver transplant evaluation procedures and extensive treatment. The only resort: a caseworker helping them jump through numerous hurdles of qualifying for state aid. Life-threateningly ill, not old enough for Medicare, unemployable but without disability insurance, my brother, the forty-five-year-old father of two young children, had suddenly become one of those cases that most of us may read about but never think will happen to us.

And then there was my mother, still in the hospital with continuing weakness and instability, an increasing risk of pneumonia setting in, and now undergoing dialysis that, yes, we'd finally convinced her was necessary and, most certainly, as planned, temporary. I had added my voice to the chorus of convincers. As Dad held the phone to her ear, I struck my final chord.

"But, Mom, don't you want to get better to see Joey get better?" *Better*, a reasonable, achievable expectation being held out to her.

As it was to Joe, even as insurance companies and state agencies haggled and his symptoms worsened. The jaundice was back, the abdominal distention. He couldn't stop itching, couldn't sleep, had no appetite. His ammonia levels were getting harder to regulate and his joint pain was diffuse. Sometimes, he had tremors. Still, as much as possible, he made trips to the hospital to see Mom. There, among the tangles of tubes and banks of beeping machines, where hearts were laid bare, and where surviving was mostly a silent, solitary occupation, perhaps there, on those visits, Joe's recognition clicked into place: This was where he might end up.

Each day eroded by what must have seemed like an endless loop of yearning and resolve, bargaining and surrender. A well of fear that seemed bottomless, a divide of fear Joe had to reach across. But reaching for what? Whom? Carol, furious after discovering the credit card charges, felt, understandably, betrayed. And surely she was scared, too. Our phone conversations now extended beyond her typical delivery of medical updates. In a rare instance of vulnerability, she recounted a night when Joe was still working. A wine rep then, he'd just spent his last day at a wine festival near Aspen. Driving to the airport on dark and winding mountain roads after a day of drinking, he'd encountered a sudden, dangerously icy storm and called Carol from the car.

"He sounded so scared, almost panicked. I think he'd been crying. He said he was afraid of driving off the side of the road. But it sounded like more than that."

Had Joe, on those dark mountain roads, confronted a hidden-away truth that terrified him? Had Carol's recognition that this episode signified something important been added to the signs she now felt she should've seen?

How easy it is to let life as we know it resume once we're safely home.

But now, with Carol unable to move much beyond her anger, who or what was Joe to reach for to get safely to his destination? As time passed and Joe continued waiting for the hopeful sign of at least being scheduled for tests, that first step to the transplant queue, it may have felt everything was spiraling down to a place where he didn't want to be, of having to abandon his familiar method of coping, saying goodbye to something he may have thought he could not live without.

Drink as remedy, and as temporary, he may have thought, as his mother's dialysis. For getting over the hump. And stopping was just a matter—Wasn't it?—of exerting your will.

But that would come later, when he'd have to submit to the telltale evaluation tests. Not when he was so anxious, scared, stressed. All the reasons lining up for that first trip to the convenience store where, on so many previous occasions, he'd stocked up on Diet Pepsi. But not this time.

II

There is planning, and then there is planning's sidekick: timing.

While preparing for my spring trip to Rome, I'd brushed up on some ancient Roman history. I wasn't tempted, however, to crack open Edward Gibbon's *The History of the Decline and Fall of the Roman Empire*, the sole text for my undergraduate ancient history course taken decades ago. Instead, I consulted the Internet, where I found a straightforward Roman history timeline, a cut-and-dry chart of dates and facts scattered with a few visual aids.

I was reminded that a timeline is just so many black-and-white, what-happened-when facts no matter how accurate or colorfully illustrated.

Search out a timeline for the eruption of Mount Vesuvius and the destruction of Pompeii and you won't find individual stories behind the burned-up bodies of people halted in their last desperate, fleeing acts. People, moms and dads among them, who'd lived their ordinary and often difficult lives on narrow streets, tending shops, raising children, putting out to sea on the nearby bay. Who became ruins within the ruins.

Like those I found online, the timeline of my brother's sudden and swift decline, that I now try to construct from the repository of memory, recorded notes, and documents, can be pared down. A timeline of key identifiable dates, an excruciatingly brief span, even if not juxtaposed against the collapse of an ancient empire.

May 22: Joe, referred to Mayo Clinic in Scottsdale, is interviewed, his medical records assessed. He's recommended for further transplant evaluation. In the days that follow, testing is ordered. Shortly thereafter, the insurance company denies coverage.

June 2: Following a seizure at home, Joe is taken by ambulance to the ER at Mayo Clinic and is admitted with intermittent confusion, tremors, and hyponatremia. In the subsequent days, he presents with textbook case symptoms of end-stage liver disease and is treated for high ammonia levels, increased confusion, agitation, malnutrition, restlessness, extreme fatigue, gallstones, pleural effusion in the lower left lung, overall weakness, hepatic encephalopathy, auto-anticoagulation, and an elevated INR rate. Possible seizure activity that could be the result of alcohol withdrawal or the worsening of liver disease, or both, requires an EEG.

June 12: Joe, in a very weakened state, is transferred to an acute care hospital for purposes of IV antibiotics, aspiration prevention, physical rehabilitation, and nutrition treatment.

June 30: Joe is discharged and returns home.

To this brief and simple timeline, what visual aid might help? An illustration of the duo tube feeding catheter inserted into his stomach? A picture of a forty-five-year-old who looks much older than he is? And who, until he's diagnosed at Mayo, had not by his previous doctors been prescribed drugs such as lactulose that were key to the treatment of his disease? Or perhaps what's needed is the reading of the EEG that reveals no active seizure activity but suggests a recurring brain disorder, a complication of cirrhosis and his disease? All possibly aggravated by his use of two antidepressants, drugs prescribed by previous doctors, but should never be taken in tandem with alcohol withdrawal?

Definitions of some words on the timeline may be necessary:

Hyponatremia: Abnormally low blood sodium levels that can create confusion and seizure and can be aggravated by antidepressants.

Hepatic encephalopathy: A brain disorder, the possible result of high ammonia levels, that causes mood and personality disorders, confusion, unusual and involuntary hand and leg movements, and, possibly, seizures.

Acute care hospital: A transitional care facility for patients with chronic illness or complex medical conditions, who are often transferred from intensive or critical care units and require continued care and extended recovery time. "On average, a stay of more than twenty-five days," according to Medicare guidelines. Pertinent if you're eligible for Medicare. Or have insurance. And is possibly shortened if you do not?

And then there are those annoying acronyms for which translations may be necessary:

INR: The measurement of time, usually in seconds, that it takes the blood to clot, the elevation of which means a simple nosebleed can become a serious problem or a fall or bump develop into a potentially fatal internal bleed.

EEG: The attachment of electrodes to the scalp to detect activity of the brain, including active seizure activity.

DTs: *Delirium tremens*, from the Latin for "shaking frenzy," experienced by less than 50 percent of heavy drinkers upon cessation of alcohol use and is often confused with liver disease symptoms of encephalopathy and hyponatremia.

A special note may be necessary as well: How no previous acronym is a good preparation for MELD, the model for end-stage liver disease, a severity index and a reliable measure of mortality risk in patients. In other words, who is more likely to die. If anyone in Arizona knew what my brother's MELD index was, they did not pass it on to me.

Buried in such a timeline, even one as brief as this, were the plans. The "Hey, I'm in the middle of a life here" plans my brother surely had. Over the years, it likely never occurred to him he'd not live to see his children marry. Surely, his dreams and goals seemed within grasp, were not fanciful or beyond his capability, were both attainable and keepable. He had years left in which to see how the story of his life would turn out.

During numerous calls I made to the acute care hospital the week I was teaching at the writers' conference, Joe spoke briefly and somewhat vaguely about some of his plans. Usually, I missed lunch with colleagues and attendees, passed on some evening readings as I juggled a three-hour time difference between the East Coast and

Arizona, and made travel plans to fly there from a Maine island as a peak summer holiday approached and most flights on small regional jets involving multiple connections had long been fully booked.

We spoke after he was showing some signs of, if not improvement, stabilization—the tremors and episodes of confusion less frequent, the fear of aspiration subsiding. We were past what my father had called hallucinations, such as the day when Joe, lying in his hospital bed, was convinced that the two of them were driving together in his car and Joe couldn't slow it down.

"He kept slamming his foot on the bed, trying to hit the brakes," my father told me.

We were beyond, too, the time Joe told a doctor who'd asked how he was feeling that the "mother ship was coming in." I'd like to believe it wasn't as strange as the doctor may have thought but was more a matter of Joe speaking Joe-ese, a kind of adult "Davey Porter moment."

On the phone, his speech was often still slow, labored, his focus limited, his topics of conversation diffuse. I'd been told he still could not hold his head fully upright. For the most part, I let him talk.

One afternoon, he said, "When I get out of here, I'm going to do something to help people. I'm not sure what, but I know I'm going to help people."

Was he bargaining? A kind of, "If only I get well, I will . . ." as he lay down his chips of good intention and new resolve?

Change was now his only choice. To survive, there would be no going back to what he once knew. Saying goodbye to alcohol was to say goodbye to his profession, to any future work in the same field, to the accomplishments and friends he'd made in it, the only thing for which he'd been trained and paid and by which he'd supported his family. Also goodbye to his champagne toast at his daughter's future wedding, to cases of wine his in-laws had encouraged and which, as

Joe toted them to their frequent family gatherings, they expected and gladly accepted.

About what he'd do to "help people," my brother was vague, but he was looking ahead to a future he was still so sure he had—examining his life, turning it over, weighing it.

Perhaps looking for those moments when the world tells us, "You are not done here yet."

Another time, in order to call him, I'd excused myself early from dinner at the writers' conference and driven out to the end of the pier where cell reception was best. A couple of fishermen loaded gear and stacked lobster traps onto their boat, an open, blunt-nosed vessel with a high bow and wide stable stern, the kind of heavy-boned work boat I've always liked best.

Joe, sounding especially tired, sighed and said, "I didn't want it to get to this."

"To what?"

"The mental stuff. It's wearing me down."

"But it sort of had to get to this, though, you know, Joe? It's a big part of the whole picture. Of your getting better." *Better.* That word we still used.

"Yeah, I know, but I hate it. All this getting into my head."

Did he mean what had been avoided? Denied? What now would have to be examined, the words, "I'm an alcoholic," held up to the light? To expose a secret long held tight to the chest, the shame of it pressed close, all that energy it must've taken to guard it. The questions he'd now have to ask himself, again and again.

One of the fishermen looked to be the same age as Joe. They also shared the same height and hair color, a similar set to the shoulders. I found myself wishing he were Joe and not a stranger. Joe, healthy, on the cusp of a new fishing season, slinging traps onto the stern, stepping nimbly, leaping without effort for a line. And how I might open the car door, walk just a few steps, having to say no more than, "Hey, you going out to set traps tomorrow?"

Tomorrow. There would be that. And perhaps a burger together at the end of the day or a plan to throw a few steaks on the grill this coming weekend. Because we could. Because we were each a part of each other's lives.

"I know I screwed up."

"You mean, drinking again?" When he didn't answer, I said, without knowing if it was the right thing to say, "Well, yeah, you did."

"And so now, here I am."

And paying the price? Is that what he meant? Is it what I had meant?

"I'm anxious to get on with it, though."

"The rehab program?"

"I'm looking forward to talking to someone."

"I bet you are," I said. Meaning without his wife's estrangement or family baggage. Meaning without us and our denials, our own deeply evaded realities. Meaning not me who didn't feel equipped, didn't have the right tools. Joe talking instead to someone who understood, whom he wouldn't have to lie to. Who would verify he's not unique in his problems, not alone in his fears.

Serious illness, I once read, was a bright light beneath which, with our minds, our "mental stuff," we chip away at the layers, as now, perhaps, my brother was doing in what I hoped were moments of expanding, sustainable clarity. But our minds were housed in our bodies and, increasingly, he'd become physically incapable. His body, his house, was failing him.

A knife blade sinks deep into timber. The carrying beam will not hold.

III

What was *not* planned was my mother's transfer to the same acute care hospital where Joe was a patient. An odd comfort for my father, certainly not because of his usual concerns about wanting to minimize driving, but as a sign my mother had improved enough to transfer in spite of it being the very place that had signified my brother's deterioration a short time before. A cruel irony that trumped any notion of convenience.

"Hey, stop by to visit Joe, and, after, you can drop by his mother's room a short walk away. On the same hall, actually, but at opposite ends, a long wide hall with a slick-tiled floor down which you could imagine a young boy from Oakdale Avenue popping wheelies and calling into her open doorway as he sailed past, 'Look, Ma. No hands!'"

Least planned was Joe's sudden discharge.

"I can't believe it," Carol sputtered. "Can't they see how sick he is?"

A discharge so totally out of sync with our expectations of what we'd been led to believe was the timeline. And with just a single day's notice. Instead of having the time to make plans, figure out next steps as had been suggested by Doctor Two of the apparent rotating triumvirate treating my brother—"Oh, Joe will be here at least a month."—suddenly, it seemed, after just two weeks, he was being ushered out.

Doc Three had delivered the discharge news to Carol and asked, "So what are your plans?"

The plans for a man who was still seriously malnourished, so weak he still needed bedside transfer assist, who still experienced tremors and whose anti-coagulation numbers were described to me as "off the charts." And for whom the regulation of his alarmingly high ammonia levels with lactulose was still so difficult to get right that my brother had confided, “Deb, my shits are now projectile,” his sense of humor still, sometimes anyway, sharp and intact.

A patient being discharged just three days after the head honcho in this trio, Doc One, a woman who’d given Joe his admitting exam and assessment, brusque to the point of rudeness, and seemed not so much efficient as unengaged, had delivered some brutal news—to, of all people, my father rather than Carol.

His numbers were bad, she’d said. “His organs are failing. How do you want us to handle catastrophic events? You need a plan.”

For my sister-in-law, this was all about insurance. “To the hospital, we’re losers. Joe’s a loser. He’s only covered by our state’s shitty aid program, and so they want him out. They’ve written him off.”

As for plans after discharge, they’d yet to take shape, her only certainty: “Joe can’t be home. He’s too sick to care for himself and I have to go back to work or I’m going to lose my job. And he can’t be trusted.”

Yes, there was that. There would always be that in her mind now.

“There’s no other way. He has to go straight to an inpatient rehab place or he’s going to drink.”

I tried to remind her, “But Joe has no car. No money. He can’t walk very far on his own.”

“He’ll find a way.”

“He seems very determined to get better and beat this.”

But no amount of conversation was going to change her mind. No alternative would work for her. To the hospital case manager, she made her position clear. “You can’t discharge my husband unless he can go right into an inpatient alcohol rehab facility. He can’t be home.”

And to her credit, she put up a fight. With the notes she and her sister, Jenna, had been keeping about what often had been conflicting reports from the three doctors treating Joe, she confronted Doc One, who'd just days before put Joe at death's door. Carol reminded her that, in speaking to Joe's father first about such matters rather than to her, the patient's spouse, she'd violated Joe's HIPAA patient privacy rights. Jenna's husband had also called the corporate office to register a complaint with the quality director.

In the administration offices, registering her protest against the discharge, Carol said, "And if we refuse to sign the discharge papers, what are you going to do? Dump Joe onto the street?"

"There's no medical reason to keep him any longer," the discharge manager insisted. "As far as we're concerned, Joe's stabilized. And if you refuse to leave, be prepared for whatever coverage you do have to tell you they are done. You'll be billed."

Doc Three chimed in, "Joe's ready to go to rehabilitation." Suddenly, the patient who'd been at the threshold of a catastrophic event was now medically stable, good to go.

Carol's efforts bought a weekend. But what the two days didn't buy was a spot in an inpatient rehab facility. Of the paltry two facilities in the area that accepted state aid coverage programs, both were full. The hospital promised to send Joe's medical records to them so that, as soon as a spot opened, he'd be in.

"It's just a question of waiting a few days at home," the case manager promised.

A plan not so much proposed as imposed. All Joe had to do was wait.

On his last night at the hospital, I called him. He was surprisingly alert. For a quick moment, I considered that maybe the docs were right. He had stabilized.

"So I understand you're going home tomorrow."

"That's what they tell me."

"You okay with that?"

"I don't know. I guess so. I don't have much choice. I really wish I was going straight to a rehab place."

"Me, too."

"I want to get on with it."

But Joe's plans were now in other people's hands, as they had been for the past few months, certainly since being hospitalized, and now included who could say how many anonymous folks at insurance companies and state agencies. Passivity on Joe's part now a condition of his illness's limitations, its mental and physical debilitations, and not the personality characteristic that had long been his go-to fallback. I had no idea how much he was being kept in the loop as other people—his wife assisted by her sister and parents—were making decisions, making plans because someone had to, and as much as I might have wanted to intervene, I was not a spouse or a parent, just a distant sister on the opposite side of the continent who had no claim to a place at that table. Not that it had rendered me totally passive during Joe's treatment. I'd observed, done research, suggested. But after years of Carol and me being at odds, I couldn't expect her, clearly in the driver's seat now, to be more open or forthcoming. Or to change her often off-putting ways, her seeking the last say and sealing the lid on further discussion.

Joe said, "I wish I knew what was going to happen. I feel so isolated."

The doctors had said, "There's nothing more we can do for him." Had Joe heard that? Translation: "They've given up on me."

"Aw, but Joe, you're not alone. We're all here for you." Once again, I was embarrassed by my response. I'd already exhausted so many clichés. The words that so easily, thoughtlessly, escaped my lips, already shameful.

"The past is past."

"What's done is done."

Even the AA mantra, "One day at a time."

But what did I know? Largely inaccessible to any of us was the new terrain my brother had crossed into.

"Everyone who is born holds dual citizenship, in the kingdom of the well and in the kingdom of the sick," the late Susan Sontag wrote.

To where my brother now resided, I had no passport. I shifted gears. "I can only imagine how alone you must feel. It has to be scary."

"Yeah, it is. Sometimes."

"Are you afraid you'll never . . . ?" I began, not knowing exactly where I was heading.

"You know what I was thinking about today? Being on Uncle Dave's pier in Michigan," Joe broke in, referring to weekend trips when I was already out of the Oakdale Avenue house, the summer before my family left it, too. Meaning Joe was only nine at the time.

"I remember I used to go down to the pier in the morning when no one else was up yet. I sat at the end and fished. It was so peaceful there. I remember one morning when it was real foggy." Joe was offering more details and specificity than anything I'd gotten from him in a long time. "I couldn't see much, but I could hear some ducks nearby. I remember the sounds they were making, little quacking noises and splashes. It sounded so nice, especially because I couldn't see them. I also heard the water under the pier. You know, little waves slapping against the wood."

Sitting in our living room a continent away, I cradled the phone to my ear and looked out to the bay. Towering cumulus had formed on the horizon, the signal a change in weather was headed my way.

Several black-capped terns kited against the blue sky with swift wing beats, plunging to dip their beaks into the water, then rise again above a sweep of bay I had become convinced my brother would likely never see. My breath caught at a sudden certainty: I was older than Joe would ever be.

"Mostly I just remember how peaceful it felt there," he said.

"Did you feel isolated then?" I asked, even though I wasn't sure that a nine-year-old could identify feelings of fear or loneliness as isolation.

"No, not really. I was alone but I didn't feel isolated. I felt, you know, peaceful."

"So go there," I urged. "In your mind, when you're feeling afraid, maybe you can go there."

Dave's pier. I hoped he would return to it in the days ahead. As he would, hopefully, to other moments I knew nothing about. Perhaps Joe as a young father, his infant son asleep against his chest. Or as a fit young man hiking a mountain, his heaviest burden the canvas pack on his back. Dave's pier. Joe speaking of it as though it were a mythological place. What our minds were compelled to hand over when unbewildering options closer to hand were dwindling. Dave's pier. Offering me the comfort of knowing there was such a place for my brother. A gift in that last conversation I had with him as a hospital patient, a brief snippet I've clung to as if it were one of my carrying beams.

A memory layered with another. With what I only learned later from my father—that in the hour before his discharge, Joe, still wobbly and prohibited from walking any distance on his own, wheeled himself down to my mother's room, where she was being visited by her niece. In the hall, as Dad arrived and approached my mother's room, he heard Joe's voice followed by their combined laughter.

"They were having a good time together," my father said. "A good time. That's what I will remember."

Man plans, God laughs. Or so the saying goes.

I've used it, often when laughing at myself, when, with hubristic certainty, I plan, overplan, carefully choreograph. About a house renovation. A trip. The book I'll surely write next. All the plans I make in a life I seem so certain will extend into the future, touch the distant horizon. Out there. Up ahead. When, I thought at the time, I'd find new ways to make my brother understand he was still loved.

And, even more immediately, when I boarded a plane and headed west. My plan, hatched in concert with Carol, was to be there to help and support Joe when she returned to work full-time, especially since no spot at an insurance-approved inpatient rehab facility had yet to open up for Joe. Correction: No spot had opened up in an inpatient setting willing to take him.

"They say he's too sick," Carol reported. "Even the place the hospital said would take him. They saw Joe's hospital records and said they aren't equipped to care for someone as sick as Joe."

We plan, no matter who or what may have something else in store for us.

For the ancient Romans, it wasn't God but the Fates who held mankind's life strings. Three goddesses spinning the threads of destinies: the span of a person's life; his allotment of misery and suffering; and the manner of his death. Ever powerful, they also passed out the good and the bad at birth. Bequeathed to my brother was, possibly, a liver already compromised, undetected over the years in an otherwise healthy man. A newborn with a susceptible liver and with what we might call a twist of fate, though certainly choice had much to do with it, directed to the very profession that would put him squarely in harm's way. As though it had been foretold.

Only on the ancient theatrical stage, by way of a deus ex machina god-makes-it-happen intervention, could what the Fates determined be undermined. Tragedy averted. Conflicts instantly resolved. A more palatable ending to a seemingly hopeless situation. Interventions that, even if welcomed, often seemed contrived. Improbable written endings that, warned Horace, should be refused "unless a knot shows up that is worthy of such an untangle."

Man plans. God laughs. The Fates heedlessly spin their threads. A mere mortal, gripped by disease, struggles for a second chance. A woman on a small island awaits an outcome she cannot plan, but who, were she writing the ending, would need no convincing that here was a knot worthy of untangle.

"I'm Not Looking for Anything."

July 9, 2007. As I remember it, a day of bright, clarifying sunlight, small breeze, low humidity. After spending a couple of hours at my desk—with work on my new book stalled, I'd been focusing instead on numerous emails—I signed off with my sister, Chris.

"Enough already. I need to go for a walk."

I headed down our lane. My presence did nothing to halt what sounded like an argument among a small knot of chickadees overhead or the red squirrel rummaging among old fallen leaves, making a racket all out of proportion to its size. Among the limbs of the maple, a quickening breeze was beginning to leak through. At lane's end, I turned onto the road.

Ours was a mile-and-a-half, dead-end road. And quiet, particularly at our end of it, where, after turning off Route 15 and driving about a mile on asphalt, it switched to hard-packed gravel. Though it may be subject to some washout after hard rain and, come winter, deep snowplow gouge, I liked the switchover crunch of hard pack beneath my car tires, the occasional ping of gravel telling me I was almost home. I liked the dense woods pressing in on either side, forming in some places a high, overarching canopy, even if the shallow-rooted spruce trees promise that at least one blowdown each storm season would take out a few overhead power lines. The woods also offered cover and refuge to my wild neighbors.

The previous summer, walking the road had been a trickier proposition. A black bear had been sighted lumbering across the road, a sighting from a reliable source—an appliance repairman working at a neighbor's, who'd been raised in Maine's north woods where, he said, "Black bear are as common as mud in April."

Quite unlike the annual, largely unattributable reports of a moose, of what's come to seem like a sort of spirit animal moving in and out of the mist. In the case of the bear, however, other reliable sightings elsewhere on the island lent more credence. Suddenly, people were afraid to walk the roads or nearby trails, in spite of assurances like the one from my pal Jim who each autumn since childhood totes his hunting rifles to a stand or blind.

"Bears are notoriously shy," he'd told me. "They're less interested in you than you are in them. Their worse offense? Messing with your bird feeders, mucking up your trash cans. And, oh boy, they can do a wicked amount of damage to them. No question, black bears barge. They aren't neat and don't ask permission. But trust me, they're not after anyone's pets." Still, even Jim had to concede that any such fuzzy profile of a bear changes if it's a sow with cubs. "Oh, well now, you're talking something different. That bear might not be so nice."

Nice. Definitely not a word that had ever sprung to mind when it came to bears. Still, count me as one of the folks who'd been excited by the prospect of a bear somewhere in the woods, even if it meant I had to be doubly sure to latch the garbage shed and haul in my bird feeders at night. I also didn't mind—well, not much—treading a little more carefully on my solo hikes listening for a nearby branch to break. Since then, there'd been no reports of a bear on any part of the island, as if, a one-season novelty, it had moved on.

Without further sightings and given recent reports of coyotes mostly roaming the other side of the harbor, our road's foot traffic belonged again to joggers and walkers often accompanied by their dogs. Once this was the domain of our beloved dog Ben, who, over the years, had been my steadfast companion on my nearly thirteen-hundred-mile drive to and from the island. A fellow resident in every rental cottage over many summers, he only got one full season at this house Bob and I bought the year before Ben's last. Still, he marked it as his territory—a place of grassy yard, bordering woods, a bluff overlooking Penobscot Bay, a world of things to sniff and watch.

In my memory's eye, he remains here still.

In Ben's last summer, our road had become the outer edge boundary of our joint meanderings, the farthest point his severely arthritic hips and back could carry him as, remarkably for a large dog, he closed in on sixteen years. Just a few years before, he'd still been a magnificent specimen of power and athleticism, an eloquent expression of nose-to-the-ground running, of a pointer doing what he was born to do. Of what I could only call a joyfulness that increased mine. In his last months, however, he wobbled, teetered, a white-muzzled senior with creaky hips and gimpy back legs. Who groaned lying down, grunted getting up, and spent much of each day in either of his dog beds. From a ten-week-old puppy, he grew into a sleek running machine, but after too short a span of years, struggled to get up a single step.

Now, walking alone, not much past the boggy hollow where skunk cabbage pushed up early each spring, I paused at the small stream passing through the culvert under the road. Here, Ben always paused, until his back legs, no longer able to hold him steady, began to shake. He looked the length of the stream where deer often came to drink, scoured the nearby woods, even though, with cataracts that in a certain light appeared like a white, oily sheen, it was hard to know just how much he saw as he gazed into the distance with a stubborn, unwavering persistence.

At the crest of a small hill, adjacent to the field, which now was spiked with pink and purple lupines, farther down than Ben and I had ever gotten the last summer of his life, I turned back toward home. Five years had passed since walking this road with Ben became routine. And even more years past the time when his daily needs helped tether me to the ordinariness of the world. By way of schedules and responsibilities, he anchored me, kept me in the moment, took me out of myself.

After his death, everything was thrown off. The road for a time was not the same. I did not know where to look.

Now, of course, I do. Or think I do. Many days, I appreciate the freedom of walking alone, not having to watch out for or interpret cues, of being freer to let my mind drift, let lines and sentences play out their rhythms with each step, perhaps discovering a way past a rough spot in a rough draft. Yet, unquestionably and still, I miss Ben, his companionship, his very being.

Much more than a candle's brief blaze and shine, he had brightened my life.

But my routine walks, including this one, had become consumed with other thoughts.

Following Joe's discharge from the acute care hospital, I'd been checking in daily with my sister-in-law. She was the gatekeeper. All information—updates on wait lists for inpatient rehab clinics, a scheduled doctor's appointment at which, hopefully, a prescription for some at-home nursing care would be written—passed through her. News about Joe—what he was eating, how he was adjusting to his meds, whether he was keeping a positive frame of mind—was not just reported, but interpreted, by her. As if my brother were wordless, a fixture in the background, transformed into a third-person pronoun. Most days when talking to her on the phone, I couldn't tell if Joe was in earshot or, worse, if their two children were, as Carol loudly condemned the hospital.

"They just wanted us out. They weren't getting enough money from the state and thought we were a bunch of losers. They pegged Joe as a drunk, and that was that."

Somewhat mercifully, the kids seemed to be spending more time with her parents.

As I listened, I was reminded of how I'd long felt my sister-in-law needed a censor or, at the very least, a good editor. As I pictured Joe in a sort of orange jumpsuit, a prisoner of his own house and, more tragically, his body's failings and its unrelenting series of depletions, I had to wonder again if Carol's quick, sweeping, and often ill-informed judgments, her blanket pronouncements and off-putting authoritarian manner, had alienated Joe's doctors and hospital staff.

On my walk back to the house, I couldn't stop thinking that this was the day she'd be returning to work. I'd be more likely to reach Joe directly. As soon as I was in the door, I checked the time again, computing the three-hour time difference I'd come to deeply resent. I was eager to speak with Joe. Our conversations the past week had been minimal. I wanted to remind him that my airline tickets were now purchased. As per the most recently revised plans suggested by Arizona events and following conversations with Carol about when my time there would be most useful, and knowing my mother, too, might benefit more now by my presence, I was departing in just a few days. In tandem with a home-health-care aide likely to be prescribed at Joe's doctor appointment the following day, I'd assist in helping him gather strength, become well enough for acceptance to a future vacancy at a rehab facility equipped to take him.

Much more reluctantly, I'd also be better able to judge with my own eyes whether it was time to press the possibility of hospice care onto Carol and her hands-on family—a new and frightening territory that my sister and I, without a template, had begun to research. Given Joe's continued debilitation and his prospects presented by at least one of the acute care doctors, no matter how inappropriately or inconsistently expressed, it should scare all of us.

I still shared my sister-in-law's outrage at the hospital over what seemed to be a premature discharge when Joe was clearly so ill. But I had to wonder, *Was this negligence, disregard, or something else?* Increasingly, I worried that perhaps the doctors had become unanimous in their assessment of my brother's condition, of a potential "catastrophic event." Had they said as much? Was hospice mentioned? Did Carol or anyone in her family ask, "Is Joe dying?"

To my surprise, Carol answered when I called. Her first day back to work and, probably wisely, she'd arranged to go in midday. In the background came the intermittent sound of running water. I pictured her at the sink. In a kitchen with, best I could recall, a center work island counter and open to a small family room with fireplace and sliding doors to the yard. Adjacent, a short passageway led to the bedrooms and, via an arched entry at the opposite end, to a seldom-used living room, its drapes pulled tautly shut. A newish, single-story house of tan stucco in a neighborhood of like-sized houses and attached, two-car garages on modest lots. I'd only been there a couple of times. Mostly, I'd seen Joe and his family at my parents' house in Prescott Valley. What I was really trying to do was situate my brother. Where was he?

"So, I just remade our bed," Carol launched in. "Again. And with the last of the clean sheets. It's that damn lactulose. They prescribed too much. He can't control himself or get to the bathroom fast enough. I want his doctor to make an adjustment to the prescription tomorrow."

"Is Joe in bed now?"

"I think so. I want him to stay there. I have to leave soon." She paused. "I hate leaving him. And he doesn't want me to go. He asked if I really had to go in. And, yes, unfortunately, I do."

"Is anyone else home?"

"The kids left yesterday. My parents took them to their cabin in the mountains. But I asked your dad if he could come by to check on Joe early this afternoon. And maybe stay with him for a while."

"And he's going to do that?"

Among the many unfortunate outcomes in the week following Joe's discharge had been my father's near absence in his son's life. On Joe's last day in acute care, Carol, angry with the hospital and doctors but redirecting it onto my father, had confronted him in the hallway as he approached Joe's room.

"It's all your fault," she accused, and without any proof, went on. "You let him drink while he was staying with you. You've always encouraged him. Do you have any idea what you've done? This is all because of you. You never understood how sick he was. And now look."

The confrontation had infuriated and overwhelmed my father, who already brimmed with anxiety and worry. Maybe he hadn't truly understood the severity of Joe's illness or hadn't wanted to accept it. And maybe he had looked the other way the night Mom was ambulanced down to Phoenix for emergency surgery and allegedly, according to Carol, he'd set an open beer on the table between him and Joe and it was unclear which of them it was meant for. But I remained confident that my father, at least in the past several months, had not encouraged Joe. He knew what was at stake.

With his tank running on empty, possessing little capacity or patience for analysis, and bewildered and encumbered by his own fears for his son and wife, he was unable to recognize his daughter-in-law's fears. He didn't understand how her unjustified accusations and finger-pointing may have been fueled by a desperate need to find fault, place blame elsewhere. As if any of that would help things make more sense, become less combustible.

"Does Joe know Dad's coming?" I asked.

"Yes. He's been asking all week, 'Where's Dad?'"

I was grateful for whatever retraction or apology had put an end to the standoff—her resolute anger, my father's adamant refusal to come to the house if she was there, about which my brother likely knew nothing. Joe would no longer be deprived of his father's companionship.

"I feel so isolated," he'd said, four words that had begun to haunt me.

"Joe and I went to an AA meeting last night," Carol announced.

This I wasn't expecting.

"We have to do something. We can't just wait for a rehab opening. I mean, if he gets one, fine. But I don't trust the insurance company. And I don't trust him. He's got to get through six months booze-free. It's a way for things to get back to normal."

As characterized, apparently, by her description of their previous day. At her insistence, they'd gone to church as a family, invited her sister and brother-in-law for lunch, lounged with her parents at the house all afternoon before they took the children north. And after, the AA meeting where, she declared, "Joe got to see people like him. Who were, you know, getting their lives back, were moving on." The meeting at which, by her own admission, Joe could barely hold his head up.

In the grand finale of what she'd considered a "normal day," they stopped at the grocery store. "Joe wanted to wait in the car, but I insisted he come in."

Once inside, Joe said he'd like some sorbet. "And oh, it was so . . ." Carol took a deep breath. "We were standing in front of the freezer case and he asked, 'Do you think I can have two flavors?'"

In my sunny kitchen on the other side of the country, I bowed my head.

I'd not yet read *Mortality* written by the late Christopher Hitchens as he was dying from esophageal cancer. In it, I marked the passage, "What citizens of the sick country do while they are still hopefully clinging to their old domiciles." Daily existence measured out by sorbet spoons.

The night did not end there.

"All day, Joe'd been complaining about his back. You know, he had an injury a couple of years ago and sometimes it flares up. But it seemed like it was getting worse. He kept thrashing around in bed, trying to get comfortable." Carol called the local fire department about 10:00 p.m. and asked for a couple of EMTs to come and check on Joe.

"I thought the EMTs could just check him out, you know, make sure nothing serious was going on. When they got here, I told them right away that I didn't want Joe going back to the hospital. I didn't think he needed to. I explained about his old back injury, how it was probably just that."

Yes, or maybe the gallbladder. Or the kidney. Or the liver.

"What a waste. Those guys were so lame. It was like, 'Why did you bother us with this?' And then Joe pipes in, tells them he's fine.

Just tired. So, no problem. They left and Joe eventually got comfortable enough to fall asleep."

"As long as you're sure it's just his back." Sure? What was I saying? Who was she to be sure? I had yet to tally up all the bad decisions, but this surely sounded like one.

"He has a doctor's appointment tomorrow, so we'll find out."

As she resumed rambling about having to get ready to go to work, I heard, somewhere in the background, what sounded like my brother's voice. It got louder, as, apparently, he entered the kitchen.

"Why do you keep talking? Talking and talking. Don't you ever stop?" he asked.

I heard a rattling sound, like something being lifted or moved across the counter.

"It's your sister. Do you want to talk to her?"

Again, the sound of something rattling.

"What are you looking for?" she asked Joe.

Something made of paper or plastic, perhaps a bag.

"What are you looking for?" she repeated.

And Joe's voice, getting fainter as he must've left the room. "I'm not looking for anything."

Getting off the call, I promised myself I'd call back later, after my father was there, mostly so I could talk to Joe. I returned to whatever blessed ordinariness a spectacular summer afternoon was offering but to which I was mostly oblivious, as I kept trying to picture my brother at the AA meeting. I knew that any image I may once have held of such a gathering, of old men, many of them chronic relapsers, filling the seats of folding chairs in a smoky church basement, was outdated.

I have to confess: I possess a general aversion for programs with spelled-out "steps," the suggestion of complex things broken down into seemingly easy-to-follow instructions that might hint at a quick fix. An easy remedy, like something emblazoned on the cover of magazines: "10 Steps to Fabulous Abs" or "5 Steps to a Better Sex Life." Perhaps this also reflects my distrust of dogma that smacks of either a New Agey, cultlike devotion to some Higher Power or the absolutism of organized religion. A longtime lapsed Catholic, I am, generally speaking, leery of, have a knee-jerk suspicion of, any "God-speak." But who am I to criticize, spared as I've been of any personal need to seek such remedy? Whatever works is all that matters. And who can argue with the astonishing number of lives saved by AA—lives of people I knew or would come to know?

My brother, I trusted, among them. Why not AA, especially since no inpatient facility spot had opened yet. *Yet*, that ever-hopeful word, three letters from which the promise of a future dangled.

But AA certainly has its absolutisms. And AA-ese is not without clichés and catchphrases. Of the steps, only the first explicitly mentions alcohol—the recognition of powerlessness over it, the acknowledgment that, because of it, life has become unmanageable for drinkers who are, demographically speaking, all over the map. As depicted in *Drinking: A Love Story* by the late writer and alcoholic Caroline Knapp, they are young and old, male and female, the neglectful and the devoted parent, the chronically unemployed and, like herself, the successfully driven, high-functioning professional.

Going through an inpatient rehab program, followed by meeting after meeting of AA—the path I still envisioned for my brother—Knapp set aside her own step-leery suspicions. She'd already recognized that to not drink wasn't a question of gritting her teeth and getting through it, as if it were a particularly difficult workout regimen at the gym. What AA gave her, already an award-winning journalist and the author of one book at age thirty-six, was "a blueprint for living." An essential lifeline. A way to take hold, to be responsible and honest with herself.

I imagined my brother at the AA meeting, an observer at the back of the room, slumped in a chair. And though he'd been hauled there by his wife, who needed this long and probably exhausting day of a new normalcy more than he was ready for, Joe, I'd like to believe, achieved his first step. I'd like to think he arrived at a place of hope and fear with the belief that there he could be safe, feel connected, less apprehensive, less isolated. A place of belonging where he might find lost pieces of himself and discover what might still be possible. Proof that he'd not heard in his bewildering and sudden hospital discharge, "They've given up on me."

Even though he may have had little choice about going to the meeting with Carol, he'd kept his promise. He'd taken the first step on the long path. He'd arrived where, in the days ahead, as Knapp describes, "You do everything for the first time." You go out to a restaurant and when the waiter's first question is, "What can I get you to drink?" you don't order wine. You sit on the sofa, watch football with all its boozy commercials, and you don't pop open a beer. You celebrate an important birthday without champagne. You question your self-worth, get nervous or anxious, sad or stressed, lose your job, argue with your wife, worry over your mother's health, and you don't seek answers and relief in a bottle.

"One day at a time" is one of AA's simple—and complex—mantras. By attending the meeting, even if sitting at the back, unable to hold his head up, Joe already had a notch in his belt. But clearly it had taken so much to get there.

"He kept slumping over on me," Carol had said. "He couldn't hold his head up. His back had become so itchy again, he kept asking me to scratch it. And every time he tensed up, I was sure his lactulose was about to kick in."

However, there he was, still on the periphery but also on the threshold of a long journey toward the promise of a life ahead. He was there among the other folks at the AA meeting still facing down their own demons and taking it one day at a time, perhaps having relapsed but who were back to trying again, learning to channel depression into humor, whose battle involved physiological realities and not just mental will. Most of whom, my sister-in-law somewhat wistfully said, "looked normal, happy." People who'd gotten further down the road in efforts to turn their lives around no matter how much roiled beneath the surface. And what did they see?

"They kept looking at us," Carol said, her tone shifting, as though suggesting their looks acknowledged, "Oh, so he's one of *those* drunks." Still drinking, still relapsing, not serious in his "I'm trying" efforts. But undoubtedly there had to have been looks of concern and the potential outreach of welcomed-in support. The recognition, perhaps a glimpse of, "That was me," or more fearfully, "That could still be me." As seekers who knew what denial had cost them, of what had been sacrificed at the altar of booze, perhaps they looked at my brother and saw what was staring us in the face. To what, with our own denials, we'd been willfully blind.

"Hi, I'm Joe. I'm an alcoholic."

"Hi, I'm Joe. I'm dying."

When I look at the photo Bob took of Ben on his last walk on a golden, late-October afternoon, circumscribed as his walks had become—a short loop around a small copse of trees just off our lane—I see the nearly white muzzle of an old, grizzled dog. I see the nubby buttons of his spine pushing through, his tucked-up abdomen riddled with small, fatty cysts, his hip bones mere protuberant knobs where once had been powerful haunches muscling him through miles-long runs. He'd come a long way to that walk, a golden-lit moment fixed now in pixel and memory. I also see that Ben was at his end. He was, after all, just two weeks shy of turning sixteen, ancient in dog years, in the often heartbreaking compression of time that, by welcoming our pets into our homes, we must accept. Our beloved dogs that are not expected to outlive us. Unlike children, who are—and who, if they don't, offer proof that something is horribly wrong, irrevocably unnatural.

Bob and I had come a long way, too. Over the years, as Ben's hips and spine grew more arthritic and his getting around more painful, we advanced in treatment steps: baby aspirin to sea cucumber supplements to glucosamine to Rimadyl. We tried a few rounds of acupuncture, which seemed to help until the day, in spite of my coaxing, Ben stood, shook himself, and needles flew off, pinging against the tile floor, his message emphatic: *Enough*. Still, we carried on, massaging his hips, draping our heating pad over his dog bed. Long before, we'd already raised his bowl onto a small stool so he wouldn't have to stoop over to eat. In the final months, I also used a rolled beach towel as a sling to hold up his crumpling hind end in hopes he might eat in moderate comfort.

For so long, preceding what would be his final afternoon, I'd refused to see or, possibly, just couldn't see what, until after he was gone, I at last recognized. All the changes, small at first but incremental, adding up, becoming more serious: the repeated stumbling; the falls on the step into the house; the inability to haul himself up onto sofa or bed or into the car; the sudden onset of violent trembling when having to stand on the vet's slick examining table; and the time when, following some wild scent Ben had detected in the neighbor's yard, he'd ventured down a slope leading to the shore but couldn't muscle back up. Tumbling onto a stretch of slaggy slate, he collapsed on his side, defeat writ large on his face.

When you see things change gradually, it's hard to measure how far they have gone.

How vivid Ben's final day remains. Knowledge . . . anticipatory grief? . . . endowed it with particular clarity, like the light that day, an autumnal luminosity so stunning that, were you able to strike it, it might ring. The knowledge that after long, serious, and often heartbreaking consideration, we'd arranged for the vet to come to the house that evening and help us usher Ben from this life. As the hours ticked past, we moved through the day with an aching finality, a "take notice" looking and watching. I'd already begun my accounting of what I'd miss. Ben in blissful sleep on the grass in the sun or sprawled there, head up, his gaze fixed on the bordering woods or out to the bay, his nostrils, spread wide, reading the salty air, its universe of individual smells dense with information I knew nothing about.

When, finally, Dr. Plor walked into our living room, Ben made no attempt to get to his feet from his comfortable dog bed. He looked up, then turned to me with his familiar gaze. In it, no suggestion of fear, no look of panic or confusion, but rather, a mild curiosity, as if it to say, *What next?* As Bob and I lowered ourselves onto the floor to lie beside him, stroking his head, occasionally putting our faces against his muzzle, murmuring our familiar endearments, Dr. Plor injected Ben with a sedative. Almost immediately, his breath slowed, his eyelids drooped, his gaze grew less focused. The second injection would make his heart stop.

A longtime witness to so many pets' bloom and wither, Dr. Plor had warned us that the end might not come quickly, but in Ben's case, it did. His eyes closed, his breaths grew shorter, then ceased. After a couple of minutes, Dr. Plor removed his stethoscope from Ben's chest and confirmed, "His heart just stopped." And then, in the remarkable way that vets treat both pets and their owners, unlike so many doctors who sadly and too often attend a patient's failing body but too little else of what makes him or a patient's family human, Dr. Plor, looking out to the bay, said, "Oh, and look, the sun just set."

Behind Eagle Island, silhouetted in black against an astonishingly gold and crimsoning sky, the sun had indeed dropped. It was at the southern end of its mid-autumn transit. Little did we know what a gift Dr. Plor had given us. How, in the years since, any sunset we've witnessed in late October in that same spot has become a "Ben sunset." A reminder of that last day, a last heartbeat, the sun after a fiery show dropping behind the horizon like the click of a lid.

Emily Dickinson called hope the "thing with feathers that perches in the soul," that "sings the tune without word and never stops at all." By contrast, ancient Roman poet Virgil declared, "All things by nature are ready to get worse."

While expectations can help shape what comes, low expectations for the future can also protect us and be only inwardly hopeful. Hope for little and avoid much disappointment. Don't broadcast hope and perhaps we won't—knock on wood—jinx it. Or maybe we oscillate between two poles. Of hope and despair, hope and hopelessness.

In *The Death of Ivan Ilyich*, Tolstoy wrote that from the very beginning of Ilyich's illness, his life had divided into two states of mind. They alternated with each other.

"Now there was despair and the expectation of an incomprehensible and terrible death, now there was hope and the interest-filled process of observing the functioning of the body." But the further the illness went, the more dubious Ilyich became in considering his sick body. More real grew his awareness of approaching death. Ilyich needed only consider "what he had been three months ago and what he was now to recall how steadily he had gone downhill for any possibility of hope to be destroyed." Even among family and numerous acquaintances, Ilyich, now bereft of hope, lay in "a solitude none more total than which there could be anywhere." He saw the chasm between those who must contend with life's decline and those who don't. Frightened and suffering, he had to bear such knowledge alone. "With eyes weary from looking, but unable not to look at what was before him, he gazed at the back of the sofa and waited."

When hopeful, we look for signs. A comfortable morning, say, after a difficult night. A day in which things seem almost normal. Hope is leaven. It helps our desired expectations of fulfillment rise. As days click by with all their oscillations, hope is, hopefully, continually restored. It may amount to nothing in the end, the wished-for result, the desired cure unobtained. Perhaps it's been unobtainable all along. But how can anyone be harmed by hope?

With Ben, there was no hoped-for cure. There were things we could and did do to prolong his life, but we could not reverse the clock. Certainly, at times, when we glimpsed the possibility of a few more good months, we were buoyed by hope. But then, in the return to the irrefutable present, it could not be sustained. By the time Dr. Plor arrived, I was without hope that Ben's life could be prolonged. I knew what the life expectancy charts of dogs dictate. My only hope was that he be eased on his way. Hopelessness did not prevent me from seeing what needed to be done: picking up the phone and calling Dr. Plor, attending to what hope could not change.

My brother, I need to believe, had not ceased to hope. In the hospital, he'd told me about going to rehab.

"Yes, I'm apprehensive. But I look forward to it."

At the AA meeting, embellished perhaps with a dollop of my hopeful imagination, Joe's gaze was still turned outward. He was still looking through the lens, I hope, of hope. But also, like Ilyich, through the lens of illness and with an acknowledgment of reality. A recognition of accelerating diminishment.

What happens to hope in the moment we recognize we are dying, and no one can change it?

What happens when a sister, far away, has to admit—one of my most painful admissions—that perhaps I did not try hard enough, did not appreciate the urgency in what had to be done or, in the very least, failed to recognize the importance of being present? A sister who, compliant, readily allowed departure delays to occur, not because she still possessed hope for a good outcome but because she was a coward. Who must admit, *I did not want to see my brother dying.*

I used to think it would somehow make a difference if I could remember with specificity what I was doing when news of my brother's death reached me. The way I remembered my walk on our road earlier in the day or my repeated checking of the clock back at the house, approximating the time my father would arrive to check on Joe while allowing myself to believe that in the couple of hours preceding his arrival, my brother, following a bad night, slept comfortably in his bed.

But what difference would it have made if I could remember whatever tasks may have occupied me while I waited to call? Whatever constituted the mundane dailyness of an afternoon that in many ways seemed like any other, without a reason to commit it to memory?

I am condemned to not knowing. To not paying close enough attention. Of letting time pass.

So let me put myself in the garden, in the hot work of what had to be done there. Or perhaps putting folded laundry away. Would it make any difference if I was sitting on the deck steps shelling the last-of-the-season peas, the dinner hour approaching? There'd be no dialogue. Bob was away and I was home alone.

To not remember specifically where I was or what I was doing seems unforgivable, but to fictionalize, make it up, certainly a writerly thing to do, seems worse. Better to cop to another failure. I do not remember. I only know for certain I was not near the phone in the kitchen, and that, when it rang, I was plucked from some task in some other place. Lifting the receiver, there was no deus ex machina intervention. Only my father's voice.

"Joe's dead."

My brother had been of this world, and then was not. Hope, that winged thing, had flown.

Endless Loop

Sometimes you do not get to understand everything.
—Marie Brenner, *Apples and Oranges*

As planned, my father had let himself into my brother's house after Carol had gone to work. "Joe," he called out. "Hey, Joe. It's Dad."

Walking through the living room, he called out again. From somewhere at the back of the house, water was running. He walked to the master bedroom. The bed was empty, and the air smelled faintly of shit. Obviously, Joe had messed himself again and was taking a shower. My father stepped around the bed and into the adjacent bathroom.

There he found his youngest child, naked and crumpled on the floor of the shower.

"Joe. Oh, God. Joey. No."

He reached inside, turned off the water. He knelt on the wet floor.

Joe was on his side, facing the back tiled wall, his knees bent, his six-foot frame somehow wedged into that small space. My father could not see his son's face. Putting both hands under Joe's shoulder and neck, he tried to turn him. He couldn't. Of course not. My brother had become, in its truest sense, *dead* weight.

Still, that did not prevent my father from sobbing into the phone later, "Deb, I couldn't pick him up. I tried. I really did. But I just couldn't. I had to leave him there."

Among the bits that would keep coming, the layering of elements that would be added in the days to come, as though in an attempt to brush in every detail of a complex portrait, to retrieve from the ruins and restore the painting beneath, my father would repeat, "His eyes were open. Like he was looking at something."

On the night of Joe's death and many times in the week that followed, he would say, "The way his mouth was, it was almost like he was smiling." He would also add, "He had a small cut on his forehead."

No one will know for sure why this was so, but in my re-creation, in the endless loop that had just begun to form, I envisioned Joe pitching forward and hitting his head on the shower faucet before falling to the floor, a picture only fully formed if I played it again and again and in slow motion. That small cut I needed as proof to believe it was a hard collapse, the evidence of a sudden and swift departure. So quick that during the moment he's alive and before the next when he wasn't, there was no time to cry or cry out, no time for pain or panic or conscious thought that he was about to die. Pure body in its final struggles, the mind mercifully shut out of the contest, to the inevitable outcome. I had to pretend the last minutes of my brother's life weren't ruined by fear.

And then in what might have been his final recounting of his call to 911, my father would also say that after he told the dispatcher what he'd encountered, he'd answered "no" to the question, "Can you find your son's pulse?"

And how she'd then asked, though he'd not understood at the time why she did so, "And when you found your son, sir, was the running water cold?"

"Yes. Very."

I take no comfort in Joe having died at home.

He had no pain meds to ease the way. He was not in his clean and comfortable bed, a benign light slanting through the pulled blinds. Worse, no one was with him. If there are "good deaths," Joe's was not one of them.

During his last twenty-four hours, my exhausted brother went to church, attended an AA meeting, and shopped for sorbet. He died on the hard tile floor of a cold shower. Any attempt at physical comfort came later—too late—after the EMTs laid Joe's body onto the bedroom's carpet and covered him with a blanket. After Carol, joined by her sister and brother-in-law who'd all rushed there from work, sat on the floor beside Joe, cradling his head in her lap, rocking back and forth, exclaiming at one point, "Oh, your blue eyes, Joey. Ever and always the bluest eyes."

Seemingly endless already, the loop I kept playing in my head, like a tape reel that gets to the end and automatically starts over again. Pieces of a picture imagined and reimagined, like the painter unable to step away from the canvas, in a seemingly perpetual state of daubing in a bit more of this, a few more strokes of that. As though, if I got it all just right, every detail of my brother's last hour, its fleeting minutes, the how and when of a final exhalation, then the ending might change.

But how endless the questions, so many without answers.

Was Joe in pain during those last couple of hours he was alone in the house? But who wouldn't want to believe he was comfortable? From his wide, clean bed, hadn't he told his wife as she was leaving, "I'm actually feeling good, propped up like this"? Was there ease for him in that moment? Had hope, perhaps, reappeared?

What, in his final hours, was he thinking? Still somewhat

comfortable, had he drifted into sleep? Had he been urged awake only by the sudden lactulose-induced urge to shit, and not quite making it to the toilet, attempted to clean the soiled floor and himself, thinking, possibly, *Thank God, it's not on the bed*, before, beneath the still warm water of the shower pouring over him, he'd been overcome?

And by what? A sudden deep and searing pain? A gradual buildup he was struggling against? If sudden, wouldn't his fall have been even harder, as though from behind he'd been smote (Where had that word come from, but yet, doesn't it seem apt?) and thus rendering a deeper wound, a bloodier gash? Maybe it was more like he slumped forward, sank slowly to the floor, grazed his forehead on the faucet.

Didn't my father say, "He was curled over on one side. Like"—he barely got it out—"a baby"? Suggesting there'd been no frantic moments, no thrashing in the shower.

Or the bed. I will be forever grateful to Joe's brother-in-law who observed, "The bed was neat. It looked slept in, but the sheets weren't tossed. They were just pulled back on one side, you know, like he'd just routinely gotten out of bed."

But couldn't it also mean that Joe hadn't been in that clean, comfortable bed for long? Barely drifting toward sleep after his wife left before the merciless urge attacked? Or some sudden sharp pain that prompted him to throw back the covers?

Always, in the background, like a Greek chorus, "When did Joe lose consciousness? Did he know he was about to die?" As if this were the most important thing. The way, as with accounts of passengers doomed on a plane going down, my first thought is to hope for an explosion, a sudden loss of oxygen, everyone passing out rather than knowing with terrifying certainty as the plane plummets toward the ground that they were about to die.

Our preferred picture of death is often presented in movies or books: a gradual fading away in bed, a clean, slow fade. The picture we all find solace in painting: comfortable, pain-eased, people you love around you, a soft light, maybe some favorite music faintly playing. When a person dies in private, when we don't get to witness death happen, it may seem less real. Maybe, even, impossible. Especially if you're only told about it by a voice on the phone, absent any physical evidence of a body in a cold shower or spread beneath a blanket on a bedroom floor. A picture beyond, possibly, imagining. Or maybe beyond ever not imagining.

What I do know with certainty is that Joe's lifeless body was lifted onto a gurney.

Just nineteen hours earlier, he'd asked for two flavors of sorbet, the request of a man not planning on being dead. And that after whoever was needed to be called in had arrived, after the formal pronouncement of death had been given, my brother was wheeled over the threshold of his house where, in its freezer, the still untouched cartons of sorbet outlasted him.

III
AFTER

All Roads Lead to Rome

"People actually *want* to go to Arizona in July?" my sister, Chris, asked me.

"Apparently so."

"Do they know it's going to be one hundred fifteen degrees there today? One hundred fifteen frigging degrees."

That this mattered little was everywhere evident at a very crowded gate at O'Hare airport where we awaited our flight to Phoenix. There was no business attire here, no "road warriors" with another mandatory destination and a single carry-on bag in which, by rote, they'd sensibly packed everything they needed. Instead, families and kids, a bevy of tank tops and flip-flops, a mishmash of toys, pillows, blankets, tennis rackets, stuffed backpacks, and bulging canvas duffels. Standing nearby, three men in golf shirts and creased pastel slacks talked handicaps and clubs, their business apparel stashed, their padded golf bags checked. When her cell phone wasn't plastered to her ear, a woman shrieked at her kids, yanking one by the elbow until he howled. Across from us, a thirty-something in a Chicago Bulls cap, stained tank shirt, and baggy shorts sprawled across two seats. He slurped whatever was left in a waxed cup the size of a small bucket, his lap covered with crumbs and drips, his fly only half-zipped. A wadded napkin and crumpled food bag littered the floor beneath him.

"Why are they here?" I muttered to Chris.

"Everyone's waiting for the same flight. It's going to be very crowded."

"No, why are they *still* here? I mean, look at some of them. Look at that slob." I tipped my chin toward the sprawling two-seater.

"Why not take him?" I said, my jaw clenched. And with such vehemence, it shocked me.

Earlier, waiting for the arrival of my sister's connecting flight from Wisconsin to arrive in Chicago, I'd passed through security, bought a newspaper, and stopped at an ATM. I offered no pleasantries, no "thank you" to anyone I encountered. I barely squeaked out "Excuse me" when I came close to running over a young woman's sandaled toes with my wheeled carry-on.

I had felt spontaneously combustible, like something in a vessel that, if unstoppered, might explode into flames, particularly if I didn't keep my eyes down and maintain my focus on just getting onto a plane. Best to ignore them . . . all the people doing their jobs, some even admirably.

"Have a nice day," a cashier had said, handing me my change.

I stared at the coins in my palm and then looked up at her and responded, "No, I will not." But she'd already turned her attention to the next person in line.

And where were all these other travelers going? Didn't they know that all roads lead to Rome? That we were all headed to the same destination, the same ending? But here they were hurrying past, rushing, as though in an emergency or, perhaps, simply out of habit, looking anxious, their incoming flight late, their connection tight. Everyone mindful of time but for whom delay meant not a welcome stay but a dreaded interruption.

As I put one foot in front of the other heading to Terminal K, the people passing in both directions had moved out and around me, as though I were standing still, a large rock in a fast-flowing stream. Or as though, cutting a wide berth, they'd recognized me as something that, if jostled, might detonate. Here were people who looked inexplicably happy. Even a young mother wrestling her toddler back into his stroller, a blond, mop-haired boy who arched his body, thrusting his head back, his belly forward. Red-faced and wailing, he kicked his little sneakered feet. She, too, looked happy.

But of course. What would my brother—my now *dead* brother—have given to be one of them? Any of them? And all so much healthier than Joe had been. Or seemingly so, even the corpulent duo reaching for their greasy bags at Wendy's.

Stopping in a restaurant concession to have an omelet, I'd taken one of the few remaining tables. The bar was packed. At 10:00 a.m. As I waited for my food, I tried to pick out the drinkers. Who, perched there with his beer or Bloody Mary or with her bead-sweated goblet of Chardonnay, had a bum liver? Who among them would be dead within the year? Had Joe been sitting among them, would I have chosen him?

It's said that we cannot imagine the loss of health until it occurs to us. And that, once it's gone, the ill are always on the other side of an invisible divide. Like me on one side, my brother on the other. And now here, in this airport, another invisible divide separated me and these people whose brother had not died.

But how could I know that? How was it possible to identify the grievers any more reliably than the drinkers? No longer do grievers don mourning clothes that publicly identify them. Yes, the ill were often easy to spot. But those the fatally ill left behind were not. Clearly, some of these people at the airport had lost a sibling. Or perhaps a spouse, a parent, a lover. Or, worse, a child. Their losses not recent but further back, and so, presumably, they were more advanced in the journey of Whatever Comes Next.

The day before, the first morning Joe would not wake to, I'd opened my eyes and resented the sunlight that revealed the landscape unscathed, the earth unchanged. No cracks had erupted in the bedrock. No boulders on the shore had been heaved. Birds had not absented the trees. Heart Island still welcomed the rising sun's golden coronation of its uppermost spruce tops. The clouds over the bay were still willingly tinged pink. Of Joe's passing, no notice had been taken.

It had felt as if I were living in Brueghel's springtime scene, *Landscape with the Fall of Icarus*, at the moment when young Icarus plunges from the sky into the sea, as depicted by W. H. Auden in his poem about the painting, "Everything turns away / Quite leisurely from the disaster." The busy ploughman working his furrows may have heard the splash. "But for him it was not an important failure." The sun kept shining on young Icarus's white legs disappearing into the green water. And the passing ship that must have seen "something amazing"—a boy falling from the sky—"had somewhere to get to and sailed calmly on."

But this at the airport was worse. Particularly at this crowded gate with its hordes of vacationers with time to spare, whose business was living, leading their normal lives, believing they had time to connect, reconnect, make wrongs right.

Nudging my sister sitting beside me, I demanded, "Why not take him?" I again gestured toward the sprawling slob. My voice cracked. "Or"—I thrust my chin at the mother still yelling at her two kids—"how about her?" I was willing to trade them for Joe. All of them.

As though from somewhere very far away, an announcement

was being made. It sounded fuzzy. I couldn't connect the words. Suddenly, it was as if I'd forgotten how to breathe.

Chris squeezed my leg. "Come on, Deb. Time to go."

We were both on the verge of tears, of breaking down among strangers I was more than willing to bargain away. We rose, slung our bags over our shoulders, clasped hands, and joined the flow crowding the jetway.

I'd never liked driving in Phoenix. No recognizable landmarks guided me. The sun always seemed to blaze overhead, so it was unclear what direction I was heading in. The roads were congested and the drivers impatient, heavy-footed, prone to tailgate. I was grateful Bob was behind the wheel as we headed to the funeral home.

This was no motorcade procession. We weren't one among a long line of cars that followed a hearse, our headlights on, a card on the dash, a small flag affixed to the antenna, giving us special dispensation to run the red lights as other drivers halted, and for a time, were inconvenienced. Onlookers drawn to the solemnity but who also turned away. Confronted by funeral processions in the middle of a bright sunny day, it might be easy to seek a comforting reminder as hearses pass: Someone's dead. I am not. But Joe was our dead, and our dead was dear. *You're damn right we should get to ignore a red light.* Today, though, there would be no hearse. No coffin. Just twenty-four hours earlier, my brother had been burned up.

Bob pulled into the parking lot already crowded, mostly with SUVs. More appropriate if they'd been wagons and buggies. Marking the death of a forty-five-year-old man would have been more normal at the turn of the nineteenth century, when more than half recorded deaths were of children under twelve and the life expectancy was forty-seven. But as it would've been then, our job today was to remember. We came to honor the ancient agreement: the remembrance of the dead by the living. As witnesses to a life, to the difference it made, we gathered to commemorate and memorialize. A name stripped of context was only a name. Rituals were crucial to a life's narrative, to the stories survivors tell.

As a child, growing up Catholic, I attended numerous wakes.

But even among Catholics today, many of whom choose cremation, there are fewer wakes with hours of visitation. Visitation. Definitely an impossibility with the dead. The dead remain dead, regardless of the talents of the embalmer. The dead's features, no matter how carefully made up or arranged, never look the way they had in life, those eyes and mouths in nearly constant motion, opening, closing, signaling, speaking. Folded hands cannot flutter up and in a familiar gesture pat a stray hair into place. Nor can the dead hoist her legs up over the coffin's lip to dance the way she did when she'd last worn the same dress. The body of the dead can only tell us they will be doing none of this anymore.

"I'm going to the viewing," my grandmother would announce years ago, even if for a fellow parishioner she barely knew. "To pay my respects," she always noted. And, not so incidentally, as I learned at an early age, to give her and my aunts something to talk about over their coffee for days.

"They did such a nice job. Millie looked so peaceful."

"But why did they do her hair like that? Wasn't it parted on the other side?"

"I never did like that gray suit."

A good friend once told me her eighty-year-old mother wanted to be taken clothes shopping. One afternoon, they headed to the mall together. There, her mother ran into some of her pals and didn't hesitate crying out to them over the clothing racks, "I'm choosing an outfit to wear for my viewing." To which one of them replied, "Good idea. I've already selected mine. A pants suit, you know, just like Hillary Clinton's."

Defenders of wakes, visitations, viewings—many of whom, it should be noted, are in the mortuary trade—say these rituals are necessary for the healthy expressions of grief and to help survivors confront the reality of death. Even, apparently, if there's no body to view, if, like my brother's, it had been burned up.

Having parked, Bob reached across the seat, took my hand, and asked, "Ready?"

Of course I wasn't ready.

I felt like a visitor to a foreign land, an impostor who'd donned the disguise of the deceased's big sister. So distant had Joe and I become over the years, so infrequent our visits or unforced conversations, that I clearly hadn't even talked about him much. Some of my friends back home, when I told them of Joe's death, didn't even know I had a brother.

I stepped into the vestibule and took a deep breath. My chest burned, as though the air-conditioning wasn't working and I was inhaling more of Arizona's blistering heat radiating off the parking lot's seared pavement.

Instead of a wake or visitation, this was a memorial service or what was increasingly referred to as a "celebration of life." The life of the dead. The life we shared with him, cherished, to be recollected in words spoken in condolence or as elegy. Or more eloquently, perhaps, in our silent thoughts. A service in which we also brushed against another of mortality's reminders that tempted us toward a small, forgivable celebration of our own life and its continuance. Not us, such a service said. Not me. Not yet.

Just inside the door, two easels held large poster board photo collages. Among Joe's baby pictures was the blue card with his tiny footprints the hospital presented new parents forty-five years ago and the profile Mom pencil-sketched of her newest newborn. Joe's kindergarten class portrait, his goofy grin exposing the first of his chipped teeth. And another at about the same age . . . what, four? five? . . . of Joe sporting a black eye, the result of an accident or scrape.

Spanning the years, Joe holds up trophy fish and, later, hoists each of his two children atop his shoulders. Elsewhere, he reclines at a picnic in an alpine meadow, poses on skis, about to take off and schuss his way down a mountain.

I wanted to linger, but first, I had to find my father. Coming from a different side of town, he insisted on meeting here rather than driving with us.

"I'm going to look for Dad," I told Bob.

I didn't get far. A short woman with graying hair and silver-framed glasses was making a beeline in my direction. It took me a few seconds to recognize her as Joe's mother-in-law. Our paths hadn't crossed since my brother's wedding years ago.

She reached out and touched my arm. "You know, your brother was very selfish."

This was her greeting. This was what she had to say to me the second time we'd been together. And, on this occasion, I could only stare at her.

She fumbled, "He could have . . . He should have . . ."

"Joe was very ill," I said, turning, and knowing I was being rude, walked away.

Did she not accept that Joe had a disease? That part of it was physiological, not simply due to a moral flaw or a failure of character?

Did she understand that if he'd lived, gotten his twenty-eight days of inpatient rehab, he'd have struggled in recovery, regardless of the number of meetings or prayers, the depth of his willpower? With a scarred cirrhotic liver that may or may not be replaced, it wasn't just a matter of Joe taking control of his life. He had a disease *and* was being treated for a liver scarred and all but shot. She had to know that. She had to know that still.

Clearly, Joe was still challenging those who loved him. How much easier it might be to talk about Joe dying if he'd had cancer or a heart attack or was in a fatal accident. To anyone who asked how did your brother die, I'd yet to say anything other than, "He had liver disease." As my response for a long time to come, it invited askers to interpret as they wished, perhaps to fill in the blanks with hepatitis, a less shameful and fault-laden cause that didn't need to hide beneath the blanket of "liver disease."

We'd all come to this occasion with our memories. Some of them, perhaps the most recent, had left us feeling raw, our skin flayed. Other memories, older and long held, simmered, were no longer so easily brought to the boil. Memories, never all good and decent, can be filled with pain, diminishment, terror, even rage. And so it was with many of us at my brother's memorial, including his mother-in-law grieving for her daughter and grandchildren, who, despite all of her religious conviction she was usually so eager to hand out, was finding it hard to forgive. We'd all come with whatever protection we could muster to hold ourselves together, if precariously, for those who needed us. Our armor protected us but exposed our fault lines, obscured our shared grief.

Even my sister, talking about Joe, had said, "We can't protect people from their own bad decisions."

True enough. Joe had made some bad decisions. And I'd been

angry with him, too. But on this day, I didn't need to think of my brother as selfish.

Memories, I once read, can lose their power to harm if you let them alone for a while.

On that day, such words meant nothing to me. This memory of Joe's mother-in-law greeting me would forever stick and harm—the first words spoken to me on this day, by a mother who was here while the still-hospitalized mother of the dead was not.

I found my father at the back of the chapel. He stood before a long, linen-draped table. Here were artfully arranged framed photographs, a guest book, and other totemic items: two heavy silver bracelets, an unadorned wedding band, a small crucifix on a chain, and a chili pepper replica in a silver plate. Also prominent were a pair of well-worn Merrell hiking boots and a cap stitched with the insignia of Willow Air, a pontoon plane service in Alaska.

"Hey, Dad." I put my arm around him. He seemed smaller, shorter, as though he'd shrunk in the last twenty-four hours. At the airport when I'd hugged him in greeting, I'd felt like a daughter needing to stand on tiptoes. Today, our roles had reversed. "How're you holding up?"

He clenched his jaw and kept looking down. I could see he was fighting back tears. He'd already confessed, "I start bawling and I can't stop. I'm afraid it will scare your mother."

The night of Joe's death, we accepted his decision not to tell Mom about her son until after Chris and I had arrived in Phoenix. But the very next morning, sitting with her at the hospital, he began to cry and blurted it out. I can only imagine what details she was given, how much Dad told her about finding Joe's naked body in the shower.

Dad had confided, "At first, I don't think she understood. But then she got tears in her eyes. 'Joey,' she whispered a few times. I could hardly hear her. After that, she didn't say anything else."

Her keening had been silent. An inner primal wail set loose inside, reverberating off her rib cage, bouncing around like a pinball before it struck the bull's-eye and penetrated her heart. And there it lodged.

"I told her about the service, but I don't know if she remembers it was today. When I saw her this morning, I thought it would be better not to remind her."

Chris and I had been letting our grieving father call the shots, including his somewhat questionable wish that she and I not go to the hospital as soon as we'd arrived the night before, even though just before boarding our plane west, Chris and I had learned that some kind of new "heart episode" had necessitated her sudden transfer back to ICU.

"If she sees you before Joe's service," he'd said, "she'll be reminded of why you're here. Better to wait until it's over."

"How's Mom doing this morning?" I asked.

"Better. She's now stabilized. I still don't know if they know what happened."

Her son died. That's what happened. Her heart cracked open.

"They're going to keep her in ICU for now. Especially, you know, considering." He banged his knuckles on the tabletop. "Goddammit, the way they should've kept Joey there . . ."

He seized up, giving words to what we all felt. Joe's doctors were culpable, had been wrong to discharge him so soon. After all, wasn't he in an *acute care* facility? The woman doctor, the worst of them, leading the charge, who had said, "He'll never get a transplant." Well, she was right about that.

Culpable, and yet not one of those doctors or a single pen-wielding insurance agent denying coverage was here today to "pay respects." Meanwhile, my mother remained in that same hospital, amidst not just beeping monitors and a tangle of tubes but the painful reminders that not much more than a week ago, her son was in a room down the hall.

My hand was on Dad's back. I could feel a sob working its way up. Rising like magma through a fissure in bedrock, through the immense, unimaginable weight he was carrying. To say goodbye to a son. And doing it solo. Because his wife of nearly sixty years, now fragile, breakable, lay in a hospital bed on the other side of town. He was here today not to bury the past but his son's unknown future full of promise and possibility. What were the limits of that kind of grief? Couldn't some sadnesses be permanent?

"Just look at Joey's shoes, how big his feet are," my father said, not using the past tense or still refusing it, as he pointed at the well-worn Merrells. "When we brought him home as a little preemie, even those tiny booties your mother knit were too big for him."

He pointed to a picture of Joe and his son posing in front of a pontoon plane. "That's when he took Matt to Alaska. He really wanted to go back there soon." He picked up another framed photograph. "I'm glad they used this one from San Diego. I've always loved this picture." In it, Joe squatted before his son and daughter on a wide, sandy beach with a long-raised pier and wave-tossed surf in the background. They're all barefoot and carrying their shoes, engaged in what looked like a serious conversation, possibly the peaceful resolution of a sibling dispute.

Where were my niece and nephew anyway? I turned to look across the long room toward the rows of seats and was surprised to see they were filling up. Apparently, folks entering the chapel had been cutting a wide berth around the back table and a clearly grieving father. I spotted the kids at the front with their aunts and uncles. That was where we were supposed to be. Bob and Chris, already there, signaled to us.

"C'mon, Dad. They want to start." Heaving a sigh, he straightened and turned. I took his arm. He leaned into me a little, as though I was the steady one, capable of holding us both up. Gratefully, muscle memory took over, propelled us up the aisle.

At the front of the room was a carved wooden altar-like platform flanked by floral arrangements and draped with a simple white cloth. I was relieved to see it wasn't ornate, neither appliquéd nor brightly colored. This wasn't the aesthetic snob in me rising up but the girl who had attended too many Catholic services overwhelmed by gold gilt and heavy brocade, while Christ on a crucifix loomed above, his side still weeping blood and with at least one suffering saint who'd been flayed or boiled or torn apart by horses looking on. Atop the plain cloth was a squat brass urn.

Once again, I was reminded that I didn't know what my brother's beliefs had become. It seemed as though he'd backed off from the extreme views he'd expressed on our ride back from Flagstaff not so many years before. And if he had, would that have helped make our path into a future relationship easier? Only once, in a phone call before he'd been ambulanced to the hospital, he referenced his church and God's forgiveness.

"I know I've been forgiven," he said.

About the pastor and Joe's service, Carol had told me, "He's going to say a few words, give his blessings."

The short man in a suit, I presumed, now stood at the front, who'd combed a few long, wispy strands of his hair to one side in a futile effort to hide impending baldness, who seemed so pale—*milky* came immediately to mind—he had to be a complete stranger to the outdoors. He looked as though he'd be more at home in a small office cubicle hunched over ledger sheets than sermons or psalms. Hard to imagine much fire and brimstone coming from him. My fear of Joe's service being highjacked by evangelical fervor all but vanished.

As my father and I made our way forward, attention shifted from a young widow and two young children, their life as they'd known it unraveling. Now many pairs of eyes were on us. As we passed people in their seats, I felt penetrated by looks of curiosity, pity. Like a member of this gathering, memory was a presence filling in the void of the newly deceased. But there was another void: the missing mother. I had no idea who among these people knew that Joe's mother was still alive. To those who did but didn't know she was ill and in a hospital, unable to be here today, to partake and witness, I wanted to explain. It was as if I needed to provide a permission slip for her absence. No. Rather to clarify I was not a stand-in. I couldn't begin to fill those shoes. Not me. Save for some of the same stuff coursing through Joe's and my blood, I barely possessed the credentials to be here as Big Sister.

Sliding into our seats, Chris and I flanked Dad.

"Is that all that's left of him?" my father whispered, urgently tugging at my arm as he stared at the urn.

Perhaps this was the first funeral service Dad had attended in which an urn, not a coffin, held the dead. Clearly it was easier imagining a six-foot man in a long wooden box. But a foot-tall brass urn? Something you could pick up and easily carry in your arms? So unlike a coffin requiring six pallbearers. Or the heavy weight of Joe's naked body in the shower as my father reached inside, struggling just to turn his son's head and feel for a pulse in his neck. An urn was not big enough to hold his son or what might've been. Or to hold a father's grief.

"That's it?" he asked. I patted his hand. "It's not him" almost slipped from my lips.

Not Joe. Not the body that had propelled him forward for forty-five years. His evanescent and combustible body. What I was to believe was not just ash and bits of bone, but something else released, returned to the world, to its sparks of energy, its veils of dust.

Carol was the first to speak. She wore a fitted, gray, sheath-style dress. Always thin, she now looked almost alarmingly skinny. Her face looked drawn but was fully made up, her eyes more heavily lined in black than usual, perhaps an attempt to help camouflage her swollen, red-rimmed lids. What rote, autopilot motions must she have gone through this morning to get herself and her children ready for the day?

As she began to speak, her voice was strong and without falter. Protectively and carefully, she talked about Joe as a loving husband and father, a good man with many interests and a wicked sense of humor. Her children, directly in front of us, sat unnaturally still. Pressed close to each other, as though buttressed, they did not fidget, look down, or away. Though I could only see the backs of their heads, I pictured their faces, how both of them must be staring at their mother, their watchful eyes following every move and gesture, checking for anything that might be amiss. To them, her words alone were not enough. Now, her every intonation, every act would be studied, dissected. She was their rock, their compass, their single mooring line in a tossing sea. It was hard to say what they'd been witness to in the last several months, what they'd heard in just the past two days, but now they must trust her, trust that this single anchor had not been dropped into mud. That it would hold.

As I listened, I thought, *She is too young to be a widow, to have her life broken into halves . . . the Before, the After.*

Too seldom, I realized, I'd seen her as anyone but my brother's wife. Or as the sister-in-law of grating, unending diatribe and explication, her views unswerving, pronounced, and flimsily based. This woman, nearly three years Joe's senior who he'd met while in college, was the only girlfriend he'd ever had. And who was, I'd long believed, a major impediment in my having a relationship with Joe. But here she was now, a forty-seven-year-old woman with whom I shared a loss.

To acknowledge I could've been in Arizona before Joe died and was not suggested I could've done something, should've been able, perhaps, to save him. Did she believe such a thing of herself? Of what she could've, should've, hadn't done? All the questions and "what if" scenarios of After.

Grief, I was only beginning to understand, was intensely individual. I could not begin to measure hers. Nor could I know the depth of her anger, the breadth of recrimination. Or to whom or what it was directed. I had yet to know how deep was the well of my own grief. Or at what level anger at myself and my failings might top out and remorse rush in.

In life, we know both affection and hostility toward those we love, but it's hard to know how to be angry at the dead. We lash out at others instead, while perhaps at the same time, we idealize the relationship we had with the dead.

For Carol, me, our families, the anger and rage—at Joe, the doctors, the disease, at God, and, if we're honest, at ourselves—could almost overtake our grief. But not now. This was the time for recollection and remembrance. Here was where we did not allow painful memories of the past to overshadow our remembrance of Joe as a good and gentle and loving man. What bound us was this loss that had catapulted us into the same pitching sea.

Likely Joe's mother-in-law sitting nearby had also, at least for a time, banked the embers of her anger, what perhaps only masked heartbreaking frustration at Joe's seemingly self-inflicted erasure, his lack of control in a struggle that might almost suggest to her he chose not to live. I glanced her way. It gave me no satisfaction that she now looked stricken.

Though my sister and I had been asked to speak, we didn't rehearse. Our roles were clear, though. We were the duo who shared a different perspective of Joe than everyone else here. We were to shed some light on the boy from Illinois, our little brother of the deep-blue eyes, who moved to Arizona at age nine and became the man everyone here knew.

Earlier, my sister had said, "You should also read a poem."

I resisted. Nothing felt right to me. Not Keats with, "When I have fears that I may cease to be . . ." Not Whitman with, "If you want me again look for me under your bootsoles / Failing to fetch me at first keep encouraged / Missing me one place search another / I stop somewhere waiting for you." More suitable for this audience, perhaps, Tennyson's "When I put out to sea . . . / The flood may bear me far / I hope to see my Pilot face to face / When I have crossed the bar."

But any insistence on metaphor felt false. Joe was not at sea. He was not a tree or the grass beneath our feet. I had no idea where he'd gone, though the consensus seemed to be heaven. Or the more vaguely described "someplace better."

In his brief remarks, the pastor had assured us that Joe was at peace. At rest. Another example for me of language that fails. A forty-five-year-old man should not be at rest, but rather, hiking in the hills, skiing down the side of a mountain, throwing a baseball to his son, tossing his giggling daughter—"Again, Daddy, again!"—into the air.

Instead, my sister and I spoke only of Joe, of the traits and characteristics of a boy who had offered hints of the man he would become. His early love of animals, beginning with a hamster that he liked to carry around in a cardboard toilet paper tube. His desire to cultivate plants launched by the careful tending of beefsteak tomato vines twisting up wire conical frames in the vacant lot next door. The daredevil with a love of the outdoors who, at age four, played hockey in the neighbor's flooded side lot rink with boys nearly three times his age until his scarf, encrusted with snot, froze to his face and forced him home. The kid for whom a classroom was never the best fit but nimbly careened around on his Go Kart and dirt bike. The goofball who effortlessly made his classmates laugh, an early proving ground for his later skill and family role as a wisecracker with oddball humor and zingy one-liners, about which, given the occasional smiles and a spattering of small laughs, many of the folks assembled were familiar.

Our little Joey, I wanted to say, the preemie growing into the size 13 boots at the back of the room with a liver that was perhaps, as the result of an erroneous blood test at birth, already a ticking bomb.

I recognized how, though specific to Joe, so much of this was not particularly unusual. Common stuff. Chaff. But as Rilke wrote in *Letters to a Young Poet*, "Even if you found yourself in prison whose walls let in none of the world's sounds, wouldn't you still have your childhood, that jewel beyond all price, that treasure house of memories?"

Of chaotic summer weekends in Michigan. Of water lapping on

a foggy morning at Uncle Dave's pier. Not worthless at all. Not gone, quite. Not if we now remembered.

I could have also said that Joe and I had enough of an age difference that he was never the younger sib that, in the crowded back seat on family car trips, I might have wanted to shove to move over and give me more room. I was already thirteen when he was laid in a crib in the adjacent bedroom and I became more of a mini caretaker—the "little mother," my father once said. For a couple of years, as part of my summer duties, I babysat, wheeling my charge around in his Radio Flyer, reading what seemed like countless Golden Books when he went down for a nap. I looked out for him. I interpreted. A high school boyfriend and I took him to Brookfield Zoo one summer afternoon, and I soon figured out the translation of "hairy stuff" he kept tearfully demanding from his stroller was cotton candy.

And then, I could've added, we separated. I went off to college and, after graduation, leased a Chicago apartment with a trio of pals. The next year, rather than follow my family to Arizona, I became the sister who stayed behind. While Joe, I realized again with a stomach lurch, headed west at the same age as his son was now.

Matt, his firstborn, a quiet, good-looking boy with his father's thick head of hair, to whom Joe was devoted and about whom, in Matt's early years, he spoke at length and with elaborate detail. The son he took fishing in mountain lakes and hiking in the hills when he was not much more than an infant and could barely hold himself upright in a backpack carrier. The son who, too often, I was told, drew his father's anger in the past year.

But was it anger? Or fear? Surely, I had to believe Joe's anger was not directed at his son but at what was happening to him. And that when he saw fear in Matt's eyes—of Joe's illness and a powerlessness over uncontrollable acts ("Why can't Dad hold his head up?") and the way Matt withdrew, pulled back, as though he were embarrassed or afraid of contagion—it must have reflected back to Joe his own fear. Or was my brother, even if unconsciously, pushing his son away? Allowing the scar tissue to start to build early, a protective layer against an uncertain future? Or was it simply, purely, physiological, my brother confused, unaware?

In the row in front of the podium, I saw two small children already cast upon the rocky road of having to understand what it meant to die. Abby, in a favorite "girlie-dress," clutched a small doll and snuggled against her mother. Matt sat ramrod straight. His eyes had not moved off me as I spoke, as though to do so was to miss a crucial puzzle piece he was fitting together into more of his father's story. About a boy like him. I was happy to see his lips were closed, his mouth relaxed. Too often, his default was a smile—almost a grimace—plastered on his face. The preemptory defense: "Who, me? I'm just fine."

The bargaining boy who, if his father would only come back, would never again have to be ordered to finish his dinner, brush his teeth, go to bed. He'd do his homework the minute he came home from school. He'd try very hard not to get sick. He would not beg for new Nikes or a 10-speed. He'd never again cry or turn away.

And directly behind Matt, the son who has lost his father, sat my father, the father who has lost his son. A connection that now and evermore would bind them.

Also up close to the front, Carol's family, a large and stalwart phalanx, less splintered than ours, stretched across multiple states. Theirs a large, united front and we, the lesser citizens, meagerly represented. The blame, if fingers were pointing, was ours to shoulder, for what lurked in our bloodlines, our inherited genetic predispositions. Still, and though I was clearly at the opposite spectrum of their political and religious beliefs, I had to concede they seemed like decent people. Their caring for Joe had always seemed genuine. He was welcomed into their midst and among them he mostly fit, though at times their seeming cohesion in the face of our family's recognized dysfunctions grated.

Once, Joe told me with a brittle, derisive laugh, "Oh, they like to think they're perfect, but, trust me, they're not. Far from it."

Among Joe's in-laws were fathers, brothers, brothers-in-law, some of them police officers and veterans, owners of guns and ATVs, the men who would more prominently figure into Matt's life now that the man he looked up to was gone, the man who'd been gone for some time, disappearing into someone who could not hold his head up, whose skin turned bright yellow with jaundice, who could no longer accompany his young son to the ballfield, and who had put up no fight when that boy, a talented player, quit.

Pull up closer, I wanted to say to him, allow me to breathe words onto cold embers, to tell you what I know about that boy that is your dad. The boy that was once like you. I saw you perk up at the story about the rafts and reedy huts he and his pals made on the banks of the narrow river behind our house in Illinois. Let my puny contributions here today matter. At least to you.

And what, looking out and beyond Matt, were the recollections of the rows of people seated farther back? None of whom I knew. Joe's friends, colleagues, school buddies, neighbors. What were their stories? What could I learn from them about the man that was my brother? Who among them wrote the sentiment on the card attached to one of the floral arrangements, "So long to my friend Joe, gone to wherever it is the good guys go when they leave the earth"? Or had entered—maybe a ski buddy?—in the legacy book, "I'll remember you, Joe, where the edelweiss grows wild and the snow is deep"?

Who are you? I wanted to ask. What can you tell me?

But then it was over. Our hour was up.

The people I wanted most to talk to, who I'd likely never encounter again, were the first to leave, return to their jobs, their children, their to-do lists. Free to resume their lives, go out into the bright, blistering heat.

But isn't that how it always goes?

Once a boy fell from the sky, and quite leisurely, everything turned away. Even a passing ship "had somewhere to get to and sailed calmly on."

Next

"This is going to kill Mom," I'd said to my sister the night Joe died.

Still weak, still hooked up to monitors, still needing oxygen assist for her COPD, and though past the need for any more dialysis and now weaned off the ventilator, my mother still had little appetite, was still unable to get out of bed and up on her walker, her muscles, already compromised since her stroke, further atrophying at what I knew had to be an alarming pace. Over the past weeks, like a Greek chorus, we'd chanted our hopeful, repetitive refrains: "Get better. Get stronger."

But what were her motivations now? We drove to the hospital immediately following Joe's service. Not surprisingly, upon learning her youngest child had died, she'd gone full throttle into reverse. Now, further weakened and compromised, she might well choose not to fight. Though we would cheerlead, she might turn her face to the wall.

Wife. Mother. Widow. What is the word for a woman who outlives her son?

ICU at the acute care hospital was on the first floor. Fortunately, we didn't have to go far into the innards of the despised place that spat my brother out.

"Look who I found," my father said, leading the way into my mother's room.

"Hey, Mom," Chris said.

She and I were carrying two of the floral arrangements from Joe's service. We'd chosen the smallest of them, hospital-room scale, and not the ones on stands that shouted "funeral" or "wake."

"I told you your girls would be here," Dad said, as Chris and I stepped forward and approached Mom's bed in what was a surprisingly spacious room, if painfully fluorescent-lit.

"Beautiful." Her whisper was barely audible.

"We thought you'd like them," Chris said, "especially the snapdragons."

She shook her head. "No. You two. Beautiful."

My smile was too big, too forced, an attempt to blunt my shock at how she looked. A two-pronged nasal cannula was feeding oxygen into her nostrils. Though weaned off the ventilator, she was wearing a trach collar. It was hard not to look at the flanged neckplate covering the incision into her trachea and the small, stiff tube protruding from it, ready, it looked like, to emit some sudden alarming wheeze or to boom forth with a voice that was not hers. Various monitoring tabs were stuck to her chest with cables connected to several monitors that intermittently beeped. The oxygen tank against the back wall hissed. As I moved around to the other side of her bed, I tried not to bump the plastic catheter bag of dark, orange-tinted urine hanging from the bed's lower side rail.

She'd aged. Looking older than her seventy-seven years, she seemed to have faded, as though in the act of receding. Her thin hair was slicked back, and with nothing framing her face, she appeared cruelly exposed. Making it worse, she had no eyebrows. They'd not, of course, been penciled in. The inheritor of my mother's thin hair and nearly nonexistent eyebrows, I'd long before wrung promises from Bob and Chris that, if I were hospitalized, "Forget the clean underwear. Give me some eyebrows!" Clearly such absence was of little concern here but did contribute to her face looking pale and stripped, and to the sense of vacancy in her expression as she lay there and listened to us, not signaling how much she was taking in. At least someone had put in her dentures.

Time slowly ticked past as my sister, father, and I made small talk and tried to engage her while her gaze kept shifting to the flowers we'd placed on a small table in the corner. Even when she directed her gaze at us, it was evident her mind was elsewhere. To me, her face said, "Things will never be the same again." Not because of her heart surgery and whatever complications had ensued, or how, with each passing day that she was confined to bed, her disabilities from her stroke intensified, but because of *it*. Of what she could not bring herself to say. Her youngest child had died.

And we colluded, steering the conversation by way of the mundane to safer terrain, trying to judge how or when to dig deep into the dangerously unstable ground of the unavoidable subject that was of course Joe. We'd yet to get comfortable with it ourselves.

"Hi there." A nurse wearing bright cobalt blue scrubs patterned with yellow butterflies entered the room. She checked the level of Mom's saline drip, observed the monitor, turned a few dials, and wrote some numbers on the white grease board behind the bed.

"So, Leona," she said, "it looks like you've slipped down. Why don't I adjust you so you can visit better?"

Chris and I stepped away and joined Dad in the chairs along the wall.

The nurse, a blond, middle-aged woman whose quick, casually efficient movements inspired confidence, introduced herself as

Valerie. Lowering my mother's bed, deftly maneuvering around the various cables and tubes, she rearranged the pillows and bed pad, her strong, capable hands shifting, lifting, adjusting.

As she gave the light blanket a final tuck, my mother raised her hand that wasn't tethered by the IV. Touching Valerie's forearm, she said, "My son died."

And the air left the room.

After it detonated in our midst, none of the three of us rushed in to pick up the pieces. Only Valerie patted Mom's arm and said, before leaving the room, "I know, dear, I know, and I am so, so sorry."

As though this were a scripted scene and my mother's simple statement a minor interruption, she again retreated behind her expressionless mask, leaving Chris, Dad, and me to resume our roles. As what? Family impersonators, banal conversationalists? What if, instead, one of us had ventured close to the edge? "Do you want to talk about it, Mom? About Joey?" But the moment had passed.

My sister and I looked at each other, not sure what should happen next. We were mindful of my father's vulnerability but clearly still hoped he'd take the lead.

Visibly shaken, Chris said, "I need to find a bathroom," and headed out the door.

My mother watched her as she left. Increasingly, it had become apparent that watching seemed to have become her chief occupation. She'd not always been such a silent watcher. But in recent years, she'd retreated, moved away from active, attentive engagement. Watching was passive, more aligned with an absence of response, and possibly a trait of depression?

For nearly an hour, she'd been taking in our words and gestures, our attempts to give her some water or make her smile. Sticking with what seemed safe, I'd talked about Maine, our renovation project, the mix of birds visiting my feeders. Chris had talked about her newest mosaic projects and of her recent finds at Goodwill that should've evoked a shared recounting of their past jaunts to such favorite bargain-hunting places together. And, of course, Chris talked about Michael, her ten-year-old son, my mother's grandson. For a moment, there was a glimmer of connection when Chris spoke about the way he'd yet to outgrow his habit of collecting sticks outside, bringing them in to be discovered by my sister in his closet, in piles by the door, or as mashed bits in the washing machine when left inside pockets.

"Matt does that, too," Mom blurted.

Standing at the foot of her bed, lightly rubbing her foot through the thin blanket, I looked into her eyes, into a deep blue that by color alone linked mother to son. I tried to find my mother, but what of her was most familiar, recognizable, seemed now to lie deep inside, fiercely guarded. I still believed she'd not found true joy in a long time, but now, it was as if she'd fallen to the bottom of a deep well, lit only by a single flickering taper, and from this far-off, dimly lit place, she was letting the world happen without her. In the world as she once knew it, where joy might still be attainable, something was missing, terribly, unjustifiably missing. Down below, she might well become accustomed to a climate of dim and muffled emptiness, and to what, out of sight, she would not have to acknowledge.

Chris stuck her head in the door. "I think one of Mom's doctors is down the hall."

I turned toward my father. "Dad?"

"You go. You go talk."

I got up from my chair. As if denial had taken up permanent residence, none of us had yet to directly acknowledge why Chris and I were in town. Or where the three of us had been before coming to the hospital today. Or where the two flower arrangements had been obtained. Surely my mother hadn't really thought they'd come from a florist or the hospital gift shop?

"Deb," she said, as I headed to the door. "Did you take a lot of pictures today?"

I turned around. "Yes, Mom, I did."

"Good." And she closed her eyes.

I am not particularly patient. In that trait, I'm most like my father.

No sooner did we locate the doctor, a forty-something man with black hair and a dark complexion who was studying some charts at the nurses' station and to whom we only briefly introduced ourselves, when I asked, "So what's the status with my mother?"

Reading his name stitched into his light-blue jacket, I instantly recognized him as Doc Two—the Nice One—of the infamous trio that had treated my brother, and who, according to Carol, "seemed to actually care about Joe and took time to explain things." The one who'd promised, she'd said, "Your husband will be here at least a month." A prediction that was short by half. Or had he been the outsider, the low man on the totem pole, the odd man out?

He explained he'd been off duty and was only now studying my mother's chart for the first time.

"I'm surprised she's down here," he said. He thumbed back through the pages. "Let's see what brought her back to ICU."

"My brother died. Joe, her son. He was a patient here, too. But then you know that."

He looked up from the charts with what seemed like genuine surprise.

"My brother died," I said, much louder than I intended. "He died. That's what happened."

"Oh, I see."

"This place discharged him. And a week later, he died. At home. Alone."

Chris took a few steps back.

"I didn't know," Dr. Nice One said. "I've been away."

"Well, that's what happened. My father found him dead in the shower. And now my mother's back here." I almost threw in, "So, you see, you don't have to consult those charts."

"I'm sorry. I'm so sorry."

"He should never have been discharged," I said, and though my threat was specious, added, needing to, "but then, we aim to get to the bottom of that."

Lost

My brother's body had been fed to the flames. An urn contained what of him remained. I'd not been privy to my brother's wishes or my sister-in-law's plans, her only vague reference a particular mountain Joe liked. Perhaps there, one day, his ashes might be let loose in the wind. But where would the grievers go?

"I feel like we need to do something for Joe," I told Chris. "I don't know. Some kind of memorial. A plaque, at least."

In a few more days she and I would board a plane and head back east. Since Joe's memorial, we'd spent most of our time at the hospital. Most recently, we'd overseen Mom's transport from ICU back up to the second floor. While we read this transfer as a positive sign, I frankly didn't see a lot of difference in her condition. She still wasn't eating and only sipped a little Ensure. She still needed oxygen. A petite but leanly muscular therapist worked on my mother's arms and legs and with a colleague tried to get her up. All they'd yet to manage was to get her sitting on the edge of the bed where, propped between them, she nearly collapsed after just a few minutes.

Using the little digital screens of our cameras, Chris and I had shown Mom the photos from Joe's service. We dwelled on the floral arrangements and the easeled photo collages, calling attention to the inclusion of her pencil sketch of Joe as an infant. We scrolled past photos of the urn, the empty shoes. About all this, she said little, as though for a mother not to speak of her son's death might mean there was still a chance it hadn't happened. When she did speak, her voice didn't project. There was no strength behind it, as if some small, reed-like instrument had replaced her voice box, its notes small and private, meant for her alone. Instead, Dad, Chris, and I talked. Our favorite subject—how much better things would be once she got back up to Prescott and, of course, back home. We talked as if this was the inevitable outcome. No alternative had yet been considered.

My father, looking tired and beat up, seemed poised to accelerate into anger, one of Kübler-Ross's Five Stages of Grief, the one at which, if I were to accept "stepped" stages and programs, I felt I might get stuck.

Dad erupted to Dr. Nice One. "I don't want my wife here. Not here. No more. I want her out."

"I understand."

"No, you don't. This hospital kicked my son out. Now you won't let my wife go."

"We need to be sure she has stabilized and is strong enough to begin physical therapy in an acute rehab facility."

"We live in Prescott. I want her up there," my father demanded.

"When the time comes, I'm sure that can be arranged. There are some very good facilities in that area."

When the time comes. Looking at my mother, it was hard to see if that time would ever come. Still, I continued to hope that word of a transfer to a Prescott rehab facility would materialize before my sister and I headed east. The fact that Joe had been in a room just down the hall still repulsed me. And yet, more than once, I'd wandered down there and tried to see inside the room he'd occupied. Smaller than my mother's and directly off the nurses' station and elevator lobby, it was a bustling, clattering location that I couldn't imagine had offered him any peace.

"What about something at the Botanical Gardens?" I asked Chris. "Joe spoke about it a lot. And you know how he loved his cactus and succulents."

We took a break from hospital watch and headed out. This was my doing, induced by a feeling that wouldn't let me go. There needed to be a place . . . some well-marked place where in the future we could point to Joe's name, speak about him, and remember him. Not a cemetery or mausoleum certainly, and though a remote, windswept mountaintop may well suit Joe and honor his wishes, I yearned for some grounded, accessible-to-the-rememberers place.

As we turned into the parking lot, the heat was already punishing. Another day headed into the stratospheric regions of 115 degrees. We'd come early to beat the heat, as if such a thing were possible. The woman I spoke to on the phone had been courteous and helpful, suggesting that most memorials were in the form of a stone bench fitted with a small bronze plaque and the name of the dead. Actually, she substituted *loved one*, clearly the go-to substitute for the word *dead* that from whatever was scripted had been skillfully excised.

As Chris and I made our way to the visitors' center where pertinent information had been left for us, I was surprised by the number of other visitors who'd elected to come here and seemed much less affected by the heat than either Chris or I. By the time we arrived at the visitors' center, we'd sweated through the backs of our cotton shirts.

The Desert Botanical Gardens, we'd read, covers a total of 110 acres, about half of which is cultivated. Its focus: the plants of the

Sonoran Desert and, in lesser amounts, desert plants of the world. The benches in question were scattered along various pathways. Oblong, backless, all similar in size and made of some kind of red stone slabs. To each, a dedication plaque was affixed.

As we wandered the paths, consulting the map and finding the locations marked for future memorial benches, we paused to look at the plants. Among them, the usual suspects I could recognize without consulting the identifying markers: barrel cactus, prickly pear, yucca, and, of course, saguaros, the tall, stately specimens that were Joe's favorites. I liked them, too, especially the ones that marched up one rocky, scrubby stretch of Black Canyon on the route to Prescott.

Gardeners ourselves, Chris and I enjoyed visiting gardens together: Asticou Garden in Maine and Morton Arboretum and Chicago Botanic Gardens in Illinois. But this was unlike any other I've ever explored. I was finding it hard to relate, to attach a narrative. Nothing linked me back to my grandmother's lilacs, my mother's tiger lilies, Dad's Peace roses. I didn't even detect any smells, not that burying your nose in a needled cactus is recommended or brushing up against a jumping cholla. Here, the names of many plants meant as little to me as the plaqued names on the benches, one of which we collapsed on, fanning ourselves and draining our water bottles.

We'd come here to consider benches dedicated to someone's memory. Once I might not have understood their point. Perhaps I did now. And these were of stone. So enduring, right?

For several minutes, Chris and I sat without speaking. Light spangled through the thin branches of a palo verde tree. The meager shade felt a little cooling, but just beyond the limbs' reach, a brutal blast of heat awaited, ready to ambush. A kind of heat that seemed capable of melting flesh, burning up stone.

A place of remembrance seemed to me important, but here? This place? Did I sense my brother's spirit here? On these structured pathways among specimen plants or farther out among the mesquite? Might it not reside among those saguaro sentinels in the canyon that, over the years since my parents' move to Prescott, had so freely, naturally, demanded my attention? And who would come here? My parents no longer lived close by. Chris and I were on the other side of the country. My niece or nephew? Presumably their paths stretched into the distant future and could take them anywhere. What significance would Joe's name have to strangers plunking down their butts? And of the available places designated on the map, we'd found none beneath trees or even adjacent to an interesting, anchoring boulder.

"Let's go," I said to Chris.

"It's pointless, isn't it? I mean, here?"

"Yeah, I just don't see it."

"Me neither."

We began to wind our way back, walking faster than we'd come.

"*Eesh*," Chris said. "I don't know how they all do it. The people who live here. This heat. The absence of green. Sure, in spring, there are some desert wildflowers and the prickly pears will bloom, but, still, I don't get it."

The landscapes she and I favored were indeed harsher in winter but they gave way to green, were lush and fertile. In recent years, as I'd increasingly made the island my home, my green had expanded to include blue. Of the ceaseless lapping of water. The ebb. The flow. The reliable certainty of the tides.

"I hate it here," Chris said.

It had been hard for my sister the past several days in ways I could not know or fully understand. She had many reasons to dislike Phoenix, to be uncomfortable here. Despite her protests, she was hauled down here in the middle of high school, leaving behind her friends and the only home she'd ever known. Her memories of Arizona were not good, attending, as she put it, a "cowboy high school," where, with a keen interest in art, she never fit in. At home, she retreated to her bedroom with earphones and loud thumping music to drown out all discord and rancor that accompanied those first years of adjustment when my parents, at least my mother, may well have revisited the decision to uproot and move west. Marrying early and abandoning any plans for college, followed by a painful divorce from an abusive husband, all of which Chris no longer spoke about much, she experienced a life here that she left as soon as she could. She returned to Chicago, as a guest first in my city apartment while she looked for a job and a place of her own.

"I wouldn't have come if not for you," she told me then.

I don't recall extending any specific encouragement. Though I knew she was miserable, I'd not been fully aware of the potential danger in her situation. At the time she arrived, I was just navigating my way after my own first and brief disastrous marriage had come to an end.

I can't say how or why I played a part in her decision to return to our native Midwest, but I'm so grateful she did. I can't imagine now if she'd not. As we approached the parking lot, I stopped and turned toward her. "I love you, Chris."

She looked a little startled.

"Seriously, I love you. I need you to know that."

"I do. I know. I love you, too."

We reached for each other and hugged. Squeezed, actually, sweat and all, as though to imprint upon one another the same message: You'd better not leave me.

We all needed this. The full-body plunge into the deep end. The cool spray of the kids' splashing as my sister and I perched on the pool's rim, our feet dangling in water that here, in the middle of the desert or at least at the center of the vast Westin resort complex where we stayed, seemed abundant, without end. Even in the shade beneath the nearby umbrellaed table to which we'd staked our claim with snacks and towels, there was something cooling just in the sound of the pool drain's occasional gurgle. Most needed, though, was the energetic, life-affirming presence of my niece and nephew, Joe's young children.

Eager to take us up on our invitation to spend the afternoon at the pool, they'd arrived—Matt in a gray T-shirt and blue tropical print swim shorts, Abby in a blue-and-green floral cover-up—quiet, a bit shy, reticent to start a conversation with two women they barely knew. Now, they were like any two kids horsing around at the pool. And they were a team. As if they'd been grafted to each other, all the squabbling their mother complained about seemingly consigned to the past, they hooked arms and climbed aboard a large air raft, then hitched up to ride the water slide together. There were glimpses of Joe in his son as Matt attempted to stack two super-sized circular tubes, climb atop them, and cannonball off. Here, in this new place, unknown to anyone but Chris and me, they were free to be kids. Any kids.

"It's probably a good thing this happened while they're on summer break and not in school," I'd said to my sister earlier. They wouldn't yet have to confront awkwardness, any unkindness or unintentional cruelty in the direct questions posed by the other kids. They were not yet The Boy Without a Dad or The Girl Whose Mother Comes Alone to Parents' Day. Not yet the kids to be shunned because, if the unthinkable could happen to them—a young father dies—it could happen to anyone.

So early in their lives, Joe's children had suffered a blow that made of vulnerability a lived fact. No wonder Matt refused to visit his grandmother in the hospital. She was just down the hall from the room where his father had transformed into someone he no longer recognized. And how must he feel in his house? While taking a shower? Just on the other side of that tiled wall was where his father died, in the very house where Matt and his sister still lived, presumably safe.

Eating our snacks beneath the umbrella, they told us about the little pet shop turtles their aunt Jenna had brought them earlier that morning. Long in pursuit of a pet, preferably a dog, they'd accepted the compromise of tiny painted turtles. They'd yet to settle on names.

"Tommy," Abby offered. "Tommy Turtle."

"Speedy," Matt said with a chuckle.

"Oh, I know, how about Tiny?"

"They aren't going to stay little," Matt rebuked his sister.

Looking at me, Abby said, "We're going to keep them until they're big and then give them away."

Matt slammed his juice box down on the table and shouted, "We are not giving them away."

Abby's bottom lip trembled. "So are we going to keep them until they die?"

Chris jumped in, telling the story of the desert tortoise that Joe kept in the backyard of their first Phoenix house and the way, later, their rescue dog Cookie sniffed around in the shrubs until she located the tortoise and barked frantically if it had gotten too close to the hole in the fence.

Abby needed to use the bathroom and asked me to take her. Past the pool, a snack bar, and a pint-size kiddie park, we finally found it. Done first, she didn't wait for me even though I'd instructed, "Wait right here for me. Don't leave." Her disobedience didn't evoke annoyance or anger. Instead, it quickly shaped into panic after I discovered she was not right outside the ladies' restroom or even within sight. Quickly, I retraced my steps, returned to a spot where I could see Chris and Matt but no Abby sitting beneath the umbrella.

I did not know where she was.

How was this possible? How could I be so negligent? Such a simple thing—escorting a five-year-old to the bathroom—and I'd failed.

I returned to the snack bar and made a closer surveillance of the tables. I stuck my head into the pool toy rental shed. I took a swing through the gift shop. I turned back and scanned the pool deck. Things were looking a little wobbly, as though sunlight itself wasn't acting right. Everything was so impossibly bright, scorched, and brittle.

"Please," I said aloud, bargaining. "Just let me find her. Return her, deliver her to me." And in return, just what was I ready to give up?

To live is to worry. That could've been my mother's motto. A credo for her life's work. But now what? Now that her son had died? Did she believe she'd not worried enough? Or that her worst worries had been confirmed?

And then, at last, I saw her. My niece. Safe. I could breathe again.

In the cavernous, high-ceilinged clubhouse, in a side alcove of deep sofas and oversized upholstered chairs, she'd insinuated herself into a small circle of gray-haired women gathered around a board game. A covey of fussing, clucking women who'd absorbed this little chick into their midst, who knew nothing about her loss or mine.

"Abby," I cried out, trying to smother the panic in my voice.

"Is this your sweetie?" the woman seated beside my beaming

niece asked. An ample woman in a white polo shirt and bright floral capri pants with, I couldn't help but note, a wide and inviting lap. "We were wondering who she belonged to." She patted Abby's knee.

"Can I stay and play, too? Please?"

"It's a word game," one of the women explained, picking up a deck of cards from the large coffee table they'd hitched their chairs around.

"Okay." I smiled at my niece. "Maybe I can help you," I added, settling into an empty, oversized chair. Jumping up, Abby wedged in beside me. "But just one round," I told her. "We can't be gone too long. We don't want anyone to worry."

An hour later, we dropped the kids at home, intact, without sunburn, their new turtles named. They ran to the back of the house where soon we could hear the distant murmur of the TV. Carol invited Chris and me to have a seat at the dining room table. Over its surface, she'd spread out albums and photos.

Here was the good stuff, the evidence of a life I knew little about. This was a gift, her offer to take a look. But it also seemed to suggest that Chris and I, not witnesses, were jurors in need of exhibits to corroborate testimony. The photos and albums once carefully tended provided proof that Joe traveled, did satisfying work, had many friends, spent time in the natural world, in the kind of places we once thought would be the territory of his chosen profession. Here was confirmation that, for a number of years, he had a loving relationship with his wife, spent time with his children, was a father for whom his children had meant everything. His short life had many moments of bounty. But absent, as in the collages on easels, in all that photographic evidence of Joe running a marathon, skiing down a mountain, raising a glass at an alpine picnic with four of his pals, kicking up a plume of dust from his desert bike, clowning around at a pool, hiking a beach with his kids, waving from the window of a small plane in Alaska, was what couldn't be seen or heard—the wisecracks, the snap of wet towels, the toasts, kisses, hugs. The drenching moments of happiness, of life spread out like a banquet, seemingly endless, everything still possible

Among the piles of photos were small, lidless boxes. They contained cards, kids' drawings, old work ID badges, newsletters, keys, certificates, concert programs, ticket stubs. Ephemera. Among it, I saw no handwritten notes or letters by Joe that might offer a window. But how would I know? Did I have any clear idea anymore what his handwriting looked like? Carol signed all the holiday and birthday cards, transparently changing the writing as she signed Joe's name. Although last December, her name alone appeared at the bottom of the "Christmas letter" sent out when Joe was already very sick but word of its seriousness had just begun to trickle out to Chris and me. A letter that dwelled more on Matt having to be removed from a private Christian school because, with Joe ill and newly unemployed, they no longer could afford it. She acknowledged the support of fellow church members and her family but made no mention of my parents, with whom Joe was living at the time. As if they were somehow to blame.

I did not possess a deep love's easy forgiveness of my sister-in-law, but I knew I would have to learn acceptance. Eventually, perhaps, but it was still too difficult.

A family, I'd once read, is its own solar system that moves through shadow and light. Its members, like stars, dazzle, explode, fade away. Whether a happy or unhappy family, functional or not, it moves in and out of crisis and contentment.

How much could this family's structure and its collective spin stretch or bend or adjust? Could it accommodate regret or forgive me my neglect?

The solar system in which I was spinning would have to accommodate so many questions going unanswered now. It would have to make room for my interpretations, absorb absences, forgive my missed opportunity to love better. But what, too, in a rotation's stretch would forgive my brother for his mistakes and bad choices, adjust for his lack of engagement, his failure to meet me halfway, extend a hand, grope for the chinked footholds in the wall between us that neither of us, with encouraging shouts to one another, had attempted to scale.

Excusing myself to use the bathroom, I drifted instead into the kitchen. From somewhere in this room, I'd heard my brother's last words: "I'm not looking for anything." And here was the phone via which, with a continent between us, I'd questioned the wisdom of Carol's out-of-hand refusal of any emergency room exam of Joe's increasing back pains. Here, too, was the freezer with its two flavors of sorbet.

And then, as I must've known I would, I found myself in the master bedroom, where I'd never been and had not been invited. Shuttered against the light and heat, the room was dim, almost dark. At the center of the opposite wall was the bed luxuriously made up with a taupe, medallion-patterned coverlet, white sheets, and numerous pillows. Was Carol sleeping here? Perhaps still trying to feel the imprint of Joe's body on the mattress? Was there a lingering scent of my brother on the pillows? And what would that be? Something woodsy? Citrusy? Musky? Carol breathing it in, holding it against the palate like a fine wine.

I walked to the head of the bed and turned around. This was Joe's view that final morning . . . the wall of louvered closet doors opposite, off to the left a tall dresser topped with a phalanx of family photos in matching frames of pale wood, and to the right, a table and lamp above which ethnic bowls and baskets had been aesthetically affixed to the wall. All in shades of sand and dark taupe. Desert colors. Had my brother had a hand in any of this?

Once, about Carol's stylized Christmas tree in gold and silver with white twinkle lights, Joe had asked, calling up perhaps the tree we'd put up those long-ago Christmases on Oakdale Avenue, "One year, can't we just have a tree with colored lights and all different kinds of ornaments?"

Was it from here that, as Carol had reported, Joe asked her his final morning not to go to work? But also, when propped up against the pillows had said as she was leaving, "I'm actually feeling comfortable like this"?

Directly off to my left was the door to the bathroom. I tried to judge the distance. How many steps had he needed? Where had he soiled the carpet? There were no stains. Had they been scrubbed, the whole carpet cleaned, possibly replaced, every trace of his DNA where the paramedics laid out his body now gone? From the door to the bathroom, I could see that all tiles sparkled, the shower so clean it didn't look used. Where was the evidence that someone had died here?

The Order of Things

At the hospital on the morning of the day Chris and I were to leave, I kissed my mother on her cheek. Her skin felt papery, as though she were being sucked of all moisture from the inside out. I grabbed some nearby moisturizer and gently daubed it onto her forehead and cheeks, navigating around the twin tubes that still fed oxygen into her nostrils, snaked around her ears, and down to the hissing machine behind the bed. Someone had washed and brushed her hair. I leaned over and kissed the top of her head. It smelled of ripe peaches.

Propped on her small bedside table were a couple of new get-well cards: one from her sister in Indiana, the other from Dad's sister, Dolores, who still lived on Chicago's Far South Side. According to her carefully penned note inside, she'd been lighting offering candles at St. Jude's, praying rosary novenas, and asking the priest to include Mom in weekly petitions at Mass. At least someone had those bases covered.

Chris pulled up a chair beside the bed. I stepped back to observe the cozy tableau that if I were a painter I might want to capture on canvas. They were making small talk, but the curve of my sister's head and my mother's upturned face suggested otherwise.

Not since my first year out of college when sharing a small city apartment with roommates and working as a glorified receptionist at a Michigan Avenue ad agency had I the kind of relationship with my mother that involved daily conversations, sharing, albeit selectively, details of my life. Before unlimited long-distance calling rates, it had been harder to stay in touch once she moved to Arizona.

In the years that followed, I lost the need to consult. About my city life, I assumed she'd not understand. I chose to hide the shambles of my first marriage and a string of bad relationships that followed. By the time, at thirty-six, I announced I was marrying Bob, she'd become a bit player in my plans and big decisions. She said little about my about-to-be husband's fifteen-year age difference, though my now having stepchildren earned me some currency.

Later still, when I told her of my decision to attend graduate school and pursue an MFA, her only response had been, "Well, you've always liked school." And when my first short story was published and I sent her a copy, she acknowledged it by saying, "I like that you named the woman Evelyn."

Apparently, that was also the name of her best friend at the time. Over the years, it had become increasingly obvious that our previous closeness and the ease of being together had frayed.

We'd never been a family of big hugs and enfolding embraces, even if, for years, my mother nurtured the belief that we were. Now, perhaps, I'd become too easily convinced that to hug her risked some tube or cable detaching, my mother so frail she might break. I couldn't remember the last time we sat so close our bodies touched. Nor could I remember a time—though surely there had to be one—when, as a child, I was gathered to her, held, my face pressed against scratchy fabric or damp apron, and eyes shut, I nestled into that sudden warmth, its familiar darkness. Did that happen? And if so, when and why? I couldn't recall. And yet here I was, feeling suddenly that I wanted to reciprocate with such a gesture.

I refused to pretend my mother wouldn't die. But did I have to assume her decline was inevitable? That she'd never go home again?

"Get stronger. Get better," we urged, and she nodded in agreement. But based on her current condition, on the devastating dose of pain that Joe's death had heaped on her, and given the weather map of sustained, unbudging lows beneath which for years she'd seemed to dwell, I increasingly acceded to the likelihood that, though this was new and foreign territory to consider, her path might well lead from acute rehab to skilled nursing to long-term care.

"Your mother calls out in the night," a nurse had informed me, taking me aside in the hall as we approached her room. "I think she's having a lot of bad dreams."

Yes, probably vivid, recurrent dreams. Hard for me to imagine what shape they took, the images that might portray what in words she couldn't or wouldn't articulate. Perhaps she sometimes woke as though in a fog. A fog without atmospheres or lusters, without an occasional lifting. A fog that concealed, in which no bell buoy or foghorn shaped the distance, offered direction through a narrow passage, or told her whether she was coming ashore or drifting farther out to sea.

Chris got up to raise the volume on the wall-mounted TV. Out in the hall, there was the usual paging of doctors on the intercom, the clatter and clank of carts. The med cart I'd come to recognize by the rattle of its one wobbly wheel. How little the sounds of the outside world penetrate a hospital's interior and the busyness of its corridors. And yet, so often, hospital corridors shaped a part of a family's history. The births, illnesses, surgeries. Elective tonsillectomies or life-saving transplants. Easy-breezy procedures or harrowing close calls. Deaths sudden or prolonged.

On the TV, Chris had found *Antiques Roadshow*, a program my mother had always loved. Even now, she seemed engaged, watching a woman waiting to find out if her $10 garage sale purchase was an authentic Tiffany lamp. But was she really watching? Or had she embarked to wherever her mind took her, somewhere her body could not go?

I scraped a chair across to the other side of her bed. I lifted her hand and gently massaged it with some of the moisturizer. She looked down at her hand, then up at me.

"Nice," she said. "Nice." And closed her eyes.

My sister went on staring at the TV, and as though finding out the lamp, indeed a fake, was the worst possible news, tears pooled and silently streamed down her face.

The order of things, we were discovering, was disrupted, out of whack. A part of our identity, like the wings of a butterfly with its intricate, identifying design, had been ripped away. My mother had lived through the death of her preemie firstborn and, many years later, her mother, a death I'd come to recognize had not been openly or, probably, fully mourned. Now, so late in life, she'd lost her Joey.

And here I sat, no longer a sister to Joe. Nor did I feel any longer like my mother's child.

In the new order of things, I could not be the child who needed comfort and guidance. I was the eldest. I was older than my brother would ever be. Something new was now expected of me.

But how could I be the comforter, the one to turn on the night-light and beat back the dark? I didn't feel tall enough to reach the switch.

After packing up for our flight home, I consulted my laptop. My inbox was swamped with unanswered emails, many of them from friends and colleagues who'd learned of my brother's death. So many well-meaning wishes. So many offers of help.

My stepchildren, now adults, some with children of their own, had been calling Bob for updates, relaying their messages of love and concern. They'd also, of course, reached out to me, often by way of emails, a safer terrain, perhaps, where words are thought out and carefully chosen and, before hitting "send," can be edited or deleted. I did not fault them for any tentativeness as they sought the right word and tone to offer comfort. This was a territory new to them. Perhaps they assumed I'd had more experience in all this.

A death was frightening, particularly when it hit close to home. In writing to me, formulating their words, they inched out onto thin ice as, presumably, they were reminded of their father's mortality. But I would not go there. Anticipatory grief, I'd come to learn with certainty, does not prepare you for the real, terrifying thing. There was no practice. And age, I'd been cruelly reminded, had so little to do with it. Death came calling whenever it chose.

"Why?" we may demand.

The simple answer: "Why not?"

Such recognitions had renewed my yearning to return to the island, to our familiar woods and tide-lapped shoreline, to the peace of wild things. Scrolling through my emails, I clicked on only a few. To a colleague and a fellow committee member who did not know I was in Arizona or why but was looking for my input on an upcoming meeting's agenda, I began to explain, "I am in Arizona. I have lost my brother." Quickly, I hit "delete." I, too, was tentative. I, too, still chose my words warily.

Dead. Die. The words we dare not speak.

Just a few months previous, a friend, having read my recent, newly published poetry collection, observed, "You write a lot about death."

"Loss," I corrected her.

"Okay. Loss. Death. Sort of the same thing."

But now I knew.

You lose your keys. You lose a credit card and go into a panic. Your young dog chases a deer from your yard and, far away in unfamiliar territory, becomes lost. Despite your best efforts, you lose a tennis match. Or, working at your desk, you lose track of time.

Your brother dies. He is dead, not lost. You will not find him in a pocket. A store will not call to tell you that he's been turned in and you can pick him up. A kind couple consulting ID tags on a collar will not return him to you. Nor will you find him being cossetted by a circle of sweet, gray-haired ladies.

Amidst a lot of hugs and handholding, Chris and I said our goodbyes to Dad.

"Go," he said, finally, throwing up his hands. "Go or you'll miss your flight."

There was little chance of that, but he'd always worried about time and traffic, the best route, all the anticipated turns and lane changes. "Remember, stay left as soon as you merge onto 110. The exit ramp you need is the first one. It comes up soon. And it's on the left."

Safe in his element, he was fretting about time, mapping out our route. I let him repeat himself for the third time. He needed to feel useful to someone. Worrying about our departure, he was a father doing what came naturally. He was not a man forced to watch the decline of his wife of nearly sixty years. The man who had already lost not just his son, but, as he had confessed, choking back another sob, "He was my best friend. My best friend, Deb, my fishing buddy."

"Go," he now instructed. "Or you'll be late."

I, too, repeated myself, assuring him we'd talk by phone as often as he'd like, that I'd be back soon, meaning what? Two weeks, two months, or in spite of the three flights it'd take me to get to Prescott from Maine, at the drop of a hat? As soon as Chris and I drove off, he'd take the elevator to the second floor and wait for one more procedure, another test result, for the one step closer to Mom returning home and to whatever would follow.

Whenever I'd left Arizona before, my mother tearing up, my dad focusing on the drive ahead of me, I felt vaguely sad coupled with a stab of . . . regret? Guilt? Of not making more of our visit? Was it relief I felt in getting away, returning to my life, to my "real self" and not some previous, more recognizable and less threatening version I needed to be in order to fit in? And so, in a way, I'd not been fully present but just managed my way through another visit? And yet I'd also felt I was leaving something behind. Something I'd again not worked hard enough to retrieve.

At the airport, my sister and I talked little, each of us lost in our private thoughts as we boarded the plane and left behind my mother's uncertain outcome, my father's battle fatigue that surely sometime soon would need respite. So much had yet to be determined. Anything could happen.

But this I knew for sure. As Chris and I buckled in and the plane took off, I was flying away from what had been my brother's home since he was nine. Away from the schools he attended, the streets he drove, the restaurants he ate in, the places where he worked, the house where he lived, the children he loved. Away from the mountains where he hiked and skied, from lakes where he fished with his dad, and from the disappearing expanses of desert he lamented. Away from the coddled cacti he planted in his yard, the garden wall and kiva he built there. Away from his clothes closet, the fleece vests, jackets, and shirts that still held his smell. The shoes and boots, so big but empty, difficult to fill. Away from the home office desk where he sat when we talked in long, rambling conversations those last weeks. Away from the busyness and noise of the hospitals, one offering the hope of transplant, another that turned him out. Away from the rooms in his house, the dark walls and decor his wife chose but said little about him. The bed so high it must've been painful for him to climb into or out of that final morning. That big white bed, his last clean place. The short but long distance between it and the shower where he collapsed. The carpet he soiled trying to get there. The place—somewhere on all that tile—where he hit his head. The floor, the drain, that small, hard, angular space.

What the Living Do

I've been thinking: This is what the living do.
—Marie Howe, "What the Living Do"

You drive in traffic. Try not to complain about the weather. Prepare pancakes but forget to flip them until they've become scorched discs. Look at your watch. Recognize you're about to be late again. Wish you'd bought hand cream. Wish you'd scheduled a haircut. Eat when you have no appetite. Compose future emails in your mind that are never sent. Realize you've read the same paragraph three times and can't remember a single word. At your desk, you stare at a blank page. You look in the mirror just to be assured that, yes, you look normal. Wonder why the phone does not ring. Hate it when the phone rings. Sleep, or try to. Wake up, remembering.

Increasingly, you resent the many ways language attempts to pretend death is not the terrible thing it is.

Gone. Lost. Passed away.

So many euphemisms and jargon. A lexicon trying to make the forever neverness of death somehow more palatable.

Laid to rest. At rest. At peace.

So many ways to avoid *died* or *dead.*

You make Monday the day by which time gets measured.

Monday, the afternoon of Joe's death. Now, counting off. One week since Monday the afternoon of. Two weeks since Monday the afternoon of. Inescapably, weeks accrue into a month.

Acknowledge there will be days like this . . . thinking you may hear his recorded voice, dial his cell phone but get only a robotic, machine-made response, "Message box is full." Whisper into the phone, "I love you." Understand there is no chance of getting a reply.

And days like this . . . the electrician stops by to talk about a proposed generator as part of your house's renovation plans. Plans for a future you are so certain you will have.

Discover, regrettably, that the ways to play the If Only game seem almost infinite.

If only geographical distance hadn't been a factor.

If only you'd gathered and pulled tighter those slender threads that over the years had unraveled.

If only in the If Only game, there were fewer occasions to need the adverbs *better* and *harder*, especially in conjunction with the verb *try*.

Vow never to tell anyone, "Time will heal," or "Life goes on." Or suggest they need a "stiff upper lip."

Reject metaphor. The sea. A wall. A flame. Whatever survivors insist they need to scale, swim through, keep alight.

Move faster through the grocery store's frozen food section. Accept that you will no longer eat sorbet.

Head Above Water

"I think I'd like to get a dog," Bob said over breakfast one morning in late July. It wasn't the first time he'd made this pronouncement since the death of our beloved Ben a few years before. But given our desire to travel, and now embarking on a major renovation of our Maine house at the same time we were considering a downsizing move into a Chicago city apartment, we both understood it wasn't the time to bring a dog into our lives. Still, that didn't prevent him from occasionally testing the waters.

"Maybe a dog *is* what you need," one of two friends offered later the same week as we finished our lunch on the deck of one of the seasonal island restaurants overlooking Stonington Harbor.

For some reason, I'd thought it was a good idea to bring up the subject. And now, I realized, this was the closest we'd gotten to nibbling around the raw edges of "So, how are you doing?" A question that, since returning from my brother's memorial service, I couldn't yet answer. Luckily, few people asked it outright. If they did, they'd likely not be ready for unfinished sentences and groped-after words, or for my complicated, looping answer that might wind up in silent, choked-back tears. A few people asked directly, "So what did he die of?" A question I still had trouble answering.

What had become increasingly clear since my return from

Arizona was that I'd become a woman of contradictions. Tired and scratchy-eyed, I yearned to sleep through the night. Awaking from a surprisingly deep sleep, I felt guilty of some kind of "How could you forget?" betrayal. Choosing to be alone, I wanted people to stay away. Alone, I was surprised people didn't call.

Lingering after our lobster rolls and crabmeat salads, as fishing boats out since 4:00 a.m. began to chug their way back into harbor, I listened as my lunch companions talked about who they'd recently seen and where, often in places and at events I'd intentionally avoided. Never mind that I'd likely have declined them, I was struck by the absence of invitations coming my way.

Maybe this was all part of what I was beginning to understand as our contemporary American desire to avoid looking at death, even if obliquely.

Like so much else, grief is privatized. It plays out behind closed doors. But without such rituals or conventions, without a guide or handbook, people are unsure how to act or what to say to the grief-stricken. Perhaps feeling inadequate, they don't know how to help.

I'd been guilty myself. I'd resorted to the carefully penned note on a card dropped in the mail or to being one of several recruits who anonymously deposited casseroles on a kitchen counter. Hanging back, we hide behind the belief, "I didn't want to bother you."

I was not previously acquainted with the corrosive powers of grief and sadness. And my family had not offered much by way of example. The mourning of my mother's mother's death decades before had seemed to commence with the announcement of her death and conclude when the funeral was over. At age twelve, I either didn't recognize my mother's private grief or was too selfish and self-involved to cast an eye much beyond my own sphere. Now I had to accept that no matter how well-intentioned, many people, perhaps not wanting to be reminded of their own painful losses, prefer that grief, death's sidekick, remains invisible. It's up to the mourners to take the lead. People wait for the signals we send.

But then there are those who know just what to do.

One warm afternoon, my eighty-year-old friend Charlotte stopped by, solely, it seemed, to sit on our deck with me, hold my hand, and let me talk. Many weeks later, when I thanked her for being present, she said, "I was ten when my mother died. I was at camp and I was summoned to the phone. My aunt delivered the news. After, when I returned to the bunkhouse, a young counselor—Betty, I'll never forget her name—came in and sat on the edge of the bed. She was, what, maybe seventeen? But she did not shy away from simply sitting and being quiet. Until, looking down at my raggedy hands, she asked, 'Shall I clip your nails?' It was a beautiful day. The sun was streaming through the windows. I was waiting for my uncle to come pick me up, and Betty, slowly and carefully and in the most gentle way possible, trimmed my nails. It remains one of the kindest, most meaningful gestures in my life."

And my friend Bruce, who earlier on the day of my return from Arizona and my brother's memorial had driven from the mainland to the island to leave at my door a small glass jar with three of the most perfect poppies I'd ever seen. At their peak, the salmon-colored petals, even in the encroaching dark, seemed almost luminous, as though from within they pulsed with light. On a white card, in his precise architect's script, a simple note: "Thinking of you."

And then there was Cynthia, who, a few days later, agreed to accompany me to a local arts organization's scholarship benefit. Bob had to be away for work, but I felt I should attend. That night, after pulling into the parking lot, she and I sat in her car, talking.

Surprising myself, I told her about how my father had found my brother's body in the shower. "And the memorial service . . ." I began.

"Yes, okay, but tell me about him, your brother," she said.

No one had asked me such a thing, but, as though I'd somehow expected such a gesture—to be asked about the person Joe was in life—my words poured forth. We never made it inside.

Gesturing toward the auditorium where the cocktail hour was in full swing, she said, reaching for the ignition, "I don't think you need whatever's going on in there, do you?"

"How is your mother?"

Perhaps this was the easier question for people to ask. And at least I was able to offer a few new facts that she'd at last been moved to a skilled nursing facility in Prescott and seemed to be doing better. How much better was hard to say, though now they could get her up and into a wheelchair. And she'd begun therapy. My father visited her every day, grasping any slender thread of promising news. I knew he also sought the support and sympathetic understanding of the nurses and therapists, even the receptionist where he daily signed in as a visitor. He'd already become a fixture, greeting other patients by name, asking staff members about their families.

"Your dad should've been a barber or a bartender," my mother once said. "He'll talk to anyone."

It wasn't easy for my father and me to comfort each other. Geographical distance was certainly a factor, but his inability to use the computer and unwillingness to learn or to connect via email or shared photos meant that, once again, we had to rely on the phone. I had hoped, as time passed, that he and Mom would talk about Joe, to support each other as they grieved. But—and this was unusual for my father—he was letting my mother take the lead, and she made only occasional reference.

Surely, if anyone did not partake in any ceremonies or customs of ritualized grief, it was my mother. Hospitalized, she'd not been present at the memorial service to hear the words spoken about her son or to receive any solace in the condolences offered by people for whom Joe's life had meaning. The mother who would've been at center stage, all eyes on her, had been absent. Unable to witness, she had to rely on our photos and retelling, our words and images as substitutes for her own. And now she wasn't even at home among the familiar places where in her mind's eye she might glimpse her son. Where, some mornings, she might find momentary joy in watching the quail bob down the hill to peck at the corn Dad tossed toward the back fence line. Her lovingly tended home where clothes needed to be laundered and meals cooked, all the customary, recognizable tasks that might, with time, reshape themselves into what was once normal, routine.

But maybe all that meant little to her now. Maybe, contrary to everything we thought at the time, she found a hospital bed a saner and safer place to retreat. Perhaps it was less scary to go into free fall if you're already immobilized and flat on your back. Maybe she was grateful she didn't have to attempt to respond to consolers. Maybe she was grateful not to have seen the urn. The last time she saw her Joey, he was alive. Now he belonged to her in withheld, deeply buried thoughts and—"Your mother calls out in the night."—her recurrent dreams.

"How is your mother?" friends and colleagues asked. I could report that, physically, she was doing better. Having moved to skilled nursing, she'd already beaten the odds. Close to 80 percent of patients in an acute care facility ICU die. But many of the women asking me were mothers of sons themselves. Their asking, "How is your mother?" meant something else.

As for me, in the weeks following Joe's death, I was often churlish, peevish. Some days, easily irritated, I possessed not a shred of patience with store clerks, other drivers, friends who were running just a few minutes late, even inanimate objects. One night, cleaning up after dinner, when pan lids wouldn't fit back into a drawer, I banged, shoved, swore, then one by one hurled them onto the floor and stormed out of the kitchen. I kicked my garden shovel when it wouldn't stay propped in the corner of the shed. I made no attempts, as I would have previously, to salvage a cake whose only crime was to come out of the oven a little lopsided.

Bob bore the brunt of it. He steered clear of loud clattering in the kitchen. He accepted my sudden eruptions. As I wrestled with a paper jam, he stepped in and rescued the printer from imminent destruction. He knew when not to interject an opinion. But then he knew better than anyone how to read the cues. He could tell the good days from the bad ones with my ramped-up nitpicking, criticisms, and a general disagreeableness favorable to sniffing out whatever might lead to an argument.

Anger, I knew, was understandable and predictable. It's ranked as part of the process in Kübler-Ross's Five Stages of Grief, as though there's an orderliness and not an unsequenced, nonlinear mess.

Anger, for a time, deflects grief. It feels better to be angry at someone or something, like the doctors and hospital I still held to blame, the insurance agents denying claims.

But much less forgivable was the anger that some days I felt toward my mother. I resented that she was not at my father's side. That she was not a fellow participant. Surviving grief was not his—our—job alone. At times, it even felt to me her absence was willed and, irrationally, that her complications and slow, precarious recovery were intended to deflect from our grief, from whatever sloppy process we each had to go through and was now diluted by our concern and worry over her survival. Worse, each day we rooted from the sidelines in a contest I wasn't sure she wanted to win.

"How is your mother?"

As a sailing friend would say to me later, someone I'd not thought particularly adept at metaphor, "There are no nautical charts for navigating through grief."

My family had sailed into new, uncharted waters and our ship had slammed up against the rocks of a beloved's sudden death. Tossed into the pitching sea, we had no choice but to strap on the life jackets and try to save another survivor, keep her head above water.

What Remains

Things are as they are in present because other things happened in the past.
—Mary O'Reilly, *The Love of Impermanent Things*

The discovery was pure serendipity.

One bright but unseasonably cool August afternoon, as I meandered home from errands by way of a lightly traveled island back road bordered by dense woods, three deer bolted from the trees, an explosion of clattering hooves and white upraised tails crossing the road in front of me. I slammed on the brakes. Just a few feet away, one of the deer paused at the wood's edge and turned toward me, before, with a tail flick, it bounded into the trees. I inched my car forward.

No discernible trail marked where the deer had disappeared. But there was an opening among the trees, and it seemed, a sort of narrow path. Not unlike the kind I sometimes found traversing our property among the spruce trees, with its telltale signs of bent bracken and moss, small, scuffed-up piles of old leaves and scattered pellets. The subtle reveals of the deer's innate competence as they high-stepped smoothly, almost silently, through the forest.

For some reason, even though I had a few groceries in the back seat, I felt an urge to follow the deer. Not that I was a fan. Deer were plentiful on the island, abundantly so. Near collisions had become commonplace. With fewer hunters and predators and more islanders planting gardens in which the deer brazenly grazed, the population had swelled. They were my nemesis. Each summer, I sprinkled dried coyote urine, dropped mothballs, sprayed repellent, rigged up fencing, strung little flags of aluminum foil strips. Still, they managed to shear the lilies, devour an entire season's phlox and asters, munch on young rhododendron buds just as they were about to bloom.

My interest had nothing to do with them. This road passed through an unfamiliar stretch of woods with what looked to be few houses. I was curious about the possible path and where it might lead. I pulled over onto the narrow shoulder and parked. What had looked like a path didn't take me far. Soon, I found myself in an overgrown thicket of young, scraggly spruce trees starved for sunlight. Low, stick-like branches snagged on my hair and shirt as I tried to find an opening among them. I couldn't imagine the deer slipping through this tangled mess. I retraced my steps, turned in another direction, and found a narrow opening I'd missed earlier. I continued on, but even here, the going was tough. How deft the deer must be to pass through what I could hardly call a path as I reached forward to part branches or step over an occasional stump or fallen tree.

I could've easily returned to the car. But inexplicably I felt compelled to continue, as though that one deer pausing on the road's edge and seemingly beckoning was a sign for me to follow. Or that, and I couldn't make sense of this, the entire encounter was meant to happen, attributable to something other than chance. But then wouldn't I have to accept the same for a loon, which, recently, for several consecutive nights, yodeled across the water precisely at 4:00

a.m., as though knowing when in my wakeful nights such an eerily tremulous lullaby was what I needed for slipping back into sleep?

Moving deeper into the woods, I was certain I'd taken the right route. Though there was no obvious trail to follow, more light filtered through the trees. Overhead, the usual suspects flitted—black-capped chickadees, chipping sparrows, a couple of rowdy jays. A repetitive *boink* directed my attention to a yellow flicker hammering a dead birch tree's bug-infested trunk, its peeled bark long ago shed into pulpy piles on the forest floor. As things opened up a little further and more sunlight dappled down, understory plants became more prolific—ferns, bracken, a small patch of bunchberry among hummocks of moss. Emerging from a rotting stump and decaying leaf litter was a small clump of diminutive white Indian Pipe. Nearby, a scattering of deer scat confirmed I'd found the right route, making me feel less like a lucky stumbler than a confident tracker.

I knew most of the island's conservation easements and had walked all of its preserves. This wasn't one of them. Walking uninvited on private property made me uneasy. I generally saved my innocent trespass for my late September rambles, after cottages and seasonal use homes were closed up, a not-so-secret practice that I was not alone in pursuing.

But here I was on a mid-August afternoon emerging from the woods into what looked at first to be someone's clear-cut path but upon closer inspection seemed to have once been an open clearing that had evolved into a field of grass, weeds, and patches of tangled raspberry canes. A smattering of young alders and birch and an encroachment of knee-high spruce saplings had also become part of the mix. Mostly, though, it was open, like a large bowl tipped to the sun, rimmed by a dense border of woods. I stepped out from the shade.

At the other end of the field was what looked to be the remains of an old stone wall. Large stones and boulders squatted, remnants, possibly, of other structures. As I got closer, I could see that, off to one side, several stunted, gnarly old apple trees, their trunks splotched with lichen, had sunk their roots into a small slope, survivors of gravitational pull, age, and neglect. Despite their meager output, a promise of autumn windfall surely helped explain this location's lure to deer.

I'd come upon an old farmstead and its remnants of stone foundations, a cellar hole, a granite step, a few planks of rotting wood, some twisted, rust-flaked wire. Nothing declared it "historic." Just a small farmstead once likely owned by an early island settler who cleared the trees, tilled the land, planted a few crops and fruit trees before turning away from thin soil and subsistence farming to the more bountiful sea.

I had no idea who owned this land. In the weeks that followed, I could've asked around or checked the tax map at Town Office. Or poked around in the Historical Society archives. But I chose mystery. I preferred not knowing.

During a string of sunny, humid-free afternoons that followed, I returned to the clearing. After a couple of trips, what the deer had barely cleaved into the woods, my feet and branch-breaking upper body helped hone into an almost discernible path.

I felt drawn to the clearing, even though it was not a spectacular or particularly historic find. Other places on the island offered more beauty. Other wooded walks provided a wider spectrum of tree species and interesting specimens, like the nurse stumps of Shore Acres, and were home to glacial erratics the size of compact cars atop which minute ecosystems of moss, lichen, and Lilliputian-sized spruce seedlings flourished. Other high vista spots appealed with their openness on a grander scale of the marshy expanses bordering the sandbar or the trail to Sheephead Island at low tide where the cove opened onto the sweep of the bay beyond. But maybe that was part of the draw of this clearing and its field—not being as open or vast.

Its view did not extend over water, past the nearby anchored islands to the distant horizon. Unlike the island's shorelines with their tidal margins' constant flux and insistent pulse and the seemingly conjoined sea and sky demanding the eye's direction up and out, the old farmstead's open field corseted by bordering woods was contained. I felt somehow protected, as if I were being held in a cupped palm beneath a blue basin of sky. Here, the passage of time lacked the insistence of the tides. In certain moments, time seemed almost suspended, the only activity the drone of drunken bees, the silent flutter of red admirals touching down among the Queen Anne's lace and jewelweed, the chitter of sparrows in the apple trees, and once, briefly, the resonant *rat-a-tat-tat* of a pileated woodpecker on a fallen spruce. Even more still and silent were the low stone walls and tumbled heaps of rocks that in collaboration with moss spoke of time.

This rock-littered and stone wall–remnanted field wasn't particularly special. Yet it tempted with its puzzle pieces that needed fitting together. A low thrown wall with irregular-sized boulders, its gaps breached by tree roots, suggested a boundary marker. Even without any capstone evidence, a straight, more substantial stacked stone declared here a portion of a house once stood. A slab of gray rock patchy with lichen marked the entrance way to a cellar hole, its shallowness suggesting, what, a root cellar? Some randomly heaped rocks being subsumed by tall grass spoke of discard, where land had been cleared and tilled to make way for a few cultivated rows that with a good season might yield more than what was needed just to get by.

Why shouldn't some twisted lengths of rusty wire suggest an enclosure for a few chickens or goats? And surely a toppled, head-high wooden post rotting beneath a stand of scraggly rugosas was right to insist, in spite of requiring a missing twin, that from it a clothesline had been strung. A confirmation that, yes, someone who cared about those she loved had once lived in this place. Someone whose clothesline display on laundry day was commonplace in her time, although, surely, her methods of sorting, in the way perhaps she held a few wooden clothes pins between her teeth, were as individual to her as were my grandmother's when, in my childhood, she rolled the wringer washer into her kitchen every Monday and, after, carried a heavy basket of wet laundry into her yard.

A ruin is a "dialogue between an incomplete reality and the imagination of a spectator," claims Christopher Woodward in *In Ruins*. Not that I'd compare the meager remains of a little island farmstead to those of ancient Rome, which Woodward explored. But a witness to any ruins—to what remains—is forced to supply the missing pieces from her own imagination. A pick-plinking archaeologist may unearth a single interpretation, one version of a story that's verifiable through carbon dating. But in the imagination of, say, a woman just passing through in her own speck of time and without the means to scientifically authenticate, there could be several.

One bright afternoon, I headed to the field with my journal and a snack. In a patch of grass bejeweled with bright yellow Butter-and-Eggs, I reclined against some boulders made almost cushiony with their pelts of moss. Drowsy with the warm light and the nearby buzz and hum, and though it was only ants crawling nearby and not small lizards scrabbling over ancient stone, I was transported to a sunny afternoon in early May, when another of my solo explorations in Rome had taken me to the Palatine Hill.

Centermost of Rome's Seven Hills, the Palatine looks down on the Forum on one side and the Circus Maximus, the ancient chariot racing stadium, on the other. Though generally less crowded than the Forum or Colosseum, it's no less historically significant. As one of the most ancient parts of the city, the Palatine's traces of huts and a cistern date back to the Bronze Age. It's been called the birthplace of Rome, particularly after archaeologists discovered what's called the Lupercal, the cave where, according to legend, a she-wolf suckled the abandoned twins Romulus and Remus, founders of Rome.

On the Palatine, where the imperial and powerful built their palaces and villas, including the home of Augustus, Rome's first emperor, the ransacking after the empire's fall was most severe. Of palaces built by the Caesars, only cellars remained. Opulent statuary vanished; marble-cladded walls were stripped. Of ornate columns that once rose against blue, mere stumps survived. Along with other large fragments, they now lay jumbled, prostrate in the grass, as if at repose in the sun after such a lengthy and turbulent past.

The Palatine can be a confusing place without a guide. There are no maps or legends at the entrance. Few identifying labels or plaques are offered along the way.

Though I recognized some surviving columns as Corinthian, I had no clue what they'd once held up. To what did some fragments of ornate marble pavement belong? Or some faded fresco decoration? Though I wandered the Palatine without much knowledge of what I was looking at, I actually enjoyed the freedom of not knowing. I welcomed what felt like a park but better—a classical landscape with ruins. Umbrella pines with deeply plated trunks and high canopies towered overhead. Thick swaths of acanthus bloomed with lavender-colored spikes. Cypress and large ilex flanked tufa and thick retaining walls. Myrtle, rosemary, and capers bristled among stone, burst forth from the crevices of bricks. Wildflowers and feathery-fronded wild fennel carpeted sunny portions of the ground, cradling architectural fragments. Ivy rambled up the vast brick arches.

For all its lack of instruction and what at times might have seemed like a jumble, the Palatine was rich with paved paths, gravel walkways, ancient brick staircases, and iron-gated terraces opening onto views of the stadium and city beyond. Places you could touch and climb. And where, on a warm spring day, a late-middle-aged solo traveler felt welcome to plunk down on warm stone with her notebook open, to rest among scarred ruins that appeared to have parked their haunches in the present but were busy contemplating the past, listening to the echo of countless footsteps and events of wars and plots, victories and conquests, losses and plagues, and eventual collapse. All the embodiment of Edgar Allan Poe's poem "The Coliseum" with "we pallid stones / Not all our power is gone . . . Not all the memories that hang upon / And cling around us."

Sprawled on a stone slab high on the Palatine, I closed my eyes and tried to imagine the lives of the Caesars, of emperors planning their next conquests, of generals hatching plots or wronged women whispering their ill intentions. What dreams might dwell in the minds of the kitchen slaves preparing a banquet's array of larks, dormice, and the tongues of peacocks? But despite the many reminders around me, of accomplishments and aspirations both realized and lost, I came up short. My imagination failed to picture with any vivid specificity what life here would've been like. Perhaps the reach back across time was too great.

Little did I know then, and maybe even more unimaginable, was that in just a few months, far from the Palatine's toppled columns and monumental fragmented ruins, I'd be sitting atop my family's ruins—my brother dead, my mother in steady decline, my father maybe only barely holding on, as if he were a subsistence farmer clinging to thin, exhausted soil. Or how, for several days in late summer, I would be oddly comforted among the meager ruins of an island farmstead, the home of people I never knew, but who had been, presumably, an ordinary family like mine. And how, engaging in puzzle-piecing together these fragments, I conferred a layer of meaning to a field being inexorably engulfed by weed and spruce, where foundation stones were sinking but also gathering to them what the wind and rain sent, getting an occasional reprieve and rising a bit with a frost's outgoing heave. All of which would, in some stretch of geologic time, eventually lose meaning. Stones becoming just stones, the field a field. The way a hill shared by the she-wolf-suckled twins and the mighty Caesars could, if untended, become a mere hill again.

In an abandoned homesteader's field weeks after my brother's death and with an imagination that could not deliver kitchen slaves or warring generals, I found it easy to picture a woman hanging her clothes on the line one hundred years ago. Although what could I ever know about the aches or sorrows that filled her house, her hours? Or what seized her heart as she hung out her young son's shirt?

And We All Fall Down

I don't have a body. I am a body.
—Christopher Hitchens

I used the railing. I was wearing sensible shoes. I'd already pulled up my windbreaker's hood before leaving the protection of the porch's overhang. There were only six steps down to the sidewalk before a short dash in the pouring rain to the car. So then was it the goodbye I called back to the friendly docent who'd held open the door for my friend Lydia and me as we left the last house of a Garden & House Tour to benefit one of the local libraries? That one lapse of attention? One of life's seconds-long, "I didn't see it coming" instances that can ripple out with long-lasting consequence? The body going about its usual business while the mind housed within it was off someplace else?

The combination of heavy rain, surprising for late August, and the painted wooden stairs may have been, as was observed later, "an accident waiting to happen." My description of it in the days that followed was, "You know, in the cartoons, the guy stepping on the banana peel?" One step and suddenly I was airborne before hitting hard, really hard. A stair tread slammed into my lower back. The pain was instant but my next breath was not. Quickly, though, I commenced a running-through-my-body-parts assessment as Lydia's lovely face hovered above me. Usually so serene, it was twisted with concern.

"I've got to get up," I gasped. "I need to see if I can still walk." Grabbing hold of her arm, pain radiated up my back and down into my legs. Though wobbly and lightheaded, I finally, wincingly, managed to stand. I took a step and then another, no matter how much my back screamed out its protests.

"Deborah, the hospital isn't far. You need to be looked at," Lydia said as she tightened her grip. Days later, she'd tell me that I fell so hard, "I thought you might've broken your back."

"Let's just get to the car," I said, certain still that if I could walk, this whole unfortunate incident would be chalked up to nothing more serious than a bad spill. But as Lydia helped me to open the passenger door, I passed out. As I did again on our brief walk from the car to the emergency room entrance.

Nothing was broken. My reflexes were sound. Traumatic shock from the fall could have brought on the fainting, as likely did my immediate insistence to get up rather than let the traumatized body go about its necessary adjustments. My orthostatic blood pressure readings taken while prone, then sitting on the edge of the bed, and, woozily, standing, told the tale.

"Wow, sixty-five over forty-eight. No wonder you passed out," a physician's assistant said as a nurse helped lower me back onto the bed. "Shock will do that, but I bet you're dehydrated, too."

Was I ever going to learn that morning coffee, no matter how copious, was not a substitute for water?

She scolded me for not eating all day. Yes, but that had been our plan, Lydia and me going to a nice lunch after the tour.

"Yes, well," the PA said, arching her eyebrows as she glanced my way from her chart. "So much for plans, right?"

They kept me for the rest of the afternoon. Another saline drip and a pain med were ordered. Before I could leave, more orthostatic readings would be required to confirm my blood pressure had climbed into friendlier territory.

"Why don't I go get your prescription filled, and if you don't have one, maybe pick up a heating pad? And I'll call Bob again in Chicago, just to update him, okay?" Lydia offered. Angel Lydia, as I'd begun to call her.

The nurse brought in a blanket from the warming cabinet. "We've got that saline drip fast-tracked, and you're probably going to feel cold." Leaving the room, she dimmed the lights. "That pain med will kick in soon."

I nodded and closed my eyes. I was in a small hospital in a small coastal Maine town that was, for hospitals, surprisingly quiet. But a hospital, nevertheless. Not anywhere I thought I'd be. Or wanted to be, particularly given the past few months. To feel comforted and safe in such an environment, to give myself over to the warmth, to what perhaps was largely attributable to the pain med, felt like some kind of betrayal. But as I felt a grip loosening, I yielded. As though a spigot had opened, tears spilled from my eyes.

For months after my mother's stroke four years before, I took no easy physical motion of my own for granted. But as time passed and I somewhat mindlessly continued to watch my diet, take my vitamins, and exercise, I returned to the easy presumption my body would be there for me. My good and reliable body with its daily accumulations of bruises and scrapes, of infections flaring then simmering, cells effortlessly replaced. The within and without that made me who I was. The flesh-and-bone vehicle by which others knew me. Surely, I wasn't alone in the many ways we disregard our body until illness or injury grabs our attention.

Within twenty-four hours of my fall and after just two doses, I gave up on the Vicodin. I'd take the pain rather than be that whacked out. Extra-Strength Tylenol took a bit of the edge off, but aspirin, ibuprofen, and any other anti-inflammatories were off the table given my allergies to them. I slept on my back, knees elevated, and experimented in finding the least painful maneuver to get out of bed.

"He's not a bone cruncher," Lydia had said of an osteopath who'd recently moved his practice to the peninsula. "He's very subtle. So much so, you may not think he's doing anything. But he's not a quack. Trust me."

I made an appointment. To a light-haired fiftyish man neatly dressed in a striped, button-down shirt and chinos, with a calm and quiet manner about whom to Bob I'd too glibly and erroneously referred to as the "bone doc," I described my fall. I also explained, as I had to the hospital's PA, that many years before, I'd been thrown from a horse and suffered a hairline compression fracture in my lower back. "In my L4," I said, my acquired shorthand, what in the briefest terms to professionals for whom such language was commonplace, immediately translated to one of my five lumbar vertebrae.

But even before that, he'd asked, just observing me entering the room and taking a seat, "Your worst pain, it's in the lower right side of your back?" To my surprised response, he responded, "It's the way your right knee is sort of cocked when you stand. Your hip line is a little off, too."

Subtle was the word Lydia used. Definitely an understatement, I thought, after several minutes of lying face up on a padded table as the "bone doc," standing on my right side, slid both hands under my back, and with just his fingertips, began to apply gentle pressure. I felt no detectable manipulation, no wrenching or squeezing, no deep probing. Nothing like what in a deep muscle massage I was more accustomed to. Through my clothes, I could only feel his fingertips pressing in various places as he slowly moved up and down my back as though it were a piano and this the *pianissimo* movement of whatever composition he was playing. After what I guessed was a good twenty minutes, and following a final virtuoso flourish of fingertips on my lower back, he assured me my injury was all deep tissue and would heal with time.

More eloquently, he said, "Your body is trying to protect itself. As though it remembers your previous injury when you fractured your L4, it's saying, 'Oh no, not that again.' With this new trauma, it's seized up around that same spot, wanting to shield it from further damage. Think of it as that region of your body needing to be convinced the danger's passed and can let go."

I hadn't told him about my brother's death or my mother's emergency hospitalization and subsequent decline, and how all that, as had been pointed out to me already, was likely contributing to "stress" or "distraction"—the proof of which might reside in the fact that on the sunny, dry day prior to my fall down a stranger's stairs, I'd actually tripped and fallen going *up* the stairs of our deck.

I wanted to book another appointment. I wasn't at all sure if this session had made any difference, but just minutes after being helped off the table, I was already missing something. Of feeling . . . what . . . *attended* to? And the deeper connection to that—what had he called it?—*region* of my body? As though it was far off, foreign, some mysterious dark hole, a Bermuda Triangle where pain and loss and what responds to hands but was out of my hands had lodged. All of which surprised me, given how I'd long been suspect of numerous practices claimed as effective for the body: alignments or manipulations or what I once heard called "resetting the circuitry." It wasn't so long ago that I'd only come around to appreciating yoga. And while I once found a half-hour session of reflexology relaxing, I was under no delusions that massaging my toes would help my sinuses or probing the outer edge of my foot would directly benefit my lungs.

"Let's wait to see if another appointment's necessary," the doctor said, handing me a sheet with a few illustrated exercises and stretches to help things along. "For now, you should listen to your body. Rest it but use it, you know? Heed it. Give it time."

The next morning, I woke to discover that somehow I'd gotten onto my side, into my favorite sleeping position. But then, trying to swing a leg to the bed's edge and raise myself up, shafts of pain shot from my lower back. The language of my body emphatic.

"Too soon," it said. "Not yet."

In the days that followed, the pain, though lessening, was still there. I felt less clenched but at times still hobbled. I carried a small lumbar pillow around the house. I needed help pulling pans from a lower cabinet or reaching for plates from an upper shelf. Rising from a chair was still difficult, and in the car, I could only sit crunched in the passenger seat, as driving, reaching for the pedal with my right foot, was out of the question. My range of movement was definitely increasing, but sometimes, just bending over the sink to brush my teeth—a small blip in muscle memory's capacious vault—caused such seizing up it was as if I'd never move fully or flexibly again.

To sit at my desk for long was uncomfortable. Instead, I got out my lap desk. Propped against pillows, I tried to return to one of the many essays I was still so sure would eventually cohere into a book. Mostly I wrote in my journal. One afternoon, I found myself musing on the word *fall*.

All the ways to fall. Down the stairs. Up the stairs. How I'd fallen in love with Bob. Or years before when I had fallen away from the church and so, I was to believe, had fallen from grace. How easy to fall for a plate of *pommes frites* sprinkled with sea salt or for sunsets over the bay and the distant Camden Hills. Countless, all the ways to fall short. To fall out of touch. To allow a relationship to fall apart, let it fall through the cracks the way words, too often, fall on deaf ears.

Fall away. Fall from. Fall into, say, depression or addiction.

So many times I had pictured my mother falling out of bed the night her stroke announced itself and life as she knew it fell away. But not once had I been able to change it, put her back in bed, take away that fall. As if there was a way to fall back.

Fall so close to *fail*.

"Heed it," I'd been told. "Listen to it." After nearly two weeks, my body was telling me to reengage with the world. And what better way to have all its shimmering daily-nesses returned to me than in the embrace, even if Mom-admonished, "Careful, kids, remember Grandma's back," of young Sam and Sarah, two of our grandchildren?

"Are you sure you still want us to come?" my stepdaughter Ann had asked not long after my return from Joe's memorial service.

"But of course," I assured her. More recently, I'd emphasized, "Actually, it's just what I need."

And now here they were with their excited chatter upon arrival, their flashing limbs running to the bluff's edge, a giggling scramble down the stairs to the shore. Wet flip-flops dropped by the door. Damp towels heaped on the deck. Specimens retrieved from the water's edge—the shells of urchins and mussels and razor clams, of dead sea stars and sand dollars—burgeoning accumulations that within just a three days' visit suggested our yard might've once been home to an Indian midden.

Aged five and nine—the recognition that they were the same age as Matt and Abby never failing to deliver a body blow—they were bright with curiosity, a pair of eager learners in how to read a tidal chart or distinguish a distant osprey by the flap of its wings. Or why lobsters shed their shells.

"Really, that's the only way they can grow?"

At the dinner table, our plates heaped with lobsters and clams, I illustrated where in the carapace the lobster shells split open and the process began. How, after shells are shed, lobsters were soft and squishy. Helpless at first, they could only flop around, their legs unable to support them. "Without their shells," I explained, "they've lost their armor. They're very vulnerable. But they find safety among the rocks."

"How long do they stay there?"

"That depends. They need to protect themselves while they're still fragile and their new shell hardens. But remember, they're also getting pretty hungry while hiding out."

Insistent on exploring, Sam and Sarah led me into my own new discoveries, as with the spiny, large-headed, and bulge-eyed sculpin, a species I'd never seen, in the lobster trap Sam helped a neighbor haul aboard his boat. Together, heading out from Trundy's Point at low tide, we discovered moon jellies spackling the shoreline—translucent, saucer-shaped invertebrates fringed with small tentacles. Having only limited motion, they're dependent on currents, much of their lives spent at the water's surface waiting for food to float by. I'd never seen so many of them—gelatinous masses, whole or in shredded fragments that hardly seemed like living creatures. Had a confluence of currents and tides brought them here or some disease or infection? Sam, seeming to share some of the same questions, squatted at water's edge and gingerly touched his fingertip to a translucent jellylike puddle.

"I guess there's no way to save them," he said, turning his gaze to the deeper water beyond the expanse of low tide mud flats.

One night, we all hauled blankets onto the lawn and searched the sky for what had been billed as a meteor shower's last hurrah. Overhead, far from any ambient light, the sky stunned with staggering abundance.

"Wow, I've never seen so many stars!" Sarah cried out.

But for all the dazzle promised in "meteor shower," we saw no storm of stars dropping from the sky, no streams of blazing light. Shouldn't such falling announce itself in a scream of glitter and light, a fiery plunge? Disappointed at first, we continued to search.

"Oh, look!" I pointed to a bright arc. But so brief and quick, both kids missed it. And then another. "Scan the sky," I instructed. "Look carefully. They're small and it happens so quickly. A streak, really."

As I lay there, listening to the grandchildren exclaim over their own sightings that came with patience and careful attention, I remembered what I'd been told. "Listen to it." And here now was my body telling me in all its usual ways, it was beginning to be hungry again.

For three days, we roamed the shore, tramped in the woods. We gathered in the kitchen, around the table, on the deck. Each day we fed our bodies, their muscles and bones, tissues and tendons, all the organs including the liver, the largest one, bigger than the heart. We ate lobsters dripping with melted butter. Clams steamed in peppery broth. Brownies warm from the oven with ice cream and caramel sauce. Cinnamon French toast smothered with blueberry syrup and dusted with powdered sugar. Feeding the bodies in which, as toddlers, we all once dwelled, running our hands over everything, sniffing, tasting. Openly staring into the eyes of strangers, reaching out to them, perhaps from a grocery cart among heads of lettuce and bagged oranges, past our own borders to pat a stranger on the arm as, already, we were attempting to make contact at the outer boundaries of our skin—to touch and be touched, make ourselves feel more real. Those warm tummies of our young, wriggling bodies our mothers pressed their faces into, the way my mother had to Joey's, laughing and growling, "Ooh, I could eat you up."

Those little bodies we reach out to catch when they fall, before, as an adult, they fall alone and from a greater height. Little bodies we too soon leave behind, growing into the bodies we may want to fix or change. Approaching adolescence, might Sarah one day soon look into a mirror and wish her hair were straighter or that she weren't so tall, not seeing how strong were her long, lean, and muscular legs ready to lead her anywhere?

Though only five, Sam knew to reach out his sturdy little arm to help me board the boat or get into the car. And, coming up to me at the kitchen counter as I whisked eggs, he seemed to know that gently resting his small hand against my back was a touch that rivaled the fingertips of an osteopath. An intuitive, deeply held gesture I fervently wished he'd never lose.

Too soon, the short visit was over. A flurry of last-minute packing. A frantic search for Sam's nightguard. The careful wrapping of their brittle sea stars and crumbly sand dollars and, as my contribution to their proposed enterprise of making a sort of wonder cabinet at home, some sun-bleached bone fragments plucked from a seabird's skeletal remains on the sandbar one summer and a pair of intact dragonfly wings.

And then they were off, the kids calling out as though in rehearsed unison, "Feel better, Grandma."

Ann waved. "Take care of yourself. Hope your back feels better soon."

Walking back to the house after watching them drive off, I paused and looked around at the bordering woods patchy with moss, my favorite boulder long-pocked with lichen, the small clearing now studded with goldenrod, an entirely different palette than what lupine had painted there just a couple of months before, and farther down the lane, beneath the sheltering oak tree, our house and garden. Things seemed ordinary in all the ways they'd always been ordinary. And yet they seemed burnished, more delineated, somehow new. It was as if I'd fallen back into the world.

"Surprised by joy." The words sprang to mind from the title of a sonnet by William Wordsworth following his daughter's death. What he'd been so shocked to discover he could sometimes forget. "How could I forget thee . . . Even for the least divide of an hour."

Grief's corrosive power can split open our carapace and force us to retreat. But then, don't we venture out, needing to? To feed a hunger not of the stomach but the heart? We begin to unclench, even if we must still embody loss.

"She kept complaining about her back," the therapist at the skilled nursing facility explained to me over the phone, my father too exasperated to call me himself. "But we can't find anything wrong with it. The X-rays and scan the doctor ordered show nothing. Still, every time we try to work with her, she cries out and makes us stop. As we've told your father, if she is unwilling or unable to continue therapy, then we have no choice. We must report to Medicare that the patient has reached a plateau and no further improvement is anticipated. Any therapeutic coverage ordered by them will cease."

Weeks after her admission to the skilled nursing facility, my father continued to believe that my mother would improve, could get as strong as she'd previously been to push herself out of bed, get up on her walker. At times, I'd readily chimed in, as he held the phone to her ear.

"You want to get stronger, Mom, right, so you can go home?"

And her repeated, unwavering response, "Yes, I do. I will."

Declining. The word I often used to describe my mother in those months. A kinder, gentler way of saying she hadn't fallen away, was not exactly failing, but had embarked on a slow, downward slope. Perhaps, it occurs to me now, *decline* may have been appropriate for what was not exactly her outward refusal of therapy but a continued—willed?—lack of engagement. Regardless of what her words promised my father and me, she, by way of her body's protests, had been declining therapy.

I still can't say what was wrong with my mother's back that kept her from therapy. Surely nothing detectable. But listening to her body, it may have said to her alone that even if she grew strong enough to get back up on her walker and one day cross the threshold of her house, she'd stagger beneath the weight of a loss that, preemptively, her body was telling her she couldn't bear.

Body from Old English, meaning "trunk," "chest," or "cask." A container. A vessel. Our upright wondrous body, home to the miracle of our individual otherness. Of what inside can be revealed by incision, pictured in a shadowy X-ray, or merely suggested by probing fingertips, but not our essential otherness. Where we hold what is tender, all the vulnerable bits within our armored shells. Or, in my mother's case, is a sort of fortress with locks and bolts on the doors.

And which my father, my sister, and I, and even a social worker, had tried to scale, jimmy the locks, but failed.

Years before, not long after her stroke, when the persistent paralysis on her right side had made it all but certain she'd never walk again without at least the assist of a walker, she'd told me about her recurring dream.

"I'm in bed sleeping, but I wake up when I hear a voice calling me from the other side of the house. And just like that, I'm able to throw back the covers, get up, and walk out of the room."

"And then what?" I asked. "Who's calling you?"

"I don't know. I only get as far as the kitchen."

Was it her dreaming body calling out to her? Yearning for its former ease? Missing its freedoms? Holding out hope, willing her to try harder? As though the body's capabilities had simply gone off for a time, were at the far end of the house? Now, perhaps, if she was still having the same dream, when she heard a voice calling, she knew whose it was. And this time, able to get up and follow it, that is where she'd gone. And stayed.

I had fallen. I had been reminded that I will fall. As will we all.

The body isn't endlessly resilient. Eventually and perhaps when we least expect it, our bodies are broken by disease, injury, a catastrophic accident we don't survive, a fall from which we do not rise. Or the cumulative fraying of old age. The slow fade. Remarkable, meantime, what it endures. How it repairs and maintains and is, most of the time for most of us, unwilling to give up, playing with what isn't known as a broken bone until the game is over, waging a battle against a disease that transforms body from friend to foe. Our unfaltering will to be.

As I slowed down and allowed my back to recover, to let go bit by bit its protection against further injury, I went for walks, in them the traces of more adventurous hikes. I returned to the garden, slowly lowered myself to my knees, weeded and pruned, the sun warm on my bared arms. I shelved my lap desk, sat in my chair, and wrote. And in the dark, hungry with desire, I reached for Bob.

Grief, like a traumatic injury, can become deeply lodged. But relinquishment, I was starting to learn, didn't have to mean we forget.

Another Day in September

A blue and gold day of stunning clarity. Of busy bird chatter at the feeders and the hum of bees wallowing among late season asters. The maples hinting at their latent simmering orange. Another day in September.

Except it wasn't.

It was another September 11, six years after the 9/11 seared into our collective memory. A day that ensured any future usage of *twin towers* had singular meaning.

9/11: The signifier of a singular event. But a date that to children born today and in the crush of time to follow will mean little more than references in a textbook, questions on an exam, the subject in stories older adults occasionally tell. The same way that for many students in classrooms and workshops where I've taught, the death of JFK has scant meaning. For them, no personal imprint on memory of a particular place where each of us who remember first learned our country's youngest president had been shot.

9/11: A day of roar and flame and the rip of sirens. Of buckling rumble and billowing clouds, of smoke and ash nearly as tall as the towers themselves, sunlight leached from the sky before revealing the unimaginable—two 1,300-foot-tall buildings gone and everything and everyone inside.

September 11, 2001, preceded the birth of my niece Abby. To her, the only signifying date, the fulcrum upon which her young life teetered, was July 9, 2007: the day her father died.

This wasn't just another day in September. And though it was as blue and gold as the one six years before, I could not dwell much on the 9/11 dead or their families grieving unspeakable loss. I was still too keenly grieving mine.

Also, as it turned out, this was the day that Obie was delivering the bench.

Since returning to the island from my brother's memorial in July, my desire to have some kind of marker for Joe had only minimally diminished. Something not in far-off Arizona, but here, a continent away, in the place where I'd first learned he was dead. I hadn't decided what would be appropriate. Nor had I gone looking.

But over Labor Day weekend, while Bob and I meandered back roads along the Downeast coast, we followed a sign for The Granite Garden posted at an intersection and found ourselves in what had once been one of the area's historic, family-owned granite quarries. Set amidst acres of old-growth forest and long out of operation, it had become home to the workshop of a third-generation offspring, a thirty-something, self-taught artist who, upon our arrival, loped toward our car.

"Obadiah here," he'd said, lowering his lanky frame to extend his hand through the open window. "Most folks call me Obie."

His sculptures and objects, as he explained, "Well, I guess you can call them 'functional pieces,'" were located in a clearing enclosed by woods that had grown up to and in some places engulfed the nearby old quarry remnants. Escorting us from the car, he pointed to a dirt track that cut through dense trees. "Have a look around," he invited. "This'll take you to the quarry and then you can loop your way back here along a path in the woods."

The setting of Obie's family quarry was almost magical as it emerged suddenly out of the trees. Whatever the signs that blasting was once done here were to my eye long gone. Nor was there evidence of large drill bits or saw bites. The only equipment left behind were a few rusted, sprocketed wheels. As though unaccustomed to any disturbance, flocks of proprietary sparrows and finches flitted noisily among the trees. Atop a wall of granite, a trio of crows, unusually still and impressively quiet—they were crows, after all—looked not so much poised to erupt into raucous alert over any threat but posed—obsidian against pale gray—for maximum effect.

The real enchantment of the place occurred, however, as we walked back through the mossy woods. Enveloped by an emerald-green canopy, we came upon several large, lichen-splotched cairns of rough-hewn granite slabs stacked among boulders. Transformed into a footbridge, a naturally bowed single slab of stone with tapering ends arched over a small brook burbling over pebbles. A little farther on, an impressive block of granite had been wedged against two large, moss-cloaked glacial erratics with flat upright sides so that together they resembled a kind of throne. In a small clearing with sun dappling down, a large stone circle appeared to be awaiting a clan of Druids. All this had been staged, intentionally placed by Obie, who obviously had a good eye. And yet it still spoke to natural landscape.

Our approach back to Obie's gallery and workshop led us past his outdoor sculptures and what he called his landscape pieces. Though some parts of his stone sculptures were polished—the veins of a large stone leaf, the eye of what, by its curved, almost abstracted form alone, conveyed *bird*—most pieces he offered for sale had only been modestly altered and assembled. A tall, columnar plinth. A round stone scooped out . . . chipped out . . . to make a bird-bath bowl. Another an oblong planter. And there was the bench.

Over the years, I'd seen plenty of stone benches in Maine—fancy carved granite types in garden centers or, on the spectrum's more primitive end, old foundation blocks balanced atop a few cobblestones. This one was different. Not a product of the quarry, it looked as though it had been hauled from the woods where it had withstood the elements, countless cycles of freeze and thaw, its making the handiwork of no human hand but the earth itself. At five feet long, about a foot and a half wide, and with a relatively flat top, this granite slab invited a human purpose, and Obie, with the lightest touch by just adding two roughly hewn stone blocks that snugly fit beneath, had transformed it.

And I'd already given it a name: Joe's bench.

It also had a place.

The summer before, to repair the damage at woods' edge nearest our house that a ground-cleaving excavator and a pair of heavy dump trucks had made while remediating some serious erosion of our bluff, I'd set about establishing a new border of woodland plants and shrubs. Here, beneath a young oak and set amidst thriving ferns and bunchberry, was where Joe's bench would go. Canted a bit northwesterly, it would take in the view that so centrally defined this place for me—the bay, the distant islands, the Camden Hills, the ocean beyond, and, above it all, open sky.

Soon after Obie's arrival, I showed him the spot. Standing there, he looked around. Squinting behind his wire-rims, he grew silent for several moments, as though, regardless of the check I'd already written making the bench mine, his final stamp of approval was required. As he gazed out at the bay, I recognized what I'd missed before: He was about the same age as Joe, and though leaner, more angular, of the same height and hair color.

"Nice," he said finally, turning and smiling at me. "So then. Here."

"Yes. Here."

After all of the previous grinding of excavator gears, the thump and dump muscle and might, Obie's quiet installation surprised me. Just one man, one small truck, and on its bed, along with the bench, a hand-built, teepee-like contraption of trimmed sapling trunks and an unmotorized rope-slung winch with which he hoisted and lowered the slab into place.

Such a solo, tranquil, and deliberate way of working with Joe's bench barely hinted at the labor that would have been required to cut, carve, cart, and move into place the immense granite blocks and slabs Obie's family once quarried. Nor, more incalculably, the labor of swarming, sweaty workers who in ancient Rome erected columned temples and palaces made of stone, the sounds of their chiseling and creaking carts echoing down narrow streets, ricocheting off the walls. But now, here was Obie, one-on-one with this stone that predated any Caesar. Joe's bench a survivor, at the very least, of this area's last glacial dunking, fourteen thousand years ago.

As he worked the winch and lowered the cradled bench into place, I realized I'd forgotten the many nuances of its long granite slab top—the irregular shape tapered nearly to a thick point at one end, the other broader but thinner, and with its slight uptilt, almost wing-like in spite of all that heft, it might try to take flight. Resembling the remnants of mysterious cave paintings speaking to the passage of time, small patches of black rock lichen bloomed atop the slab, a sort of comingling among a verdigris of light-green moss that splotched the stone. Stepping away to gain a better perspective, I noted how, for all its bulk, the bench had an admirable, natural gracefulness.

It also didn't escape me that the bench's top resembled a stone tablet that, if properly honed, could be incised, like a grave marker. I could almost imagine it being the last surviving specimen of some primitive avenue of stone slabs once erected upright in the earth, markers announcing that here was where someone's bones were buried, sacred ground, a place of contemplation and healing. An answer to the human need of memorializing the passage from life to death.

In *The Dominion of the Dead*, Robert Pogue Harrison asserts that across time and the spectrum of human cultures, one imperative has remained clear: "to dispose of the dead deliberately and ceremonially." Be that a corpse, bones, relics, whatever the remains. More than a desire, it is by way of our human natures an obligation, perhaps even a traditionally mandated duty, one in which Sophocles's Antigone, for example, risked her life attempting to bury her brother rather than leave his corpse to rot outside Thebes's city gates.

The event of a death remains unfinished until remains are disposed of ceremonially, claims Harrison, and not doing so means the "deceased person is fated to remain, in effect, *undead*," the grievers yoked to an open-ended, unreconciled state. In *The Iliad*, until Hector's corpse can be retrieved, Hecuba and Andromache may well lament and ululate, but their grief remains "dysfunctional and ineffective." In *Moby Dick*, Ishmael refers to the whalers lost at sea as the "placelessly perished." The unmarkable sea possesses no gravestones. And though memorial tablets erected on land by grieving widows may pay tribute, Ishmael exclaims, "what bitter blanks in those black-bordered marbles which cover no ash."

More than one thousand victims of the 9/11 attacks were not identified. Despite months of careful sifting and myriad forensic technological tools and computer programs, identities could not be authoritatively assigned to what was recovered in the rubble. Words not usually associated with the human body had to be employed: *Obliterated. Pulverized.* And, even more unthinkably, *vaporized.*

Horrifying enough that in the minutes before the towers' final fiery collapse, terrified people escaping the flames, suffocating smoke and steel-bending heat, stepped into shattered windows one thousand feet aboveground and jumped. Plunging and tumbling, their arms outstretched, shirttails and open jackets flapping, billowing, they resembled from a distance puppet bodies, all strings cut, not the loved and cherished bodies of brother or father, mother or son. Even more unfathomable was to consider that, among the smoking, twisted girders and charred remains of the towers that smoldered for weeks, bodies reduced to mere atoms mingled in the white, dust-choked air with equally atomized computers, desks, carpets, and glass. Bodies of the dead that became dust, some of which blew out to sea and settled on the Atlantic and not by way of a commemorative sprinkling of ash performed by those who loved them, by, say, a mother who once held her son to her breast.

The only certainty for families of the unidentified dead was the location where their loved ones perished. Meager consolation after the days of posting photos and heartbreaking Missing Persons flyers on New York streets, of visiting all the hospitals, of turning away from a screen's unrelenting loop of images before finally having to accept that their loved one wasn't coming back. Nor, apparently, the least bit of a death's physical proof evidence.

Regrettably, humankind's long history of warfare and brutality has delivered to us fields of carnage, remains never to be identified or returned, a legacy of limbless, headless torsos with all clothes blown off, scattered arms and legs that in a nightmarish dreamscape seem to be waiting for someone to gather and reassemble them, put the dead back together. Of what is beyond assemblage . . . bits of bones, bloody bundles of fabric and flesh, body parts blackened and charred like pieces of wood, minute human particles splattered on walls that only the stiffest brush can scrub away. All almost impossible to imagine, what by the inconsolable must be refused.

From a distance, the thousands of markings on the long, polished, black granite panels of the Vietnam Veterans Memorial, better known as The Wall, look like the stone's texture until, up close, they materialize into the nearly fifty-nine thousand names of the men and women who met their deaths in Vietnam. The cumulative effect is staggering.

A stupefying chronicle of loss, this memorial to the fallen whose bodies, or what remained of them, were sometimes identified and returned for burial and cremation in places across the nation or, more sadly, were not. When "missing in action" became "presumed."

But by including every name, The Wall insists on singularity. Each inscribed name represents a life of particulars, especially to the kin and comrades who press their fingers and lips to the incised letters that evoke an individual presence.

I'm reminded of Homer's Odysseus. Until he returned home alive or his corpse was returned to his family, he was in effect "undead." Odysseus's mother, Anticlea, who died of grief awaiting her son's homecoming, confesses from the underworld that her longing "took the sweet spirit of life from me." Unable to either embrace or bury her son, "she died in spirit before she died in body."

My brother's body did not go missing. Following his death, there were rites and ceremonies, his urned remains—"Is that all there is?"—on display at the memorial service. But my mother was not a witness to Joe's lifeless body slumped in the shower. She was not present to reach out for one last caress before he was wheeled away. At Joe's memorial service, she was the one missing. She never saw the urn.

Merciful, I'd long thought. But was it? Those denials of proof? Unable to embrace Joe in sinew and bone, see one last time the flesh that was her youngest child and not being able to physically participate in the service, in the ritualized send-off to whatever afterlife she held in her head, had her spirit, like Anticlea's, begun to die? To learn to believe the dead one is dead did not come naturally. But how much harder still if the unnatural had happened and your child preceded you in death.

I didn't recognize it at the time, but I was beginning to understand that no matter how painful our commemorating rites and rituals and our witness to the mortal remains, they can maybe help us separate from our loved dead and secure them a place in the afterlife of our imagination.

I have asked myself if there was a photograph of Joe in my mother's hospital room. Given my father's general reluctance to talk about his son's death and his "Your mother's not strong enough" and "I don't want to upset her" beliefs and her repeated refusal to open up to a social worker or seek counsel from clergy, any mention of Joe seemed to have been banished, any conversation skirting anywhere near deemed off-limits. I have to ask, too, if we failed by avoiding any talk about Joe's death or offering her any evidence after, if not of the urn itself, at least the photographs of it, the obituary and memorial program. Maybe she'd needed an image of her son brought into her room, or his voice by way of his favorite Neil Young CD, every belted-out word of which Joe knew by heart.

Yes. The circumstances of her fragile health and physical limitations. Yes. The confines of a skilled nursing room she seldom left. Yes. Amidst Abby's crayon drawings, the get-well cards, and photos of grandchildren, amidst all the clutter of myriad necessities—the oxygen tank, bottles of hand sanitizers, soaps and creams, boxes of latex gloves, bolts of gauze, an array of elastic arm protectors, all of which seemed forever beyond any effort to stay tidied up—what kind of commemorative shrine might we have constructed for her?

Surely my mother didn't need a photo to conjure her son from memories. She could reconstitute him from thin air, and in some confused moments maybe even expect to see him again, not by way of illusion or dream but literally see him walk through the door or, upon waking, discover him sitting in the chair opposite her bed. Surely my mother grieved. But how did she mourn?

Within days of Obie's installation, it was as if Joe's bench had always been here. I could see it from any window on the south side of the house or when coming up the drive or walking our lane. Of the earth, but with a human stamp on it. A reassuring presence.

I knew my mother would never see it. Weeks later, however, I did show her a photograph.

"Look, Mom, here's Joe's bench," I said, holding it out to her as I sat beside her bed.

When she didn't reach for it, I moved it closer to her face. She appeared neither puzzled nor pained. If anything, her expression was one of detached appraisal.

"You know, it's for . . ." I stammered, "for remembering . . ." Then blurted, "So what do you think?" as though it was only dawning on me that what had been missing were questions. We'd not been asking my mother enough questions.

She raised her hand toward the photograph, but rather than take it, she tapped at one corner where I'd captured a bit of the nearby perennial bed.

"Are those asters?" she asked. "I always liked those purple ones."

For my mother, Joe's bench clearly had little meaning. It did not move her to say anything about Joe or even change expression. With the right questions and proddings and with photographs as prompts, were we even capable of excavating her sadness? Hauling it into the light? Which then would hurt less?

For so long, I'd wondered if one reason she refused to talk about Joe was to keep alive the notion her son might not be dead. But if I could address that version of myself now, I'd suggest that perhaps it was a way for my mother to take control, to possess her pain. Perhaps to all our efforts, she was refusing commonality, telling us, "My grief is nothing like yours." Saying, "No one else can hurt in my womb. No one else can remember the feel of pushing my son into the bright and unsafe world where, in the days that followed, I almost lost him. A difficult birth and now this impossible death. That child, oh that child, gone. Let me not be violated by sympathy, by what the rest of you think you know."

Saying, "You need a bench. I do not."

To most folks, Joe's bench likely appeared—and appears still—as an attractive element aesthetically placed in the landscape, a focal point drawing the eye to it and nothing more. Similar, perhaps, to the way in Rome, among cheek-by-jowl pagan temples and modern office buildings, juxtaposed with Renaissance palaces and pizza kitchens, I often gazed on ancient fragments and had no idea their origin or intent, though surely their stone spoke to me of survival, of enduring time's passage.

On the bench, no plaque or incised name would ever appear. But just as each chiseled letter on The Wall seems encrypted, a code decipherable alone to those who know the person represented by a name, so, too, Joe's bench was encoded by way of my memories of my brother, my desire to preserve a presence, honor an earthly absence. The bench helped me memorialize and commemorate. But it was more than that.

Rootedness, I recently read, was for the ancient Romans an ideal, and very much tied to ancestor worship. If not diligent in carrying provisions to the tombs of their ancestors, they ran the risk that their forebears would not become protecting gods. Families kept sacred fires stoked, made of them a hearth that, once established, could not be moved except for unforeseen necessity. By way of belief and hearth, they thus became as fixed to the soil as to the altar itself.

I no longer lived in my ancestral home. Nor would I ever again. There would be no gathering around the hearth of Oakdale Avenue in a Chicago suburb. And though my family had lived in Arizona for years, I felt no connection to it. The desert Southwest was not home to the meaningful places of a life I'd once lived with them.

In her short story "Face," Alice Munro writes, "In your life there are a few places, or maybe only one place, where something has happened. And then there are the other places, which are just the other places."

Joe did not die here. He never looked out at the bay from the bench. But here was where I first learned he was dead. Here was where I had to start to absorb grief. Here was where I was being reminded that, for a place to become special, it required encounters and obligations. And acts of human grounding. Here was where I'd begun to ask, "How can you call a place home unless in it you've had your heart broken?"

On an island far from my native Midwest, where no branches of my family intertwined, I was increasingly putting down roots, incrementally binding myself to what was no longer a setting but an embraceable knowable landscape within a community of shared history, traditions, habits, and, already, a chunk of my personal past. A place that was becoming home, regardless of its absence of a sacred fire. But which now had a bench.

Long after I'm gone, the stone of this bench will endure. Long after our renovation plans are accomplished, it'll outlive our house, just as, all over the island, grave markers, some with their names eroded away, will remain after houses and their inhabitants have long vanished. Eventually, Joe's bench will lose meaning. It will become again of the earth and its continuum. But for a time, it will be a necessary memorializing gesture. A personal landmark that has helped define, make of my island place, my hearth. A human marker of who remembered, and who for a time was here.

Bridging the Divide

The evidence was everywhere. I didn't need to consult a calendar to know that the autumnal equinox was behind us. With colder days of diminishing light winging our way, we were headed toward winter.

Hard to remember June's early green wonders or midsummer's bright palette of promise. Most recent to exit the stage were the sulfur yellow of tansy and goldenrod, that golden dazzle so abundant in field and roadside it seemed intended to feed our eyes, as though we were capable, like human solar panels, of storing such brightness for the dark days ahead when winter winds howled.

Up in the trees, the color wheel had irrevocably tilted from simmer to blaze to smolder, to what, as leaves unhinged, must fall away, just as the forest floor's ferns and bracken had no choice but to surrender to their rumpled, brown collapse. Much of my slumping garden was now no more than spent blooms and tattered crowns, seed heads blown and gone. Only late season asters and snakeroot had the genetic makeup to hang on until the first killing frost, when they, too, would sink back to earth.

All of it telling the same story: Everything dies.

If ever a season spoke to our mortality, it's autumn. But autumn, I was being reminded, also brimmed with a restless, wild energy.

The army of red squirrels who'd weeks before made fast and frantic work of our big red oak's acorns had become equally obsessed with bolstering their nests. For weeks, warblers gorged at my feeder, small bright chips fueling up for their journey. Even more of a hazard than usual, deer stepped into the roadways, lured by an orchard's windfall. At least we had none of the mainland's black bears getting cheekier this time of year with feeders and garbage bins. And though just days before, ospreys, heeding their internal urgings, had emptied the skies above Heart Island and were now en route to South America, seabirds of some heartier type had settled on the bay, perhaps recklessly fooling with the calendar or knowing something about what was coming that we with our clocks and barometers did not. As it seemed my neighbor might, gauging by the size of his woodpile that daily, with no apparent end to his zeal with chopping block and axe, increasingly towered toward potential topple.

I wouldn't be around to know. Count me out as a hearty type. At least not hearty enough to ride out the winter in our house. A native Chicagoan, I was no stranger to the brutalities of a mean winter, but in a house without insulation or central heating? With no way to keep the water pipes from freezing? By this time next year, some of that would be remedied by our contractor undertaking our renovation's first phase. In autumns to come, I could, if I chose, forge into the winter along with the red squirrels fleecing their nests and the eiders and loons seeking deeper water less likely to freeze over. I'd join my neighbors and fellow islanders huddled around our small community's collective fire, my voice added to the choir grousing about the weather.

In autumn, year-rounders hum with their own wild energy, folks who know firsthand the wisdom and necessity of preparing for a long Maine winter. Who make and fix, rig and rerig, preserve and freeze, and, maybe, among a few throwbacks, stock a root cellar. Who fork up mineral-rich wrack at the causeway to heap onto their over-wintering gardens, some of whom, as owners of old, drafty Capes, will also stack hay bales against foundations. Folks who know when to pull up their traps and shrink-wrap their hauled-ashore boats.

Though on a much smaller scale, and one of privilege, not necessity, I'd become a small cog in the wheel of all this cyclical island energy as I went about my annual end-of-season to close up house and garden. Though I was still days away from cleaning out the fridge, suspending phone service, covering the furniture, sprinkling an ample supply of mothballs in the cellar, or asking our plumber, Lewis, to bleed the pipes, I hauled emptied flowerpots and the Adirondack chairs to the garage, made runs to the dump, closed our post office box.

And one early morning, with a foretelling chill in the air, I began my annual assessment: a mental checklist not documented yet into my journal or downloaded with photographic evidence. A calculation of how the summer had measured up to my plans, the promises that had been fulfilled or had come up short. The new trails I planned to hike, books to read, recipes to try, people to have over for dinner. All the pages I'd been so sure would be written at my desk. What of the trellis I'd planned for the sprawling climbing rose? The invasive march of wild sorrel I vowed to conquer? All of which, in another end-of-season ritual, would find its way into my journal as a list titled, "The Summer Of."

Typically, I'd have included our grandchildren's visit, my fall and injured back, a trip to Monhegan Island. But instead, I spilled out:

The Summer Of

Joe's death
Mom's decline
Long hours on the telephone
Learning to live with grief

And for the moment, that was as far as I got.

As a word for a named season, autumn is a relative newcomer. Fifteen hundred years ago, Anglo Saxons marked time's passage with just one season: winter. In the Middle English of the eleventh or fifteenth centuries, the year was divided into seasonal halves: summer and winter. By the seventeenth century, spring had replaced the earlier widespread use of Lent as a season. And by the eighteenth century, autumn, a Latin word, took over what had been previously known as harvest. Eventually, but only in the United States, fall began jockeying with autumn and seemed to have gotten the upper hand.

In late October, look to the bare-branched trees and the ground beneath them and it's easy to see why. And, when resetting the clock, who isn't helped by the friendly reminder, "Spring forward, fall back"?

Maybe I wasn't considering much of this on the day that I headed into the garden to finish the last of my cutting back and mulching tasks, a day so unseasonably warm we seemed to be in a late September pause, when even the trees looked like they had doused their burn and ceased their slow undress. A good day to work in the dirt, to be engaged with the earth. Working among the remnants of another season, I pulled up the stakes where July's sweet peas had twined and the purple, big-as-pie-plate blooms of clematis clung. I plunged my pruners into one of the hydrangeas. I yanked out much of the lamb's ear that had succumbed to fungus and the liatris that had never flourished despite repeated transplants. I sidestepped the coneflowers, their seed heads not yet spent, recalling how, so unfussy and reliable, they'd again attracted clouds of red admirals. Perhaps next summer, I'd plant more of them and get the same results.

We gardeners tend to be a humble lot in spite of our delusions of grandeur when, as a long winter takes its toll, we huddle inside, crank up the heat, and dream big, our narrow, cultivated beds suddenly ballooning to dimensions rivaling Sissinghurst. We know that for all we protect against white flies, Japanese beetles, leaf miners, and thrip, for all we may manure, water, transplant, divide, and trim, no outcome is ever guaranteed. I'm helpless against many of the myriad forces that determine a garden's outcome. A feckless agent who, even come January and unable to get my hands in dirt, will attempt to cultivate the weather by fretting over snow—too much or too little—and over strong winds, limb-threatening ice, gnawing voles that burrow through drifts, or perhaps, a sudden warm blast from the Gulf that coaxes tender buds to pink up too soon.

Yet, come spring, for all the vagaries of weather and what I can't control, life erupts and blossoms appear. Without my doing a single thing, white snowdrops stipple the forest floor, skunk cabbages push through the crusty snow, trees leaf out. Nature can be cruel, but mostly, reliably, it's generous. It fulfills its promise. And, in my garden, it offers proof that I know what I'm doing, have done the right thing. Or at least it colludes in the illusion.

Years ago, after I'd gone from apartment city dweller to suburban homeowner, I decided to plant daffodil bulbs in my front yard. As a novice new to the enterprise of homeownership and, most definitely, garden-making, I was eager to undertake what I'd been told was foolproof. At a nearby garden center, I browsed through the selections marked "Dutch Bulbs." Not known to me at the time was that none of our familiar flowering bulbs were native to the Netherlands. They're descendants of the Middle East, of early bulbs mentioned in most translations of the Bible. But because a Viennese ambassador returned from Turkey with bulbs that eventually made their way into a botanical garden in Holland, fields of bright tulips have ever after been quaintly partnered with churning windmills. More elemental and crucial to my undertaking, however, was what I had to learn about planting bulbs.

"Be sure the root end is at the bottom. Like this," a helpful garden center employee demonstrated, after I'd mistakenly referred to the entire bulb as a root. As for any final advice about planting, she instructed, "After digging the hole, just add a dollop of bonemeal."

"And faith," I said, with a small laugh.

Which probably needn't have been said, given how, as I was soon to understand, faith was as necessary to the gardener's arsenal as pruner or spade. As was desire.

For what is a garden, whether it's a small plot on a bit of land or something grander, but a wild place we try to shape to our desire? That, with our time and care and a garden's tolerance for intrusion, is transformed from the imagined into something real.

As I plucked and pruned and heaped blackening remnants from my garden onto the compost pile, hungry gulls squabbled on the shore. Amidst a flurry of wings, jays and juncos duked it out at the feeder. More than just being active and restless at this time of seasonal shift, it was as if we all knew what was coming. Living beings united in tenacity, possessing the embedded, intuitive drive to survive, though particularly for us humans in our post-lapsarian garden, mortality casts a long shadow.

"How can you hide from what never goes away?" the ancient Greek philosopher Heraclitus asked.

From death that is always present. Concealed in the dark bottom of a pocket, hidden in a winter morning's metallic taste of impending snow. Awaiting in the empty meadow with its wind-bent grasses, in the chilly gusts tossing leafless branches overhead. But without such a taste of darkness, without such downward pull, would we appreciate as fully life's evanescence?

On an afternoon in late September, I needed go no farther than my yard to find the evidence. Among the *memento mori* everywhere I looked was the "yes" in spite of the darkness. The "yes" because of the impending darkness. Of death that, Wallace Stevens wrote, "strews the leaves / Of sure obliteration in our paths," yet, beautifully, evanescently, "makes the willow shiver in the sun."

I had never planted bulbs at our Maine house. Because, I'd always said, I didn't arrive early enough in spring to see the crocus and daffodils bloom, and any later-blooming tulips were totally off-limits, given the palate of our local deer population.

But now I reconsidered. Years before, I may have needed a nursery employee's assistance, but as I've come to discover, each time I've worked in my garden since, my mother's hands live in me. As do my grandmother's. Each with their garden knowledge. As do their lilac hedges, peonies with a phalanx of ants marching among the pale petals, tiger lilies stalwart against a white fence, tall spires of hollyhocks cheerfully camouflaging a cinder alley, and the purple of my mother's irises, her devotion to them unflagging, even after her move to less iris-hospitable Arizona. On my knees, digging into the thin layer of our planet we call, simply, dirt, they live within me.

And within my pinprick of a garden, which, though often seeming to me a refuge, a still-point buffer against the bustle, was a part of the surrounding whirl, the hum beyond its borders of a vast, cyclical world, whether I was here to see my buried bulbs bloom or not.

On the night before my scheduled dawn departure to drive back to Illinois, I made a final round of the house, checking once more the closets and drawers and cabinets, locking all doors and windows, pulling the shades, emptying the refrigerator. Rather than preparing for a journey, I felt like I was untying knots, freeing a boat from its mooring. Or for a non-boater more at home in the garden, as if I were uprooting myself, preparing, once again, for transplant.

In previous years, I'd almost always felt a tug at this time of the season, as though my ancestors had been nomads or I was a migrant bird with an internal urge to lift and go. This time, though, I had to fight the urge to stay on the island, to burrow in, the way that, on these colder nights, turtles and salamanders were already claiming their spots deep in the muddy banks or my neighbors were stacking firewood, hauling up their traps, hunkering down. Here, I'd begun to think, in this place where inescapable seasonal shifts seemed more clearly defined, I might find better instructors for how to grieve. In this house where I first learned of my brother's death and hauled back to it from Arizona the pain of that loss. And where, on my last night before driving off, I gathered up and boxed the talismanic objects—a key chain, a small-framed photo of Joe at nine, his sommelier's silver-plated cup, a pebble from his garden—which, on a dresser top, I'd made into a type of shrine. To what had become in recent years a repertoire of ritual, I added this new and necessary gesture.

At its root, *dwell* means to linger or pause. But dwell also implies permanence, a continuity in a specific place. Where, over time, our rituals develop. Where our meanings and attachments, our experiences and personal landmarks, accumulate. Through encounters and obligations, we come to know and are known. We erect memorials. We house the fragile and fugitive bits of our self and try to protect what we fear may be lost. Witnesses to the visible erasures of the seasons as they come and go, we become a part of continuity and of endings. Of deaths that accentuate a place's ability to outlive us while generations succeed one another like leaves on a tree. All the crucial particulars that make a house, a place, home. Here, increasingly, *dwell* in this sense applied.

"If we could drive into heaven, it would probably look like this," my sister once observed as we drove over our island's suspension bridge on a day so thick with fog the towers and support cables had been engulfed in gray. The only thing visible as we ascended the steep approach, my car hood pointed skyward, was a scrap of pavement directly ahead of us, discernible solely by its bright yellow centerline.

"A leap of faith," I said, accelerating. Though it wasn't exactly. I'd long before notched my belt with countless bridge crossings. I'd come to know in my body the sudden lurch, the quick ascent, and then on the other side the smooth descent, not unlike the way a loon, no matter how clumsy and noisy its laborious wing-whapping takeoff, returns to the water, setting down with barely a ripple, the maneuvers surely borne in tissue and bone.

Built in 1939, the Deer Isle–Sedgwick Bridge spans the Eggemoggin Reach, a wide, navigable arm of the Atlantic. The bridge's main span is nearly 1,100 feet long, rises 98 feet above the water, and is supported by 213-foot towers and bundled, twisted-strand steel cables and diagonal cross-bracing stays. For most islanders, the bridge was and remains a welcome substitute for a ferry dock. It's hard to imagine life here without it, even if residents bristle at the suggestion that the bridge makes us less of a "real island." Umbrage is taken, too, at one guidebook's description of the bridge as a mere "vehicular connection." Boosterism aside, our local pride in our bridge is probably tied into, at least partially, the admiration we all generally possess for man-made objects of strength, for what can withstand the forces of wind, gravity, heat, of currents, battering surf, decades of heavy use. Structures that are stronger than we are, that more than compensate for our physical inabilities and, though we seldom express gratitude for them, hold us up, transport us across water, enable us to ascend and span.

Unless you're traveling by boat, you cannot arrive or depart our island except by way of the bridge. Normally, you can't linger on its narrow lanes, especially if you're being tailgated by a refrigerated, lobster-packed 18-wheeler barreling toward market. But at dawn on an early October morning, as I made my way off the island at the end of another season, I stopped on the traffic-free bridge. From its apex, I could see pink light easing into the eastern sky, the Eggemoggin Reach spread below me in startling stillness, the tree-studded shores on either side darkly silhouetted. I paused on the bridge for one last look but also because I was reluctant to make this end-of-season "crossing over," the island expression used mostly when you only plan to be gone a short time for mainland errands. *Crossing over,* a euphemism that too many times in the weeks after Joe's death had been painfully forced on me.

My car was packed with clothes, food, books, files, and more. None of it was about to challenge the bridge's posted load limits, but, as if my journey were by sea and not a series of toll roads and turnpikes, it felt as if my car in its hold held heavy ballast. Something to steady the course for what ahead was still unknown and uncharted, the ways in which I'd yet to grieve. And there was the weight of loss. A griever's loss I had in no way anticipated and was now being added to losses, big or small, that over time accumulate. Losses that were never of equal weight.

I hated to admit it, but the loss of my dog Ben had weighed more, laid heavier on my heart, than had the death of my remote grandmother. The loss of my island house, its gardens and our land, would surely weigh more than if we had to give up our Chicago house. But how, as I paused atop the bridge, could I dare consider, even if only fleetingly, that the death of my brother might weigh more for me than my ailing mother's? Safer, if not just easier, was to wonder how the loss of Joe surely weighed heavier on her than her premature firstborn who had lived only three days. More difficult was to question whether the death of one of his daughters—me or Chris—would've weighed less for my father than that of his son.

How could I ever know what loss—losses—weighed most on my brother in the end? A loss of hope or belief? The loss of the "second chance" he'd prayed for? All the losses that ate away at whatever he'd thought the rest of his life might look like. All that he'd once had and known.

There are losses we can leave behind, that stay with cobbled shore, among an oak tree's branches bared in winter or atop a stone bench mantled with snow. Others we must carry with us. Not just the talismanic objects from a dresser top shrine, but the losses that reside within us: my childhood Oakdale Avenue neighborhood, our redbrick ranch, its floor plan imprinted in body and brain; a failed marriage; the losses of a beloved dog, a job, a coveted assignment; and, by the mere passage of time, a former agility and grace. And now, my brother and my own loss of a second chance. A loss of opportunity. As if their aim is to strengthen bones, help develop new musculature to carry us forward, losses must be endured because we are living, still here, still able to love, remember, be of the world, put words on a page.

There was no detour for where I had to go. Just like to drive off the island, there was no other route. I had to cross this bridge.

In its simplest sense, a bridge is a connector, but it can also reconcile two opposing sides, even link two seemingly irreconcilable polarities. Between leaving and returning, holding on and letting go. Of staying still and moving ahead.

In "Change's Purchase," Jonathan Farmer writes about poet Alan Shapiro, who also lost a brother and a crucial part of his identity.

"All of a sudden, I was nobody's brother."

Farmer notes how Shapiro claimed that grief is a privilege. A person had something important enough to grieve. He cites Shapiro's poem "Joy." In it, as Shapiro is headed to his dying brother's bedside vigil, his young daughter accompanies him part of the way, singing and pirouetting beside him. He notes her spontaneity, the animal-like candor of her movements, his young daughter resembling not the lion pouncing, he writes, but the stumbling antelopes swerving, leaping, running to escape. And how, even after they've managed to get away, after the fear and the relief, the antelopes continue running, driven only by the joy of it. He suggests it's possible that any one of them was also running away from where their fallen loved ones lay. Running all the way across the wide savanna and into fresher grass.

The poem's short lines are small bursts of energy, like a scrambling herd zigzagging down the page, over that empty but fecund white space waiting to be filled. As though the words themselves are spanning the polarities of fear and relief, between devastation and joy, joy and grief. Running toward life and the hungers that are necessary and sweet, even if they must accompany terrible loss. Or *because* they include loss.

I headed over the top of the bridge, that place where on a day of high wind or when heavy trucks are coming from either side, it's easiest to feel the bridge's movement. The place that during the bridge's construction decades before had sent designers back to their drawing boards to correct too much unwanted motion. That pivot point spot in the bridge between coming and going and where, to maintain stability, ballast may seem the most necessary. But perhaps that's exactly what wasn't needed. Didn't I want motion?

Seemingly weightless, antelopes were able to leap up and, after escape, turn back to life. Loss and life not so much opposing poles but more like land masses a bridge might reconcile, link. I hadn't escaped anything life-threatening on island or savanna but, increasingly vigilant, I had a growing awareness of harm being close. Of more loss poised to pounce from the shadows. I also knew, as I descended the bridge to the other side, the road ahead like a white page I had yet to fill, that though my heart did not wildly pump like that of a fleeing animal, it still wanted what it had always wanted. Which was everything.

IV
(EN)DURING

In Between

Back in Chicago, I surprised myself, acknowledging Joe's death in an essay I was writing with a seven-word sentence I hadn't expected. "My brother died with his eyes open." Stated with authority, a matter of fact. I now had currency in the domain of death and grief. No longer was I a mere visitor to the terrain of loss.

In Chicago, I received a call from my father, who told me that, the night before, his neighbor stopped by with the news that his son, "the exact age as Joey," had had a stroke, fell, and hit his head. He was brain dead by the time he reached the hospital. In my parents' living room, two fathers embraced, sobbing.

In Chicago, I inquired about upcoming orientation sessions for patient care volunteers at Midwest Palliative and Hospice Care. I was impressed by their comprehensive services, so many that Joe should've had. They asked why I was interested, and I told them about my brother's death.

In Chicago, they said, "Too soon." Six months their magic number. Six months following a death. "Shall we put you down for training in January or maybe February?" they asked. Meaning that, by then, six months after, I'd be . . . what, exactly?

Over lunch at a favorite city restaurant, a friend suddenly

reached across our table and said, "I'm so sorry for what you've been through." As though I'd come out the other side.

In Chicago, I returned to my study where things were exactly as I'd left them nearly five months earlier. The lamp on my desk, the calendar tacked to the wall. The empty spots on shelves where books I'd transferred to the island were now returned. But it wasn't the same. It all belonged to Before.

In Chicago, I resumed leading a poetry reading group. Before emailing the poems we'd discuss, I added Philip Larkin's "Aubade." I reread the passage I'd already read so many times before. "The good not done, the love not given, time / Torn off unused . . . / An only life can take so long to climb / Clear of its wrong beginnings, and may never." And, for reasons unknown to me, I added Auden's poem "September 1, 1939," noting that one of its famous lines, "we must love one another or die," he later revised to "we must love one another and die."

In Chicago, as October wound down to my scheduled departure for Arizona, my father called. "Your mother has pneumonia and it's not looking good. You may not want to wait. Fly out here now."

From Chicago, I flew to Arizona, perhaps to see my mother for the last time. In the aftermath of Joe's sudden death, the world had become a more frightening place. I no longer knew what to expect. Although I had to anticipate I may have to look down at my mother and feel sick to my stomach, knowing she was going to die.

I flew to Arizona to see my mother, but now, in this distant Southwestern state that had become my brother's home, I was again obsessed with the relentless imaginings of his last hours in bed, of those minutes he'd made his way to the shower.

I flew to Arizona to attempt to do for my mother what I failed to do for my brother.

I flew to Arizona to see my mother as she lay dying. But as I approached Prescott, passing the Comfort Inn, Safeway, and Leff-T's Steakhouse & Grill, places that had begun to take on new meaning, my father called my cell phone. The antibiotics and respiratory therapy were working. My mother was suddenly doing better. The prognosis had become less dire. The message: Your mother won't die today.

In her room at the skilled nursing center, with its palette of nondescript neutrals and a waxed tile floor smelling faintly of disinfectant, in a room with a sink and counter cluttered with the now-familiar jumble of stuff essential to her care, and blessedly, with a window that merely looked out to a snippet of grass and wedge of parking lot but did let in some natural light, my mother, while waiting for us, had drifted off to sleep. Since I'd last seen her, her skin had sunk closer to the bone. More black blotches bloomed on her skin. Her hair seemed to be disappearing. Fortunately, her dentures were in so that her face didn't look ravaged, caved in, defenseless to pain. There was, of course, the nasal canula delivering oxygen, an IV, the old PIC line, remnants of the trach collar. A bag of urine hanging from a bed rail offered evidence the catheter was still in place. But new on the scene: the wheeze of a pump for her new bed hydraulically outfitted to reduce the threat of bedsores. A bed so ponderous that for now it had ruled out the possibility—another small blessing—of putting another patient into what was meant to be a shared room.

In her room during the next hour, we gathered, having come, or so we believed, to see her one last time. When my sister walked in, my mother's mouth dropped open in a silent gasp. She looked scared, then stunned, not needing to say that in Chris's striking resemblance, similar in height, features, short-clipped graying hair, she thought, at first, she was seeing Joe.

In her room, somewhat rejuvenated by our visit but increasingly bedridden and still slogging her way back from the brink of life-threatening pneumonia, my mother looked at peace, almost happy, far removed in her head from what surely would be her next move. And though it was a mere transfer to the opposite wing, from skilled nursing to long-term care, the distance from what she'd once known as home was incalculable.

In my mother's room, her eyes moved slowly from face to face. She said, "I have you all here."

No one spoke to the obvious. But in the silence that ensued, her eyes sought mine as though needing verification. Yes, her youngest child was missing. No, this was not the way it was supposed to be. And no, there was no bargaining, no quid pro quo. Her dying would not bring back Joey.

In my mother's room, I tried to tidy up. At the sink, I began to pull out flowers from a vase that had been sitting on the sill and drop them into the trash can.

"Why are you throwing those out?" my father asked.

"They're dead."

"Not yet."

In my mother's room, trying to avoid what might tug her into the past, I stumbled. "Hey, Mom," I said, "you'd be proud of what a good job Dad is doing taking care of the house."

"You're scaring me."

"Why?"

"Because he won't need me."

In my mother's room, as my five-year-old niece in her pink-striped dress and blue flower-petalled flip-flops stood beside the bed, her fingertips tracing the raised veins on my mother's bruised hand, I said, "I like your necklace, Abby."

"I made it when my daddy was still alive."

In her room, my mother kept looking at the clock on the wall, as though needing to confirm she'd gotten through another day.

In Arizona, at my parents' house, I slept in the bed where Joe had slept for several weeks during the last months of his life. In that small house backing up to the foothills and open grazing land, where the only interruptions in the nighttime quiet were the yips of distant coyotes or the occasional rattling of the fence when roaming javelina wild pigs came down the hill and tried to break into the yard. In the bed where Joe once told me he'd slept his best during a terrible time.

In Arizona, my father and I discussed "arrangements," what now consisted of my mother's imminent transfer to long-term care. Once her Medicare coverage, including its onetime catastrophic benefits, ran out, we'd have to consider the state's available financial assistance, and given all that program's complications and hurdles, consult with someone to guide us through the intricacies of covering costs for my mother while not rendering my father so penniless he couldn't continue to live on his own at home.

In Arizona, I wasn't at the point yet where I could show off my wisdom, my knowledge of acronyms, the newest among them SNF and AHCCCS. Language that had not yet grown comfortable on my tongue. I was still in foreign territory, my skills as rudimentary as the first time I visited Italy and could barely make it through an Italian menu or ask for directions to Rome's Termini railway station. I was not yet ready to speak authoritatively with the medical front line caring for my mother and show them what I knew. "Hey, you're not talking to an idiot here." But I did prostrate myself by becoming the model relative who reiterated, "I know you are busy," and "I so appreciate your time." I learned to pepper any request or inquiry with "my mother, my mother" because then nurses on sore feet or doctors with bulging charts may, through a daughter's not so subliminal messaging, be reminded of their own mothers for whom, of course, they'd want an extra dollop of care.

In Arizona, standing at the kitchen sink in my parents' house or brushing my hair in front of my mother's mirror or sitting in her armchair, I was reminded of all she could no longer do: wash a dish, stir a pot, dial a phone, strap on a watch, file her nails, write a check, apply lipstick, make love, lower herself onto a toilet.

In Arizona, in the bed where Joe had slept, I dreamed of him. More accurately, I retrieved a long dormant memory of the morning when he was still a crawling infant and someone had lifted him out of his crib but forgot to close the door to the basement stairs. As I had come into the kitchen, I saw only the nubby-bottomed footpads of his blue onesie as he crawled around the corner to the top of the stairs. I cried out, raced across the room, arms outstretched, but he was already in free fall. In disbelief, I watched as his little body tumbled and bumped, again and again. A fall quick but interminable. At the bottom of the stairs, he lay sprawled on a small rug, utterly still and terrifyingly silent. But by the time I clattered down to him, he let out his first howl. He thrashed, flung his arms, his eyes pinched shut. As if he were a mere rag doll, there was not a spot of blood on him. Nothing appeared broken. I ran my hand over his silky head because I'd been taught that the skull, the fontanel, was a baby's most fragile part. About the fall, my mother would say in the weeks after, "He could've cracked his head open." And though it seemed he hadn't, long afterward, I checked his head, running my hand through his eventual toddler's brush cut, needing still to be sure there was no small fissure through which something unforeseen and irreparable might erupt and a chasm form. For weeks after his fall, with each crack in the sidewalks where I pushed his stroller or in the dry, caked dirt beneath our favorite park bench, I was reminded of my brother's head, how, perhaps, something inside, invisible to the eye, had split apart, been weakened. A dream, a memory. There all along, waiting for me to discover it as if with the plink of an archaeologist's pick. But needing no archival restoration, it had merely waited for witness, to be remembered. In far-off Arizona, where I'd been witness to too little.

In Arizona, in the park adjacent to the skilled nursing facility, after helping my nephew with his homework, he and I and his sister took a walk. Abby gathered fallen sycamore leaves into piles. Matt wandered ahead, aimlessly whacking at things with a fallen branch—tree trunks, benches, a trash can, a patch of spent mums. As if each thing was something to be brutally conquered.

In Arizona, I was back in Prescott, where not long after my mother's stroke four years before and after my father's treatment of a staph infection in his spine, he'd had to recover at a skilled nursing facility so wretched that in the parking lot after leaving him there, I heaved up my lunch. Where, returning to my parents' house, I waded into a slew of phone calls, meals to fix for my mother, clothes to wash, cluttered closets that hadn't been touched in years. In the spare room with its easel and fat paintbrushes my mother had long stood upright in empty Maxwell House coffee cans, familiar tools she'd never use again because, shortly after the stroke, though she could, she would not pick them up again. For several days during my father's recovery, in the house I could not bring him back to yet nor promise him when I could, I became mother to my mother. At night, I tucked her in, pulled up the covers that slid so easily over the thin nylon nightgowns she still preferred, stroked her hair, doused the light. Tucked her into the bed where my father, now the healthy one, slept alone.

In Arizona, after saying goodbye to my mother and promising I'd be back soon, I drove to the Phoenix airport and passed a car with a bumper sticker that read, LIFE HAPPENS.

Or it doesn't.

Or it ends.

I flew back to Chicago from Phoenix, the city where I'd lost my brother. That city where I'd never felt at home. Where I may never have been fully present and where time meant waiting to return to where I belonged.

I flew back to Chicago as one of the kind of people my mother used to talk about when I was young. Someone with money enough to travel, dine in nice restaurants, buy clothes in small shops, get good haircuts. About whom I was to become, and though she provided no specific instructions, had pointed me down that path.

I flew back to Chicago on a plane cruising at thirty-seven thousand feet above the planet's geology with its promise that the world, though it may change, would continue. Far below me, rivers, at least one of which, in its creation, had assumed various positions before adjusting, settling, establishing itself, defining the channel in which it would come to flow, carve out a place for itself.

I flew back to the city in which I'd stayed behind when my mother moved on. Where I came to invest in believing her dreams in moving cross country never materialized, but I, the gal on the go, the smart one, staying put, got away.

In Chicago, I returned to my desk, not ready to write about any of this except in my journal. I wrote in pencil as I always do. With pencil, words aren't so set in stone, allowing for, maybe even encouraging, erasure. But the pencil dulls, is sharpened, sharpened again. Used up, it eventually disappears.

In Chicago, I pressed pencil to blank page. Once, my mother held brush to empty canvas. I noticed how my hands had become so like hers—long, thin fingers with small nail beds. Nails trimmed and clean but never polished. Twin ridges of prominent knuckle bones. A pentimento-like emergence of sunspots like small, pale tiles. Knots of branching blue veins. In tasks I had learned at her side—ironing or tacking up a hem or whisking an egg with a fork—I saw my mother's hands. As I see them now, writing this, pressing lead to page.

In Chicago, I found myself waiting for the phone to ring with another piece of bad news. How long did it take to accept the loss of normalcy, to brace for whatever lay ahead? For the way, no matter how authoritatively they're given, facts were open to errors and contradictions.

In Chicago, I tried hard to be in the present. The elusive, perpetual motion present. A mere matter of seconds. The amount of time it took to raise a glass of wine, pick up the phone, close a door, strike a piano key, walk through a shaft of light, take a breath, say goodbye. The present that was "on a precarious ledge," as Samuel Johnson said. That "leaves us as soon as it arrives . . . and is known to have existed at all by the effects it leaves behind."

In Chicago, as elsewhere, I had once believed life would end. But I'd come to understand life did end.

In Chicago, I was still my mother's daughter. I would always be my mother's daughter.

Memory's Charge

The memory of your past becomes your past.
—Stephen Dunn

It was a late afternoon of strikingly clear sunlight streaming through the narrow window above our heads.

It was a rainy morning, and the light through the window overhead a dull pewter-gray.

The day was hot, the air uncomfortably humid.

The day had not yet warmed, the air in the basement cool.

Wanting something, I called down to my mother, and getting no answer, descended the stairs to find her.

Wanting nothing, I wandered downstairs and discovered her doing laundry.

The washing machine was running. Something inside clunked, occasionally banging against the side.

The washing machine was not running. The only sound the swish of sudsy water, the scrape of a brush against wet fabric.

My mother was bent over the laundry tub, hair up, face sheened with a light film of sweat.

Her hair was down. It obscured the side of her face.

But yes, she bent over the laundry tub, scrubbing a pair of pants, a muscle-memory task she performed multiple times each week.

And the only light, whatever light there was, came from the narrow window above our heads.

As if tides ebb and flow within our brains, bits of our remembered past are carried in and out like flotsam and jetsam riding the currents. They arrive from places where memories develop, are stored and retrieved, the products of countless neuron firings, silent pinging charges. They bob to the surface at unlikely moments or are driven to the shores of consciousness as though by a cold nor'easter. Some memories, with the near certainty of a tidal cycle, return again and again. If each time a little changed and embellished, if each time our remembering is a little different from the last.

All of us are a sum of our memories. Of what, in stunning clarity, our minds choose to hold onto, but also of what we cannot in fine detail restore or fully retrieve, carry into the light from, say, a dimly lit basement, even if we instruct ourselves in the tangible moment of now to remember.

I did not instruct myself to remember one summer afternoon just a few months shy of my fifteenth birthday. I still can't say whether I'd been purposefully driven to find my mother or had aimlessly encountered her in the basement. The certainty is this: I stood beside her at the laundry tub in a room that was not really a room but a carved-out space of singular function and so unlike our house's pleasantly habitable spaces that she'd worked so hard to create and maintain.

What does it matter if her hair was pinned up or falling across her face? If it was late morning or early afternoon? Haven't I, in all the versions I've reconstructed since, allowed memory's sidekicks—imagination and invention—to fill in the blanks, try on different options? Perhaps it's never been as easy as my effortlessly imagining her in water ballet competitions at Palmer Park Pool years before I was born. How, in a flowered swim cap, like Esther Williams, my mother arched, glided, and, lithe as a seal, submerged into a balletic trick as though at home in two worlds, none of this close to what I'd actually ever seen her do, but in my mind's eye is performed with enviable enjoyment and ease. Or how, after, she hoisted herself out of the pool, smiling, giggling, her arms beaded with water droplets as if bejeweled.

Likewise, I've never had to work hard at conjuring up the rest of our basement separated from the laundry tub by a partitioned wall my father installed one winter, then added knotty pine paneling, tiled the floor, built a wet bar, put in a fireplace. He transformed half the basement into a "rec room," a place where I spent many adolescent afternoons as I lip-synced the *West Side Story* soundtrack, belted out Petula Clark's "Downtown," joined my sister to watch TV reruns of *Gunsmoke*, wondering if Kitty ever snagged Matt, or why on *Bonanza* there were no women in the Ponderosa household.

Regardless of the lack of accurately remembered details—and who can say, after so many years passed, what within our memories is truly accurate—the Laundry Tub memory sits on a prominent shelf. It requires no dusting off. It's central, I've come to believe, to my relationship with my mother. Of course I did not know this at the time. I had not yet pulled out repeatedly our exchange that day as she pre-scrubbed my father's work pants. I'd not yet turned it over, examined it, run my fingers over its rough edges, pressed it into my palm like a well-worn souvenir, a long-dead spider encased in amber, visible but no longer able to harm.

Laundry was not always considered women's work. As pointed out by Maureen Stanton in her essay "Laundry," the Old French word *lavender* meant "to wash" and was equally gendered. Later, in further evolution, the word *launder* referred to a person of either sex who washed linen. Still, laundry has long signified a chore done almost exclusively by women.

Consider, as Stanton suggests, that after automatic washers made their debut in 1937, Horton Washers promised their machines would "keep wrinkles out of your face and keep you youthful." Whirlpool's early slogan was "Saves Women's Lives." In washing machine ads, the only male on the scene was the repairman. And consider, too, that even with automatic washers at your disposal, back in the day of soiled, ammonia-reeking cloth diapers soaking in large tubs, you could count on a baby going through some five thousand diapers before being potty-trained. A staggering number, although I'd hate to have to calculate the poundage of dirty clothes my sibs and I tossed with abandon into the laundry baskets, giving little thought to the fact that it wasn't through magic our clothes appeared clean, folded, and neatly stacked in our drawers or that another fresh towel lay ready to be pulled from the shelf, perhaps even tempting us to bury our noses into its fragrant folds just as the ads suggested, the message, "Clean laundry signifies love."

It's hardly surprising that so many of us have early memories of the women in our lives doing laundry. In my childhood, Monday was Laundry Day, or so my grandmother had decreed. Not yet able to afford or possibly refusing to spend money on an automatic washing machine, she rolled out her wringer washer, the washboard, and bars of Fels-Naptha soap. If I happened to be visiting her on Laundry Day,

I'd often perch on a chair nearby and watch how her fingers ominously flirted with the wringer.

My mother had a wringer washer, too, a bulky thing she hauled from the pantry into the kitchen of our South Side Chicago two-flat, my first home. From my booster seat at the kitchen table, I had no view of her fingers jeopardized by the heavy rollers. What remains most clear are color and sound . . . the washer's pale-green enamel, its loud *clunk* and *clank*, the churning of the wooden rollers, their little snap when the last bit of pant leg was pulled out.

Color and sound also seem to be the foundation of what I believe is my earliest memory, a kind of Virginia Woolf-ian "first memory." In "A Sketch of the Past," Woolf claimed, "If life has a base that it stands upon, if it is a bowl that one fills and fills and fills, then my bowl without doubt stands on this memory" of Woolf as an infant lying in bed in a nursery in St. Ives, the waves breaking on the beach beyond the window, a yellow blind being blown by the wind against the sill, its little wooden acorn pull scraping across the floor. A "moment of being," as Woolf called it, perhaps more impression than memory.

If I'm endowed with a "moment of being," I believe it to be this: I am propped in a painted wooden high chair at the center of the kitchen, our flat's biggest room. I have a clear view of the print wallpaper, a pot on the stove sending up puffs of steam, a pair of gauzy tieback curtains. Sunlight has found our kitchen window and falls across the white table and the floor's blue, brightly patterned squares. A wide swath reaches my mother's feet where she stands at the sink, her back to me. Her hands, I somehow knew, or now feel certain, are moving through sudsy water. I cannot see her face, but I distinctly hear her voice. Pre-language, and still a pint-sized container of pure physical sensation, I had no idea what she was saying.

But the mere sound of her voice, the tumble of words, their

cadence and tone, was like a current that not only washed over but filled me. In a memory my body retains, I was being held by my mother's voice as surely as if she were rocking me in her arms. Soothed, comforted, identified. The sound of a voice, and so unmistakably hers, that in the way seals or seabirds gone hunting return and locate their young by distinctive cry amidst a large colony's cacophony, I could recognize my mother by her voice alone.

Impression or memory? What does it matter?

Or how exactly it became embedded within, that subliminal knowledge, the reassurance of my mother and me at home together, sole companions, as if no world lay beyond that sunlit kitchen, regardless of the large paned window, the door that opened onto the gray-painted porch stairs, the weedy vacant lot next door, the hard-edged streets and sidewalks of our tough neighborhood beyond.

One of a life's many fragments, a significant remembered moment by which we each are shaped. And though we do not know it at the time, may suggest, in the words of Nabokov: "Everything is as it should be, nothing will ever change, nobody will ever die."

"Mom, what's wrong?" I may have asked in the basement as I approached the laundry tub. Or maybe, "Are you all right?" Or possibly, "Is everything okay with you and Dad?" This last question fueled by the especially rough patch my parents had been going through, strains that I assumed mostly involved money matters. Deep silences followed by sudden eruptions.

"Blowing off steam," my dad called it, as if he were only a volcano in some distant land.

About his disappearance one night after storming out the door, I'd asked the following morning, "Where's Dad?"

My mother's only explanation was, "He's at your grandmother's."

Which didn't sound good. But maybe it did, a little? That being apart for a time might solve things? Eradicate the charged field we'd been walking through? All that corrosive uncertainty, the worst kind of a child's worry.

Many years before, I'd absorbed that one of my roles was to make or try to keep my mother happy. Simply being of the world was no longer adequate. Though it was not something we talked about much and got little mention, I already knew there had been a child before me, a premature firstborn, a son named Craig who lived only three days. My birth following his death had bestowed upon me special status, as though not just my birth but my survival seemed almost, to some of my family, divine. At the laundry tub, however, we were long past the mere fact of my existence being enough.

My mother had been crying.

I'm certain of this. Or do I need to remember her as crying so I can view myself as the comforter who stood beside her at the laundry tub abutting our basement's pocked concrete foundation wall, the only light not from the pull chain bulb but the narrow-pane window above our heads? A meager light, although, in many of my recalls, it seems to bathe my mother in rich golden hues, as though she were a subject in a Vermeer painting, *Young Woman at Window Doing Laundry.*

Whatever I said, however we got to what followed, I can't say.

Perhaps it was by way of an opening. "You and Dad don't seem very happy together." Said, possibly, with the naive confidence that, in my advancing teen years, I'd gained not just a burgeoning vocabulary but a certain sophistication about how things worked between adults. Or didn't. Surely, I'd already recognized some fault lines, had noted ways in which sometimes my parents seemed ill-suited for each other. And hadn't I recently learned about the divorce of a classmate's parents? An experience that, by all the evidence she and her younger brother presented in the hallways between classes and in a shared chem lab, they had managed to survive. Which is not to say a possible divorce of my parents was what I had in mind. Besides, in my father's Catholic family, even among the less devout, any such solution had long been nonexistent, emphatically refused.

Whatever the preamble, and no matter how much I puffed up with a teenager's ill-placed self-assurance, I was not prepared. Following a long exhalation and in a clear, enunciated voice, my mother said, "You know, I was pregnant when your father and I got married."

This had not existed anywhere in the script I'd imagined. A teenage daughter concerned about her parents wasn't supposed to know—be told—this. Not now. Not here.

Suddenly, it was as if I'd shrunk, had become not just smaller, but less protected. I pressed my thighs against the cold laundry tub for support. Any of my attempts to cross the threshold into a worldlier, more adult understanding evaporated, the last remnants disappearing with the recollected whispers of girlfriends clustered around a locker, talking about one of "those girls." The fast girls. The got-herself-in-trouble girls. Like our high school's latest dropout who'd "gone away to have it."

"But she did get married."

Correction.

"She *had* to get married."

At the laundry tub, as I stared at the concrete foundation wall that had seemed so solid, seldom-used words like *fraud* and *sham* popped into my head. What was I supposed to do with this information? What was my mother trying to tell me? That she hadn't loved my father, and so now, nothing that happened should surprise me? Including, perhaps, her desire not to be here? Without any warning or notice, I'd become complicit. Forced upon me something I didn't want to know, shattering my portrait of my parents, of my father, a man she may not have chosen to marry. Maybe hadn't truly loved. Though no one was asking me to, I didn't want to choose between them.

"So you *had* to get married," I finally managed.

"No, your father and I were already talking about getting married. This just changed things."

"Changed things how?"

"We got married sooner."

"But did you really want to marry him? Did you love him?"

"Of course."

"But why tell me now?" This I feel rather certain I didn't ask but should have.

At some point, doing the math, I'd have figured it out myself: My mother's pregnancy predated her marriage. A computation I'd make whenever I got around to wondering more about who my mother used to be before she belonged to me. When I'd eventually give more thought to that high school graduate, a typist who for a short time rode the train to the city, wore kick-pleated pencil skirts and trim Peter Pan–collared blouses, her hair swept up with tortoiseshell combs, perhaps even then smelling like Pond's cold cream. The young woman who became my mother still on the threshold to whatever her life might have been. And which may not have included Dad, me, us, this.

Certainly, my mother's basement confession—how I'd already begun to think of it—made some things leap into sharper focus. The framed wedding photograph on my parents' dresser . . . had I ever questioned the lack of a veil? Had I ever missed before the heft of a padded leather wedding album on the bookshelves? Had the day my parents married been as somber as the picture I was beginning to paint of it? An occasion without pelted rice, a four-tier wedding cake, all the pomp I'd come to understand was part of such a celebration when, as a four-year-old flower girl for an aunt's wedding, I'd carried a little basket of rose petals and posed for photos beneath an arbor of silk wisteria. None of this, I'd failed to see, had been a part of my mother's experience. No brimming, joyous moments of tossing the bridal bouquet, cutting the cake, no reception with dance band and forks-clinking-against-glasses toasts. My mother uncelebrated, passed over, her premarital pregnancy making her in her staunchly Catholic mother-in-law's eyes blemished and thus undeserving, while in her own family, she became again the middle child who went unnoticed, especially as plans were already underway for the long-planned and triumphant wedding of her unpregnant sister Hazel. And yet in the wedding photograph of my mother in her tailored suit with a gardenia pinned to her lapel, she looked happy, didn't she?

I was old enough to have thought of all this before we stood side by side at the laundry tub. But, self-centeredly, I'd apparently more or less considered what happened in those years preceding me just a prelude to my arrival.

Standing beside her, years past—and now suddenly long past—the days when just being beside my mother had felt calm and safe, I did not know yet that my mother's single-sentence utterance I carried up from the basement into the light, like a crucial piece of evidence needing further examination before a final verdict, would become pivotal in our relationship. Instead, within moments, it became more of a catapult vaulting me back not just to the young girl perched beside her on a counter stool at Kresge's sipping our Green Rivers, or the adolescent following her up the escalator to the foundation department at Gatelys to buy my first bra, but all the way back to the infant in a high chair in a light-flooded kitchen who had not known what her mother's words meant. For all I knew, it could've been a painful admission, but I had felt in it only safety and certainty.

To all the reasons that had prompted her to take her fourteen-year-old daughter into her confidence that summer afternoon and any subsequent regret in doing so, I was still oblivious. I was still busy making it all about me, my desire to refuse any notion that my mother's real life may lie elsewhere, unclaimed. Or to consider the possibility that her dreams had not included me. I did not see her weariness as she bent over the laundry tub, her shoulders, as I've painted them since, slumped forward as though she were attempting to shield her midsection, her body not so much bent over in physical labor as beneath a heavy weight. I want to believe I was a comforter who knew what to do, said something she needed to hear. Or that I touched her in some meaningful way, my hand on her back, my arm around her pulling her closer. If I did, I can't summon it. Nor will I go easy on myself and imagine I did.

Afterward, our family's life on Oakdale Avenue resumed, more or less peacefully, although whatever tensions existed between my parents still seemed to simmer. As if I'd equipped myself with a seismograph, I detected subterranean rumblings, minute fissures spewing forth occasional plumes of smoke. My parents had never been shy about bickering in front of us and this remained unchanged, as did my mother's frequent sighing, though that was many years away from sounding bone deep. It might've all seemed normal, and often I felt it was. The footsteps and door closings, the drone of TV news and sitcoms, the clatter of dishes at another meal were all the mundane actions of a middle-America family in 1965 heading into the future, going about daily routines, marking time's passage, the accretion of ordinary moments that comprise a life. And yet, as a young teenager still bruised from the weight of what I'd felt forced to carry up the basement stairs, still absorbing my mother's wish, whatever the reason, to make me her confidante, it felt as though a tremor had shifted our house a little off its foundation.

Surely, I must've watched her more closely, searching for some new encrypted gestures that suggested she was not where she was supposed to be, checking to see if some secretly coded words were being passed between my parents. And though I was on the lookout to check if anything had changed or might be about to, eventually it seemed nothing was especially different, as if what had happened long ago, at the cusp of their married life, had been absorbed, was now nothing more than mere footnote. Just as in the basement where she'd not displayed a shred of overt, deepening resentment, had not slammed the dirty clothes into the washer or banged shut the dryer lid, she likewise, on many Sunday afternoons, calmly set a pot roast down on the table and her deepest yearning seemed to be for a peaceful meal together, unlike what we were to understand had been her family mealtimes when her father still drank.

As before, I joined her shopping the sales tables at Gatelys. We watched each episode of *The Fugitive* together on Tuesday nights. I alone expressed interest in going to the movies with her to see *The Agony and the Ecstasy*, proud I had a mother who knew something about Michelangelo even if that still didn't seem as impressive as our neighbor who'd once asked me to babysit so that, going solo, she could attend a late afternoon screening of Fellini's *8½*.

I'm quite certain my mother and I did not specifically talk about what was revealed in the basement or why, as if, by mutual agreement, we'd declared the subject taboo, perhaps neither of us feeling equipped to take the next step, whatever that might've been. It was almost as if it had never happened. Though I didn't consider if it was possible she didn't give it a second thought.

"I need a window in my kitchen."

This I distinctly remember my mother announcing. It was 1973. We were standing in the kitchen of the house my parents rented after their surprising move to Phoenix the previous year and now were embarking on a search to buy a house there.

I was two years out of college, had a job in Chicago, shared a city apartment with two friends, and still had no intention of relocating to the desert Southwest. Using a chunk of my savings, I'd flown out to visit, and in that kitchen of dark cabinetry and harvest-gold appliances, my mother said, "I need a window in my kitchen." Not want. *Need.* And so clearly recalled because I'd so seldom heard her use that word when it came to herself.

Perhaps she's also needed the kitchen window of our redbrick ranch on Oakdale Avenue, a vantage point above the sink that afforded her a view nearly the length of our block with its neat, postwar brick bungalows, mowed yards, and well-tended flower beds, a few young maples planted after the ravages of Dutch elm disease, a cluster of neighborhood kids, hers among them, who rode bikes, or on summer nights, played Kick the Can beneath the streetlight. A window as a mother's lookout, a place to watch for incoming danger. But was that what she sought looking out? Or did her imagination stretch, take her farther? As if something had been lost.

How will I ever know what she may have been looking *for*?

And that narrow window above the basement laundry tub? Just

as the window in our two-flat kitchen in what I believe is my earliest memory seems essential to my remembering it, so, too, is the basement window to my Laundry Tub memory. For all I can't call up but attempt to embellish or revise with new details, the window over the tub remains constant. Though the exact words and gestures of a long-ago summer afternoon may have evaporated, the window above our heads with its framed, meager view of only the sidewalk, a porch railing, and some languishing marigolds hasn't slipped away.

If I were an artist and wanted to give this memory a permanent home, I might be tempted to do a collage, a selective shaping of broken and incomplete images and half-recollected fragments. However I'd represent it, I would have to include the window.

"We store in memory only images of values," claimed essayist Patricia Hampl.

Images of what was as essential to our understanding as a "flat fact." My mother flatly stated that she was pregnant and so they married. A fact that remains. But so, too, is the window that all these years later still sheds light on the meanings of a long-ago memory, an image that in all my recollections I've never been tempted to swap out.

But what is absent, ripped from my scrapbook of memory, are so many specifics of the years following our basement encounter. My time at home in my final years of high school before heading off to college, when, I've long been convinced, my mother's confession helped hasten my desire to get away. This coincided, of course, with the time a daughter naturally and increasingly feels the need to break free of her mother. When rivalry rears its head. Increasing tensions between us could be considered normal. Still, her admission may have made it easier to pull away.

Armed with the excuse that my mother was no longer the person I'd assumed she was, I felt justified in pursuing my own desires, the consequences for which I was pretty sure I'd pay a lesser price.

Unlike some of my friends, I did not keep a diary, though, like theirs, the pages would likely have been filled with boyfriend angst. Nor did I write in anything resembling the notebooks that for years now I've attempted to maintain, having been convinced, as Joan Didion claims, "We forget all too soon the things we thought we could never forget." We forget who we were or "lose touch with some of the people we used to be." The selves we were then that help us know who we are now.

Oh, snippets float up, like floating particles trying to attach themselves to a particular memory. The mind attempting to shape a mess of fragments into details. What we arrange to make sense of the things that have happened to us, the small building blocks of our life's story. Overmatched by time, we're forever engaged in memory's struggle against forgetting. And who can say why it's the odd bits we often remember: the smell when my mother and aunt played chemists in our kitchen with Clairol hair color and foil wraps, the sounds of my father tinkering under his truck's hood, and the White Sox game playing on his radio as I roller-skated past the open garage door, the picture of me sitting at the kitchen table urging someone—my mother?—to pay attention to the instructions for building an underground bomb shelter, in part because they'd been given to me by my friend Doris whose father was, impressively, a science teacher.

Or why, for example, the memory of someone we meet briefly or with whom we have a chance encounter stays with us, while something clearly of more importance vanishes.

Like the balding, middle-aged man who often strode past the

glass entrance door of the office where, for several months after my college graduation, I worked as a receptionist.

One morning, he opened the door that was just a few feet from my desk, leaned in, and said, "You know, you're going to permanently put creases in your forehead if you keep raising your eyebrows like that."

And yet I can't recall the specifics of frequent phone conversations with my mother during the same time period, even though a coworker claimed, "I can always tell when you're talking to your mom. You two chat like girlfriends."

Giving punch to Woolf's claim, "Things I do not remember are as important; perhaps they are more important."

In contrast to our girlfriend chatter, I'm reminded of what my father once declared about my mother and me.

"Oh, you two could fight like a couple of sisters."

Maybe he'd been referring to my last high school years I have trouble summoning or the summers I lived at home during college. I doubt, though, he knew much about the afternoon my mother confronted me with her discovery of my recently obtained birth control pills.

I'd just returned home from my summer job in the city to find her standing before my open dresser drawer where she'd returned some clean laundry. In the room I still shared with my sister, in its latest incarnation of blue-and-white with cafe curtains at the windows and twin beds covered in chenille, she demanded, "Who gave these to you?" She held up the disk of small white pills. "How'd you get them?"

I snapped out something about this being none of her business, and that I was, after all, nineteen. "Besides, what's the big deal, anyway? All my friends are taking them." I'd never admit that I'd actually felt queasy when I'd popped the first one into my mouth.

"You have to be careful. There's so much about all this you don't know."

I think I may have laughed, meant to mean, perhaps, with a not-so-oblique reference to her basement confession: "Really, Mom? You of all people are telling me this?"

I held my hand out, our eyes locked, each of us defiant, as she calmly placed the disk in my palm. Turning toward the open drawer, I made no attempt this time to conceal the pills beneath my underwear. For a moment, as she handed them over, it was as if my mother was the one to provide them to me instead of the male doctor before whom in my papery gown I'd trembled when explaining why I thought I needed them, dreading not any physical side effects but that I'd be thought of as "easy" and expecting some kind of lecture. But the doctor, seeming not the least bit fazed or concerned, wrote out the prescription. Yet, in handing me back the pills, it felt for a moment that my mother had been the one to equip me so that I might achieve some of what I believed she'd wanted for herself. That she provided a means by which to both protect and carry me into the real world when the time for passage arrived.

But I'd robbed her of that possibility. It never crossed my mind that embarking on my own to the doctor, I'd denied both of us of an important conversation but also a significant occasion when, perhaps, as she may have wanted, we'd have gone to the appointment together, my mother playing an important role. Shoving my dresser drawer shut, I shrugged off a mother's legitimate concerns, of being scared for a daughter naive to think she was now fully equipped and protected but ignorant of the many things a flimsy disk of pills could not protect against. A mother who was, I thought at the time, resentful of my freedoms. Who may have heard, "See, Mom, I am not going to be like you." Not once did I see her—of this I'm pretty sure—as a concerned, thirty-nine-year-old (only thirty-nine!) woman in a changing, perhaps bewildering world.

It was 1969 and I a Know-It-All college student, the first in my family, who'd vowed never to be backed into a corner, wondering what might've been. As a country, we'd moved past our mourning of JFK, had buried his brother Bobby as well as Martin Luther King. We were sending more and more troops to Vietnam, where casualties mounted. We'd just witnessed Woodstock and increasingly listened to Betty Friedan. I may have once been boy-crazy, particularly when it came to achingly handsome Scott Davis, but I was not sex-crazy. My fantasies were still G-rated. Though I may have been a child of the times, I can safely attest I was not a late '60s "flower child." Still for the most part a dutiful, somewhat conservative daughter yet to embrace much of the counterculture, I did not sit in, burn my bra, smoke weed, buy bell-bottoms at military surplus stores. The only peace symbol I brandished could've gone unnoticed on the lower corner of my three-ring binder.

I'd said goodbye to the dizzyingly quick transitions of a basement memory's young teenager, the yin and yang of demanding to be treated like an adult and still yearning to be shielded. Now, as though it were some brave act, I spun a disked dial and swallowed what I thought was not just protection but a guarantee of freedom. Doing so, I'd be different from my mother and, presumably, an entire generation of women like her.

I don't believe my mother meant her shared intimacy in the basement years before to be a kind of cautionary tale. But had it propelled me, made it easier to declare, "I will not be like her"? A "get out of jail free" card liberally used once I was away at school and for years after, long after a teenager's or a Know-It-All college student's narcissism had run past its expiration date? One that helped justify some of my poorly judged choices, including, before I was even thirty-six, a failed marriage and a brief affair with a married man. My victory was I hadn't been trapped.

A window is not a mirror. A mirror reflects back to us our image, perhaps what we want to see. Or what we wish was there but isn't. Seldom, if we're honest, can we say we see the worst bits of ourselves, meaning not just a stubborn cowlick, crooked teeth, a lack of eyebrows, or poorly applied makeup.

Were my mother and I strangers standing side by side in front of a public restroom mirror, washing our hands or dabbing on lipstick, we'd have looked just like two women, any of our physical similarities purely coincidental. I'd have no laundry list of reasons that I as a daughter did not want to be like my mother. And she'd not have a running tab of all the ways I'd disappointed her, the most stinging, "You're too selfish."

If it were still possible for her to join me one morning when, typically, my first cup of coffee in hand, I stand before a window looking out, watching birds congregate at the feeder or light creep into the sky, trying to assess the incoming weather while, possibly, playing with a poem's lines in my head or worrying over a new essay's clunky transitions, we'd have no idea what the other was thinking, over what terrain our minds independently roamed. Perhaps one of us would remember a time when something beyond a window prompted us to rap on the pane or to touch fingertips to glass, or with a crystal-clear memory shard that inexplicably and repeatedly returns, recall the way we'd once noticed how, on a particular cold morning, the condensation of our warm breath on the glass, like effervescent evidence, shrank, vanished.

"Oh, Mom," I might be tempted to say to her, "imagine if windows had memories. Or could read minds."

Or what if we turned away from looking out and away, changed the direction of our gaze and, rather than looking elsewhere, faced each other, saw one another as two women possessing our individual dreams and disappointments? Narrowing our gaze, our vision might broaden. As though the window had been unlatched, lifted, and was open to new vistas and possibilities. What, then, might we ask one another?

In "Memoir with a View," Sue William Silverman notes that a window was a favorite motif of Romantic painters. The female subject of German painter Caspar David Friedrich's *Woman at a Window* looks out to a near and distant landscape. Transforming window into metaphor, as Silverman suggests, juxtaposes an ordinary life against a backdrop of events, seen or unseen, in the larger world.

Even earlier, in the 1600s, Vermeer often depicted his female subjects contained within a domestic space but with a nearby window or the suggestion of one and the world's presence beyond. Pouring a pitcher of milk or reading a letter sent, possibly, from some far-off place, his young women are seemingly constrained by domestic life. Most notably, and typically from the nearby window, they are bathed in a golden light not surprisingly the color of amber that critics maintain accentuates a notion of containment.

Yes, it can be argued that the woman looking out the window in Friedrich's painting represents longing, the feeling that all the action is taking place somewhere else, who wonders, perhaps, *How do I escape?* Likewise, many of Vermeer's female subjects may appear restrained within a room. Engaged in a mundane, solitary task, they yearn to extend beyond their domestic constraints. But another way of seeing them is that these are portraits of the self-contained. A woman pouring a pitcher of milk is silent within the tumult of her deep, inner commotions. Likewise, the young woman with a water pitcher who is either opening or closing the window shutter to the world beyond is engaged in her own thoughts, the unshared secrets no one knows about, regardless of whom she'd married. No one is in the room telling the young woman in blue reading a letter what to think or answer for. The emblematic world map painted on the wall above her head is not needed to symbolize the world beyond. Isn't it already clear how, engaged with whatever her letter contains, she's been transported, is both here in this room and is not? These young women who may or may not be wives. Or mothers.

If I wanted to paint my mother as a nineteen-year-old in a room with a window, I might choose to depict her in the small dormered bedroom in my grandmother's—her mother-in-law's—house where she and my father lived for a short time following the death of their firstborn. Here, silent and alone, she sits in a motionless rocking chair, her arms and lap empty. Light from a small adjacent dormered window spills over her like a mantle. Outside, a dove perches on a nearby rooftop. Here is where she surely grieved.

But was there a rocking chair? Was there a dove?

Perhaps the rocking chair is a detail of my creation. Perhaps it resembles the spindle-back maple one in which I distinctly remember my mother rocking my sister and brother years later. As for the dove, I am relying on what I'm certain she once told me—or was it my father?—about a dove, or might it have been a pale-gray pigeon that came to perch near the window for several days after she was released from the hospital? But isn't this always the case? A moment of time with details, real or imagined, from which we construct a story or daub paint onto canvas?

Eventually my parents walked out of my grandmother's house into their future together, still Leona and Joe, not Deborah's parents. Presumably in love but probably scared, too. My mother and the young man who'd almost literally been the boy next door, the handsome guy with a thick head of dark hair and a chipped front tooth who made her laugh, the spontaneous one, subject to impulsive and sometimes regrettable decisions, though perhaps that was not hinted at yet, and who, when my mother's father was drying out, suffering hallucinations and serious DTs, had helped to hold him down, these two walked out and away. They walked away from the house to which they'd brought shame.

When, not long ago, I asked my father about that time, he'd reluctantly confessed—obviously some rememberings were still too painful—that his mother "sort of, you know, held it against your mother."

"She didn't accept her?"

"I suppose you could say that. At first, anyway."

I didn't think to ask him what his mother had thought of her son and the role he'd played, the blame and guilt she'd assigned to him, her sonny. It was surely a question that might've opened something of more value than my trying to imagine when and where my parents first had sex, and if one time was all it took, timing, as proved over the years, seldom working in their favor.

What my father conceded, I added to what I already knew: My mother never saw her firstborn. For three days, at only six-and-a-half months, Craig struggled in whatever preemie ward existed in 1948. The prognosis wasn't good. Though not expected to live much after birth, Craig clung to life for three days. But not once did my mother, who was having to grapple with her own delivery complications, see him. "It's better if she doesn't," seemed to be the prevailing medical wisdom, a barbaric practice that I've been assured since wasn't uncommon. Nor was, apparently, the absence of my parents' collective protest. Only my father was to hold their son. Just once. When, in the back seat of my grandfather's car, he rode to the cemetery, on his lap Craig's lifeless body in a small coffin ". . . the size of a shoebox," he once memorably said.

So perhaps I've been right all these years, painting my mother as a nineteen-year-old alone with her grief, with a loss she may have even felt she'd somehow brought on herself.

Many times over the years, my mother said, "I wanted to go to art school." Implicit to my ears in her failing to do so, I heard, "But I had you kids instead." My sibs and I the "instead," the obstacle to a choice she'd been prevented from making. Never mind that there seemed to be no evidence, photographic or otherwise, that in high school or the year after graduation, she'd shown any desire to enroll. It had always been easier for me to picture her in Palmer Park Pool than with an easel tucked under her arm. Still, it was selfishly unfair of me to ascribe a singular reason for her not enrolling. Of the many reasons, the lack of money, not just time, had to top the list. And to her credit, she did eventually take art classes at a community center, her instructor, Mr. Ponsen, clearly talented and with several one-man shows under his belt, though I remember him most clearly as the first man I'd ever known to grow hair in his ears.

Occasionally, I'd ask, "So you'd rather have gone to art school than have us?"

Not surprising, her quick reply, "Of course not."

I became convinced not to attend art school had not been a freely made decision but one thrust upon her. And thus, the wellspring from which all other subsequent failings and disappointments bubbled.

And isn't that often the thing with dreams? We hold onto them, long after possibilities have gone the way of falling leaves, of a truer self that circumstance, choice, or chance has prevented us from becoming.

For years, I believed the "what might've been" defined my mother, explained her life's increasing unhappinesses. Going to art school burnished into the bright and shining accomplishment she'd sacrificed.

As I watched her grow older and more discontented, I often returned to the basement memory as though it was my wellspring. What I'd learned there, coupled with her "I wanted to go to art school" admissions, was proof of potential embitterment. Increasingly, I recalled the many times as a teenager and then before I left home for my city apartment and she headed west, before I played a part in letting geographical distance embrace emotional distance, when I'd wanted her to be happier, had even wished, if that was what it took, that she'd cross the threshold, choosing at last what beyond the window were glimpses of a different life that could've been hers.

But a window is not a door. Even if the door is a Dutch door, like the one that I'd failed over the years to paint into any image of the past. But suddenly, here it is—another feature of our Oakdale Avenue redbrick ranch that, like a laundry chute and a block glass bathroom window, had made our house seem more special than our neighborhood's tiny, postwar bungalows. I can't say if my mother's wish for such a door was as emphatic as her need for a kitchen window, but its inclusion in the house plans was, according to my father, "your mother's idea."

And here it is, retrieved from memory, in our maple-cabinet kitchen, a wooden door leading to our house's rear entrance. A split door that when its top half was unlatched and open, let in light, a view of the porch steps, our street beyond, while the closed bottom half cut off passage, kept the house's inhabitants contained. Half window, half door. As though it was possible to be half in, half out. Which, were it an object in a painting of a young woman at a table, might be as emblematic as Vermeer's world map.

But a window is not a door, not even a half door. My mother stuck with the window. She looked out, perhaps with longing, but she didn't go out the door. And though I may have fancied myself her booster had she chosen to leave, that decision would have been devastating to our family in ways too impossible to imagine now. It was I who went out the door. In ways that went unspoken, were largely unencouraged, and perhaps often misunderstood by both of us, she pointed out and beyond the window even if she didn't show me the door. Even if she didn't hold it open, did not summon me across the Dutch door threshold, she unlocked it, kept it ajar. As much as it was my choice to go, hers was to stay.

But I recall only once when she and I ventured back into the territory of the basement confession where, perhaps, the metaphors for laundry might apply. It was during my parents' visit to Maine in the summer of 1990. My mother had recently stopped drinking. She'd lost weight and looked healthier, if somehow shrunk, smaller in scale. I'd noted how, since their arrival the previous day, she was smiling more. At the fish market, she held up a lobster and joked. She cooed to our dog Ben, spoke aloud to the birds at the feeder. She hummed. She seemed to be genuinely enjoying herself.

We were sitting side by side on a bench near the mail boat pier in Stonington, the small town at the southern tip of the island where the year before Bob and I had begun to rent a summer cottage. In a white sweatshirt, jeans, and tennis shoes, with a print scarf jauntily tied, headband-style, over her thin, loose curls, she was gazing out over the Thorofare to large domed Isle au Haut, tacking down the horizon seven miles away. It was late morning and the full lobstering fleet had yet to thump its way back into harbor, but a few boats at the nearby co-op pier were unloading their haul. Gulls circled, screeching overhead as the occasional smell of bait wafted our way. A couple of kayakers quietly paddled by.

Awaiting my father, who'd gone to buy tickets for the hour-long scenic cruise aboard the *Miss Lizzy*, she and I had been sitting quietly in the sun, enjoying the view, snapping an occasional photo.

"I never should've told you about your father and me. About, you know, my being pregnant," she said suddenly.

I turned toward her. Her camera now idle in her lap, she continued to look out at the water, as though she'd been assigned to watch for any incoming stormy weather, or scanning the surf, was ready to summon whatever of her swimming skills still remained to jump in and save someone from going under.

"You were too young," she said. "I shouldn't have burdened you like that."

Still staring at the harbor, she said, "I loved your father."

"I know, Mom."

"You shouldn't think—"

"I don't." I reached for her hand, as though I was again a mere teenager struggling to know what else to say. But now knowing that she did remember it, too, shouldn't I have felt something more urgent? Especially if, as I'd long thought, that afternoon in the basement had been so defining? Or as the years piled up and I never expected a moment like this, had it become no longer necessary to me? I'd already accepted that for all their shortcomings and obstacles, my parents, no strangers to hardship, were still together. Both of them stayed, endured, compromised, and best I knew, loved one another.

"Mom," I began, "you don't owe me anything. You don't need to apologize."

"Actually, Deb," she said, turning toward me. "I think I do." Her voice wobbled but sunglasses hid her eyes.

An apology. Necessary and absent, which, in her mind, perhaps, I'd over the years exacted a price.

"Okay," my father said, striding up with our tickets. "They're already starting to board." He reached for my mother's other hand, urging her up. "Come on, you two, let's get good seats."

I still wanted to know: How did my mother remember that afternoon in the basement? What of it had lasted for her? And why had she said anything now? But my father grabbed her hand and I couldn't ask. And maybe, too, I still needed to hold onto some part of my version in which I'd so heavily invested for so many years.

It never came up again. Nor whatever that day on the pier had triggered my mother to haul it into daylight after so many years in the most unlikely of places. Perhaps her decision to do so had a connection to her recent attempt to stop drinking, some requisite piece in a multi-stepped program. Or maybe it was an effort to set the record straight, how my parents being together was no mere accident or an act of duty. Just a few years later, her stroke precluded, if only in her mind, any further travel. They never returned to Maine, not even after Bob and I bought our own island house. It was as if on the pier that summer afternoon, I'd witnessed the water parting, swallowing up a singular opportunity, and all evidence of it.

Instead, post-stroke, I traveled west a couple of times each year and watched her struggle with her physical diminishment. Increasingly, she grew quiet. Never chatty or possessing a loud voice, her words were fewer, softer, unprojected. Eventually, in their last house, the woman who loved windows closed the blinds on the window looking out to the yard and the hills beyond, positioned her chair with its back to the living room window and its view of the street. Less and less, I heard her voice that once had held me. Words that had been spoken to me alone. Words real, not imagined, my aunt once telling the story of the summer morning she came up the back stairs to our two-flat. Having heard my mother talking, she entered the kitchen and found only my mother and her infant daughter.

Now, years later, my mother's retreat had only grown deeper, especially after her transfer from skilled nursing to long-term care. It was as if she'd become lost in grief at another son's premature death. And who could say what else? She'd sunk into the silence where our stories, as Hampl has written, "live their real lives, crumbling into the loss we call remembrance." No longer did caregivers urge her to have dinner in the dining room or attend any of the scheduled activities. Seldom did she want to go through the process of being hoisted from bed into her wheelchair and transported to the lobby with its picture window views of the distant mountains. Sometimes, though, she'd turn her head toward her room's window with its slivered view of the parking lot, perhaps her mind no longer roaming as much over what might've been but over all that she'd lost.

Watching her, I wondered if ever, lying there, she descended into the basement as though into some excavated ruins, carrying up to the light some fragments, small bits and pieces linked by invisible threads. The shape that she, too, had made of things, what she alone knew. Just as what I have long carried up into the light—fragments, really, without any benefit of carbon dating or scholarly confirmation—was my version solely, and open to interpretation.

Recently, working on an essay, I had to reacquaint myself with the definitions of *flotsam* and *jetsam*. Too often, I've used them in conjunction, almost as if they were synonymous.

Both words refer to debris, but there are distinctions, differences in meaning both subtle and significant. Under maritime law, flotsam refers to debris or wreckage in the water that is not deliberately thrown overboard but is the result of shipwreck or accident. Flotsam wreckage generally stays afloat and can wash ashore in some distant, unexpected place long after a ship has sunk. Jetsam is the debris of what is deliberately thrown overboard from a ship in distress. Shortened from *jettison*, jetsam is discarded to lighten the load, stabilize the ship, save it from going under.

We all have memories of the past, bits of which, washing ashore, surprise us. Or pieces that we've had to jettison in order to survive. But the past doesn't always let go so easily or deliver to our shores the bits we need to embellish, expand into stories trying to tell us something. What, if we were pitched overboard, are the floating bits we may need to hold onto, used to justify our actions, the untruths we've told ourselves?

All those pieces that, being remembered, become reality, become, possibly, our wounds, our capacity to wound, granting us dispensation to be selfish or neglectful.

Not Out of Sorrow but Wonder

Bob and I had long-standing plans to return to Rome during the Christmas season. Back in spring, we'd agreed to rent an apartment where we'd stayed on previous trips. But now with my mother's deteriorating condition, I was no longer sure we should go.

"Of course you should go," my sister said. "But I know how you feel. It's like we're on hold. You know, waiting to see what happens with Mom."

This trip. Our Maine house renovations. Bob's and my discussions about how we wanted to live in the future and where. Suddenly, to think about, to plan things further out than a few days seemed impossible, as though it were some kind of betrayal, or worse, a temptation of fate.

Dad added his voice to the chorus of encouragement. "You should go. What are you going to do here? Your mother will be fine. I'll be fine. Carol and the kids will be driving up. Go."

Even though we'd celebrate with the kids, grandkids, Chris, and her family after our return, and though my family was decades past our making a mess at the kitchen table cutting out Christmas cookies, hanging the embroidered red felt Christmas stockings from the mantel, carefully setting out the white, pearl-lustered nativity figures my mother had made, and at dawn, staggering into the living room to a heap of painstakingly wrapped gifts beneath the tree, I felt torn. I'd long ago gotten used to not being with my parents at the holidays every year. Now, I was about to board a plane, feeling that getting away—wanting to get away—didn't seem right. Nothing about this Christmas, the first without Joe, was going to be routine.

Almost immediately, it became apparent that this trip to Rome was a type of pilgrimage, a return to where, just eight months before, I'd been so unmindful of my brother's illness. And perhaps no place declared this more emphatically than Piazza di Santa Maria de Trastevere.

As Bob and I made our way across Ponte Sisto and dove into the twisted, narrow streets of Trastevere, the sky was deeply overcast, the air saturated with a raw, cold mist. In the piazza, not unsurprisingly, none of the few outdoor tables at Bar Marzio were occupied, though small clumps of bundled-up tourists milled about the stepped, octagonal fountain taking photos of the cathedral's nineteenth-century mosaic facade, the balustrade parapet, and campanile. In the arched portico entrance beneath the entablature, a gypsy woman crouched, dozing on a piece of cardboard.

Months before, on a late morning in spring, with sunlight so dazzling even the shadows had looked bright, when all the buildings' shutters, now buttoned up, had been thrown open, I'd sat among strangers, languidly sipping a cappuccino and planning my day, a woman so seemingly sure of herself. How naively I'd indulged in contemplating anticipatory grief, particularly about Bob, our lives together, whatever time we had left. This time in the piazza, my grief was not anticipatory. No preemptive loss, but the real deal. And this time Bob was with me, my hand in his, making even more ludicrous any suggestion that anticipation might prepare me, give me a head start on grief. As though practice were possible.

Together, we entered Santa Maria. I was still smug with my knowledge that the cathedral's twenty-two supporting marble columns had been ransacked from the Baths of Caracalla under the pope's directions in the twelfth century. I still had interest in the restored mosaic vault in the apse, the nave's soaring coffered wooden ceiling, the intricately patterned Cosmatesque tile floor. I again wanted to get the best photographs without using my flash. But this time, I was more focused on the simple, life-sized statue at the back of the church—St. Anthony of Padua in his plain brown robe, the saint known for granting wishes. Elevated on a marble pedestal and wooden offering box, the saint as statue held an infant on whom, with bowed head, he lavished his gaze.

Most notable to me, however, were the slips of paper piled at his feet, heaped in his hands and the crook of his elbow. Most were of plain white paper, but some were lined, torn from small spiral notebooks, a few in bright colors as though to attract more immediate attention. And all folded over, their petitions secret. Here is where in spring I could've scribbled an entreaty, "Please, heal my brother." Now I had a second chance. As always, I carried in my tote bag a pencil and small notebook. But I didn't know what to write.

Nearby, Bob kneeled in a pew: my surrogate pray-er. Next to me, above a small brass offering coin box, banks of votives flickered, candles lit in the memory of the dead, one of which, just minutes before, as I'd lowered my camera, I'd watched Bob light. With my pencil poised, "If only I'd known how to love better" sprang into my mind. Instead, I hastily scribbled, "Please take care of my family." I tore out the page, folded it, dropped it at St. Anthony's feet, and as though I'd been engaged in a subversive act, quickly stepped away and waited for Bob in the portico.

Outside, in a more persistent rain with a colder bite in the wind, he and I hurried across the piazza and through the arch into tiny Piazza Calisto. We headed to one of our nearby favorite restaurants. For here, too, was Rome. A wood-paneled room, a fire burning bright and warm, classic Roman cuisine, a celebration of the pasta I swoon over but seem incapable of copying at home. *Cacio e pepe.* So simple and yet so perfect. Happiness compressed into just three ingredients. Enough. More than enough.

Mostly in those first few days, we spent hours walking, just walking. Rome's streets, the "Art Museum of the World," I'd once read. A museum without a roof, controlled climate, or archival glass display cases, and subjected to thousands of tourists each day, to dropped cigarette butts and engine pollution. Without docents or guards, a living, breathing museum open to hordes of feral cats among the ancient ruins of Largo di Torre Argentina, the archaeological site just steps from where Julius Caesar was murdered. A museum where we could sit on a first-century parapet or stand beneath a beam of sunlight streaming through the oculus of the Pantheon built by Hadrian in AD 117.

We walked the length of Piazza Navona with its outdoor Christmas stalls, musicians, and mimes, all overseen by Bernini's massive, muscled river gods. We went out of our way one afternoon just to climb again a small church's familiar twisting ramp of worn stone stairs and landings with their primitive stations of the cross besides which stems of flowers were occasionally strewn and which, at the top, deposited us into a square notable for its elevated view of Roman rooftops and the distant pine-spiked hills.

Uncharacteristically, we eschewed maps and allowed ourselves to get lost on winding, labyrinthine streets where we passed small *osteria*, their windows steamy from pots of boiling pasta water and where in tucked-away alleyways, long battalions of motor scooters were parked handle grip to handle grip in so precise a way as to not seem Italian. We discovered walls so covered over with layers of bright graffiti, they had been elevated into a kind of street art. We sidestepped trash spilling out of cans, the result, perhaps, of another strike being called or a batch of would-be pensioners "going for a coffee." As we paused before a small, quasi-official-looking building, a door opened and a pair of loud Italian voices erupted, each interrupting the other and speaking faster than seemed humanly possible, engaged possibly in a quarrel with another civil servant in another *ufficio* with indeterminate hours of operation.

We wandered into small churches we knew nothing about but that we now knew probably contained another example of a *presepe* (a nativity), so ubiquitous a Christmastime staple that, even though I'd not been to Rome in December before, I surprised myself not to expect such a thing. Now, I began to seek them out. I favored the smaller presepi, rich in detail, and imagined scenes within a larger context—a stable manger with its customary angels, shepherds, and barn animals foregrounding an entire village of tiled-roof houses, a baker tending his oven, a cobbler, his hammer poised above a pair of scuffed boots. My favorites were the unexpected ones in the window of a fancy candy shop, a presepe with all the trappings entirely molded of dark chocolate, and in a gourmet food shop, another nativity, this one carved into a giant wheel of Parmesan cheese.

As we walked, we were swept into the press of people, noise, and commotion. Beneath our feet, the past thrummed. It was hard not to be mindful of time, of age. Walking behind two American women climbing the stairs to the Campidoglio, I heard one declare, "I like Rome. Everything's older than I am."

Another time, I was reminded of something I'd read the night before—a researcher requesting a book from the Vatican library received a note, "Missing since 1530."

We walked among other tourists but also Italians who seemed indifferent to Rome's almost endless range of beauty and surprise as they went to work, swept their steps, performed routines of daily living while trying to survive in a crowded city that had endured over centuries but now strained beneath rising costs and the burden of its aging population while being commandeered by an onslaught of visitors who arrived with their personal visions and expectations of what Rome should be.

So much of this city, the bulk of it, some have claimed, lies underground. Like a mushroom's mycelia. Or like us, each of us walking, talking, toting our cameras, stopping to look, eat, catch the bus as night closes in. What we see of one another but a mere fraction of who, inside, in our subterranean hidden pasts, we truly are.

Inexorable. A word that sprang to mind at the end of another long day as Bob and I slowly wound our way back to the apartment. A word that, when it comes to time, Rome had long exemplified to me. How mindful it made me of time's relentless advance, the impossibility to alter or resist it. The vast expanses of time and my small, blink-of-an-eye speck within it. Not long before this trip, I'd reread some of Natalia Ginzburg's essays, including "Fantasy Life," in which she claims that at a certain age—certainly mine and likely those of the two women mounting the steps to the Campidoglio—we begin to think more of what we had and won't have again, of what we've done and won't do again, won't have the chance to do, no matter how deep our desires. Who we've been. Who we'll never be.

"In this way," Ginzburg writes, "we come to know inexorability." We are more tempted to replace certain facts in our past by other facts, to "emend our lived reality." Doing so, we may embrace what we now know is impossible—those second choices, the lost opportunities. But, she exhorts, "Throw out emendation. Swear a kind of allegiance to whatever has happened." All of it, like time, clear, real, inexorable.

One night, back at the apartment, I scrolled my way through the burgeoning collection of presepi images on my camera. I noted that, as was the custom pre-Christmas Eve, the mangers' cradles were still empty. Infant Jesus had not been born yet. But I could only think of him as missing.

Another night, I woke in the dark, confused. For a moment, I thought I was back in my bedroom on Oakdale Avenue where some nights when I woke and thought I may have been roused by my infant brother crying out, I tiptoed into Joe's room. Standing over his crib, I'd watch him sleep, his small, active body, its animating presence now still, and amazingly, miraculously, breathing, just breathing.

On the morning we set out for St. Peter's, Bob said, "I thought you didn't want to return to St. Peter's. That it would be too crowded at Christmas."

True enough. But I'd decided to return for a reason: my mother.

"Just think of it," she'd once declared years before, the page of an art book open on her lap. "Marble. Hard stone. How could he do that?"

She was referring to the *Pietà*, to what is considered Michelangelo's finest sculpture. The subject matter is familiar. The Virgin Mary holds the dead body of Christ, her son, after his crucifixion and his removal from the cross. Remarkably, as my mother noted, Mary's garments are less like marble than cloth with multiple folds, curves, and deep recesses. Never mind that, as critics point out, such draping folds were necessary to disguise the disproportionate sizes of the two bodies, the near impossibility of this small woman being able to cradle the body of a grown man.

Most of us do not take in such corrections or that Mary appears so impossibly youthful for a mother of a thirty-three-year-old son. What most of us see—what surely my nonreligious mother saw—are not holy subjects so much as a mother confronted with the reality of her son's death, even if he appears to be merely asleep in her arms. More impressive than fabric folds is the exquisite tenderness Michelangelo was able to evoke from stone.

The *Pietà* had long represented something important to my mother, more than just a masterful work of art. A framed, two-dimensional rendering of it that she'd bought somewhere hung in my parents' bedroom for years. Later, after she'd begun to work with oil paints and attempt portraits in the small workspace she'd carved out for herself in the basement, she painted Mary's veiled head and her downward cast face, as though she'd zoomed in on it with a camera and cropped out the rest of the subject matter. It was one of her better efforts, evidence, I've come to believe, of her own felt tenderness toward a young woman who'd lost her son. A portrait that hung with prominence in my parents' Arizona living room.

As I stood in St. Peter's and contemplated the swarm of people crowding around the *Pietà*—since 1972, when it was attacked and badly damaged by a mentally disturbed man wielding a hammer, the *Pietà* has been protected behind bulletproof glass—Bob asked, "How are you planning to get up there?"

Pressing into the crowd, I slithered in between people, using my short stature to step in front of taller viewers raising their Point-and-Shoot and phone cameras above their heads. Finally, I worked my way close enough to take a photo of the *Pietà*'s entirety if I chose to. But this wasn't about being able to say I was here, I saw this, and even had photographic evidence to prove it. I'd come only to witness. As if with a second pair of eyes. As I looked, being jostled and trying to tune out the noise, I saw not anguish exactly on Mary's face but a painful sadness. What some have called serenity, I saw as resignation, an almost necessary, if nearly impossible, acceptance. For several minutes, I lingered, for my own indulgence but also as if this had been part of a promise to my mother I was determined to fulfill. This, at least, I could do.

Leaving St. Peter's and emerging into bright sunlight, rather than cross the piazza, Bob and I walked the south Colonnade among Bernini's massive, masterful pillars. Atop them were statues of saints, a gesture that still felt to me unnecessary, the pillars themselves, the play of light among them, more than enough. As we made our way back across the Tiber, I said, "There's something else I need to see."

This time, Bob opted to peel off and return to the apartment. Solo and with a singular purpose in mind, I headed to the Capitoline Museum. Thanks to previous visits, the galleries had become somewhat familiar. Still, I'd forgotten how tucked away the Hall of the Galatian was. Finally, after several wrong turns, I found it, a small domed gallery with travertine walls, a black-and-white marble floor, and best of all, several large windows flooding the space with natural light. Some admirable marble statuary and busts rimmed the walls, but elevated to eye level on a large marble pedestal and stealing the show at center stage was the *Dying Gaul*. I'd come for him.

Created in the first or second century AD by an anonymous artist and thought to be modeled after a Hellenistic bronze dating to 220 BC, the *Dying Gaul* is a life-size, powerful depiction of a fatally wounded soldier who's dropped to the ground in his final moments. His face is contorted in pain, his deep wound visible. In the fighting Gallic style of the time, he's totally naked, save for his shield. Any imagined battlefield where he'd put up a long and difficult fight drops away in the quietude of a light-filled room where I bent down to look into the face of a man who knew death was imminent.

Where tenderness had been central to the *Pietà*, here it was pathos.

Hours before, I'd greeted the morning without a prescribed plan for the day to come. And though serendipitous, it now seemed intentional. A mother mourning her dead son. A dying son, naked and collapsed, dying alone.

"Here lies one whose name was writ in water."

We literary types likely recognize these words. Chosen by English Romantic poet John Keats before his death from tuberculosis at twenty-six, they are inscribed on a tall, rather plain and impersonal monument erected by admirers years after his death. It's found in what has come to be called the Protestant Cemetery that lies just outside Rome's walls in the shadow of Cestius's first-century pyramid tomb, which, though weed-chinked, mottled by lichen, its blocks darkened by weather and pollution, seems almost impervious to time. There is no fancy entrance to the cemetery.

After Bob and I climbed down from the bus that lurched its way to Testaccio, we walked up a narrow, pot-holed side street and through an arched, gated doorway into a relatively small space on a steep hill bordered by a part of the ancient, ivy-draped Aurelian Wall. Most of the cemetery is chockablock with headstones and tombs, some quite elaborate: a woman carved in marble, collapsed in grief, her body draped over a large headstone; a defiant winged angel astride a large plinth; and sculpted into a stone tablet, a father and his children weeping as the veiled mother is led off.

Clearly Keats's gravesite, though it remains the one most visited, is no match for these, nor is that of good friend and fellow poet Percy Bysshe Shelley, who's commemorated by an even plainer, undecorated slab sunk into the grass on an upper slope.

But more than the gravesites themselves, it's the parklike if somewhat overgrown and under-trimmed landscape that attracts many visitors. The cemetery's a rare thing—a walled oasis of quietude in a crowded city of heavy traffic. Unlike the thronged Pantheon and St. Peter's, it's almost tranquil, something I hadn't recognized I missed until we meandered beneath the towering cypress trees and umbrella pines that, on a sun-polished if somewhat blustery December day, creaked.

Writing about the Protestant Cemetery in his book *In Ruins*, Christopher Woodward claimed, the "promise of continuance is not in the angels or cherubs or the stiff crosses but in the fecundity of Nature." Nature, which, even in December, was evident in the brittle blue dome overhead, in the creaking cypress, small birds flittering among them, in the unclipped hedges and grasses bulging between pavement stones and monuments, in the ivy attempting, as Woodward observed, "to efface the letters of a name." Reminders within these ancient walls that we, and the things we make, decay, die. Here was evidence of continuity and fleeting transience.

In his poem "Tombstones," A. R. Ammons wrote, "The chisel, chipping in, / finds names the / wind can't blow away / . . . stone holds / what time let go." But, as Keats was perhaps suggesting with his chosen inscription, there was hubris and futility in having your name chiseled into stone. We may as well write it in water. Facing death at twenty-six, he knew, as we all come to know, death was not a predicament we chose. Not to be was not an option we got to refuse.

I've long been in the camp of Rousseau. "He who pretends to look on death without fear lies." Regarding death, poet Philip Larkin called it that "special way of being afraid." I was no stranger to the primal fear of my own inevitable nonexistence, but rather than succumb to thoughts of death's certainty from which none of us is exempt, I found myself wondering, *What do I believe? What do I want to believe?* As I looked at Bob wandering a footpath up near the wall, stopping occasionally to study the names and dates of particular headstones, and whose earthly time, like mine, would end, too, I recognized that something was still trying to tell me that belief in an afterlife can help.

Not surprisingly, after my brother's death, no one asked me, "Where do you think the dead go?" And I offered up no suggestions, having long believed the curtain comes down, the lights go out, end of show. Even so, at times I secretly indulged in imagining an ultimate Big Beyond I'd long been convinced didn't exist. Where our best selves, put back together and made whole, live on. I recognized the need that if only to ease our terror when we peek over mortality's edge and find an abyss, we may well seek solace and comfort in the belief we'll be reunited with the people we love.

How easy, really, to imagine heaven as some numinous place where, in gauzy light, our dead loved ones are corporeal. Softer-edged and less substantial, they're still largely as we once knew them, able, once our own earthly days are over, to hold out their arms in welcome. Did faith in such an afterlife help you fear death less?

Larkin, notoriously atheistic, declared religion was created to pretend we never die. But even many churchgoers, Bob included, don't religiously adhere to what form an afterlife takes. They may believe in God but not a heavenly hereafter. Perhaps the loved one somehow "goes on." Or, as Ammons puts it more succinctly, "What is gone is / going on with other / going things."

Does this kind of belief help us accept that we will never be with those we love in the same way again? Never again to sit together over a cup of coffee, walk the shoreline, throw our heads back in laughter, hug, hold hands. Never again a brother in his earthly appearance with small scars embedded in his scalp, the chipped front tooth, the chewed cuticles. No more one-liners, a screwball sense of humor, the lopsided grin. Those blue eyes. No meetup place that allowed for such a thing.

I was suddenly reminded that, months before, Michael, a friend from Chicago, had called me after hearing my brother had died. He'd just lost his father in a car accident. As we were saying goodbye, Michael recounted how his young nephew, after being told his grandfather had died and gone to heaven, had asked if he could see him.

"No, we cannot visit him there."

Two days later, after the funeral, Michael was getting ready to fly back to Chicago and his nephew said, "Uncle Mike, when you are in the plane, maybe you can look in the sky for Grandpa. He's always so slow. Maybe he's still on his way and hasn't gotten to heaven yet." And though my friend and I shared a small laugh, the silent yearning we each felt before hanging up was palpable.

In spite of all mankind's accomplishments and achievements, our scientific powers and logic, the specifics of an afterlife are largely beyond comprehension, but open to imagination and interpretation. Perhaps it's something intangible and vast, of matter and energy infusing time and space with being, something capable of making stars that give light and tides that answer a moon's tug. Some after-existence that even the unreligious types like me might consider. In which, after a name is effaced, an essence is not erased. Still, it's hard to believe that anything can be better than this: a sun-sparkled day in December beneath a bright blue sky, a brisk wind in the pines, Bob walking in my direction.

If anything, I know gratefulness for my one and only earthly life. Some nights, in bed, after a long day of mental and physical exertion, when I set aside the book I've been reading, switch off the light, stretch out beneath the covers and find the perfect position to welcome sleep, and I feel so good, so perfectly comfortable, my body not firing off any warning signals and Bob peacefully asleep beside me, when I am filled with such well-being and the promise of another day to come, I hear myself say, "Please, let me have many more nights like this. Many more years. Please." Uttered to whomever or whatever is in charge, is responsible for pulling all the strings, for the rolling of the dice another time, and with a single swipe, could wipe the board clean. Is this a prayer? If so, I am still so unfamiliar, I do not recognize it.

When No One Was Looking

I'd taken the shuttle bus from the Phoenix airport to Prescott enough times to know that the driver's exiting Route 69 at a convenience store was an uncustomary stop.

"I'm picking up one of our relief drivers," he announced. "This'll just take a minute."

But suddenly one of the women sitting somewhere behind me wanted to get off to use the restroom even though we weren't far from the scheduled stops in Prescott. Of her companion trailing behind her, equally as giggly and, given her size and age, just as inappropriately dressed in a tight fuchsia tank and brightly flowered capri pants, she asked, "You have to go, too?"

"No. I want to get some chips."

"Oh good, get me a Pepsi, too, okay? Need money?"

The doors wheezed shut behind them. The bus idled in the sun, the air-conditioning cranked up. Only mid-May and the temperatures, even up this far from the valley and not yet midday, had already surged. Fortunately, the half dozen or so passengers who were also forced to wait had no urge to begin squawking into their cell phones.

Ordinarily, I'd get a rental car at the airport, but my father had convinced me to take the shuttle. Either way, the route had become all too familiar. From the airport and heading out of Phoenix, the freeways were choked with traffic, the city's sprawl gobbling up more and more of the desert with cheek-by-jowl housing developments, resorts, irrigated golf greens, water parks, an array of indistinguishable shopping malls, big-box stores, and fast-food franchises. Regardless of the different ecological habitat, it was becoming one of the seemingly countless landscapes that had been bulldozed, paved over, rendered featureless, as if our nationwide aim was to make places so indistinct and homogenous that at the sight of a Red Lobster, Olive Garden, or Best Buy, we'd feel oddly comforted.

It still amazed me how far out of Phoenix you had to travel before things opened up, offered swaths of natural, indigenous landscape. Now it only occurred past Anthem, a newly created community that by way of a developer naming a complex of outlet stores The Village seemed meant to help make it one. Beyond that, I looked forward to the approach to Bumble Bee and Black Canyon City and the fat prickly pear and saguaro cacti marching like sentinels up and down the canyon's slopes cut through by the highway. And then, just a few miles farther, where the road leveled out flat as a tabletop, was the place that, not knowing the correct terminology, I had always considered a mesa. But today, nothing seemed distinguishable, not even the northern horizon and the mountains beyond Prescott. Like magnets, they usually commanded attention, as though each of us heading in that direction couldn't resist their pull.

The driver returned to the bus with his colleague, who hopped into the passenger seat up front. But where the heck were those two women? I looked at my watch. We'd only been here five minutes. But suddenly, in the face of my personal urgency, the delay seemed endless.

I didn't need to review the timeline that, since leaving home, had continued to replay in my head. On May 8, my mother was diagnosed with shingles, and the consensus by everyone treating her was this now tipped the scales. Three days later, she was officially admitted into hospice "comfort care" and I began to take my cues from the nurses. I also began to hatch a plan to warm my father to the idea of trying to get Mom transferred home under hospice care. There'd be no need for a Hoyer hoist to lift her out of bed. She wasn't going anywhere.

But only a week in, her decline accelerated. And then, suddenly, it became urgent. The head nurse called.

"Things are progressing much, much faster than we expected. It now appears your mother is 'actively dying.' You might not want to wait."

And here I was, at 11:00 a.m., having caught the earliest flight out of Chicago.

And here came the women, laughing, hoisting their chips and drinks to reboard the bus just as my cell phone rang. The bus doors wheezed shut again and the driver pulled onto the highway. I hunkered in my seat, nearly crouching over my phone, and quietly answered the call.

"Deborah, it's Bill, one of your mother's hospice care managers. I'm so glad I got you. We've been trying to reach your father."

I asked if they'd called his house, knowing, but not wanting to know, that I should be asking why they were trying to reach him.

"Unfortunately, we had to leave a message on his recorder." Bill paused. "I know you're on your way but I wanted to reach you. I am so sorry. Your mother passed away about half an hour ago."

"So my father doesn't know?"

"I'm afraid not. Not yet."

But of course he wouldn't. As usual, wanting not to be late, he'd probably left the house early. Way earlier than he needed to. That had always been his way. My poor dad, no doubt already parked in the first drop-off lot waiting to pick me up.

So, this was it. One day, you complain of "stomach pains." By nightfall, they are worse and it's hard to breathe. An ambulance takes you to the hospital where they test for a possible "GI problem." Early the next morning, you have a heart attack and need surgery to repair a bad heart valve and to bypass three blocked arteries. You never go home again. Instead, your life narrows from hospital to acute care to skilled nursing to long-term care, none of which is home, your address a bewildering set of acronyms: ICU, LTAC, SNF, LTCF. A year since being admitted. Ten months since your youngest child was found dead in his shower.

And just six weeks since my last visit, which now seemed a lifetime ago. A "life" time. Which is to say, the last time I saw my mother alive.

We'd celebrated my parents' sixtieth wedding anniversary. My father had placed a congratulatory ad and their wedding photo in the local newspaper. We'd laughed at her choice of a celebration dinner: a Burger King Whopper she barely nibbled and a milkshake rather than a chocolate Ensure she sipped through a straw. And though things looked grim, we all, if somewhat naively, still attempted the language of hope, just as we had with my brother, all plans and vows and pledges spoken in the future tense.

I squeezed my eyes shut, turned my face to the bus window, and pressed my forehead against the glass. How was it possible that our life's most significant moments could pass invisible to the people around us? To the driver and his colleague quietly chatting in the front seat. To the women, still inexplicably giggling behind me, their occasional shards of laughter piercing the air. Those women whose need to pee and get a drink caused a delay that was in no way responsible for my missing my mother's last breath, but who to this day I hold accountable. Their crime: being so blissfully unaware.

"Need help?" Dad asked from his open car window.

"Naw, I got it."

"Your flight okay?" he asked, as I settled into the passenger seat.

His eyes looked bloodshot, the eyes of a man not getting much sleep.

"Right on time," I said. "And not too crowded."

He reached for the ignition, but turning toward him, I put a hand on his forearm. "Dad, it's Mom. Hospice has been trying to reach you. They left a message at home and must've just missed you. Mom, she . . . she died, Dad."

"When?" He was looking out the window. "When?"

As if the exact timing was at the heart of something, as if, perhaps, he should've just known, felt it, felt the earth shift a bit beneath his feet.

"About forty-five minutes ago."

"I was on my way here. I stopped for gas. I . . ." He banged his fist on the steering wheel.

"Want me to drive?" I asked.

But he needed something to do, something requiring his full attention, maybe absolving him of any requirement to speak.

Since getting Bill's call on the bus, I'd been wondering if the caregivers had been as forthcoming with Dad, had used the same words about Mom—*actively dying*—and if he'd taken it in, known exactly what that meant. Or had he simply not heard it? Or dismissed it? My father, who'd gotten so good at talking around my mother's condition, not directly about it. Not for the first time, I asked myself why he wasn't with her. It had probably never occurred to him to stay at her bedside through the night. A man for whom such a difficult thing might not have been possible. But I, also an absentee, was not the one to judge.

Suddenly, he blurted out, "Yesterday, when I left her, I told her it was okay. I said that. I bent down and kissed her. And I said, 'It's okay. It's okay, hon. Joey is waiting for you.'"

As I approached my mother's body, "Oh" escaped from me of its own free will . . . one long exhalation. My father's grasp on my arm tightened.

Among my first thoughts: *So this is what my mother will look like dead*. But like a lid clicking shut, a shift of tense: *So this is what my mother looks like dead*. As if her skeleton was trying to push through flesh, her cheekbones about to emerge, her facial skin stretched, attempting still to conceal the skull. Her mouth gaping partly open but uncontorted, without grimace, the evidence I needed to think of as an absence of struggle, of her body having given up, yielding. Was, simply, done. But her hands, the skin even more splotched and blackened than the last time I'd seen her, her fingers a bit curled in on themselves, her adept, slender fingers that had cradled, cooked, and created, were still beautiful. In them, a gracefulness yet to be fully extinguished.

As my father moved in closer, collapsed on a chair beside her bed, I went around to the other side. I reached out to cup her face with my palms and bent down to kiss her cheek and forehead. Beneath my lips—Was this possible?—they still felt a tad warm and somewhat clammy. Half-closed, her eyes appeared to be staring at something on the ceiling. But they were not the eyes of the living.

This body that wasn't her. But was. My mother who'd slipped from *is* to *isn't*.

Gratefully, I saw that someone had brushed what was left of her hair and reinserted her dentures so that she looked more recognizable, a gesture my mother would've wished for, too. Pressing my hand over hers, it was clear that someone had rubbed lotion into her hands and arms. For the first time since entering the room, I started to cry. So close to the end, she'd known a human touch.

Beside me, my father was stroking my mother's leg through the blue patchwork quilt that had been spread over her—a gift from hospice volunteers, I was to learn later.

Choking back another sob, he said, "I'm so glad she looks peaceful. Her suffering is over."

I couldn't imagine what he must be feeling, having lost the person he'd loved, married, and lived with since he was nineteen, but I could well understand if there was some relief that it was now over. "It was the same thing with her mother," he'd recently told me. "Remember how much your grandmother suffered her last year?"

Actually, I didn't. I was twelve and my grandmother had become someone I didn't recognize. After her leg was amputated due to complications from diabetes, she became confused, not knowing who my sister and I were and often blurting out something strange. She scared me. But for years after her death, my mother recounted her mother's heroic struggle against a series of mini strokes, a host of other maladies, embellishing it with details in order to permanently affix the story of her mother's unquestionable sacrifice into the family canon. And so it had been especially surprising when my father reported that, a few months ago, out of the blue, my mother had said, "At least she didn't have to bury any of her children."

"Here, Dad." I pulled up a chair. "Why don't you sit alone with Mom for a bit? I'll be out in the hall."

"No, it's okay. You sit. Maybe . . . I don't know." He wiped his eyes, stuffed his red bandanna handkerchief back into his pocket. "Maybe I should go sign those papers they have for me. But you stay with her, okay?"

How quiet her room was now. No special bed pump wheezed. No oxygen machine gurgled. This was the first time in almost a year I'd seen her without a PIC line. I pushed up the sleeves of her gown. Gone were the tape and elastic cuff that had held all her tubes and needles in place. No catheter, no bag of urine hung from the bed rail. The detritus had been cleared out. It was just my mother and me holding her hand, rubbing her fingers, surprised to find them still somewhat pliable.

I'd like to say that as I sat with her, a pervasive spirit, an essence in the room, was still present. But all I felt was an overwhelming absence. My mother's body that had once held her dreams, her secrets, and imaginings, had once, just barely twenty years old, held me, was becoming an empty vessel, a husk. But I refused to think of it that way.

Was it only then that I better understood why we sit with the dead? The bodies of the newly dead, their irrefutable reality.

We sit to express love, show respect, continue to bear witness, and perhaps more important, help usher our loved one from this world. The "departed," we say, as if they have only now embarked on a journey and we are here to see them off, say our goodbyes, be sure they have someone on the shore waving as the anchor is heaved. But here, too, is where we seek comfort, continue to remember, help usher ourselves back into the land of the living. Where we lament, and begin, or perhaps continue, to regret.

The night before, what would I have done at her bedside? Someone who was not her daughter rubbed lavender-scented lotion into my mother's hands, maybe wiped spittle forming on her lower lip, held a wet, warm cloth to her brow, played soft music from the bedside cassette. Someone not her daughter monitored her breathing, noted the body's contractions, knowing perhaps they were involuntary, a sign not of pain or struggle but the body shutting down. Who may have asked for more morphine to be administered in the hours of my mother "actively dying," the process that still seemed to me more a relinquishing, a surrender, although that is to suggest, at a certain point, we have any choice.

I was struggling with what to whisper to her. What singular sentences I'd not already uttered could ever adequately express my gratefulness for her being my mother, for giving me the gift of life, welcoming me so unconditionally, making my happiness central to hers for so many years? This woman now dead. Gone. How to say goodbye?

And what would I have wanted from her? To tell me I was a good daughter? To tell me that the time I'd carved out for her from my presumably busy life had been enough? That she understood how the geographical obstacles prevented us from . . . what, exactly? Did I want to hear that she'd felt loved and respected by me, that she'd not felt taken for granted? For what would I have said, "I'm sorry"? Did she forgive me my absence here in her final hours? Would I admit that I didn't know how to tell her goodbye? Surely I'd have emphasized again my abiding gratefulness, as I did now, whispering to her.

And again, as I did now. "I love you."

All these months and I never asked my mother if she was scared. I was afraid to.

And now, all that was no longer possible. The woman who'd given me life was gone. Her earthly journey that had begun seventy-eight years before was over.

In the hall outside my mother's room, Bill, present, prepared, but keeping a respectful distance, said, "Whenever you're ready, we can call the funeral home folks and have them come for your mother."

Following his final private moments, Dad emerged from Mom's room, more red-eyed and a little wobbly. I took his arm, as though my new family role was something I'd practiced. "I think we're ready, right, Dad?" I asked and nodded to Bill.

Earlier, he'd offered us, "You may want to stay to see her taken away."

"I don't," Dad had blurted.

But I did. I think I did. Surely I did? But we left. We left my mother.

We walked away from the room where, as I left the last day during my trip here in April, I turned back at the door, dwelling a few extra moments, and said what? Is it possible to have forgotten what was exchanged in those last moments I saw her alive?

The brittle proof: There are endings around us every day but we do not recognize them. In seemingly ordinary moments stripped of urgency, we pay attention, maybe close attention, but not to the right things. And now I was leaving again, walking down the same hall where, the month before, I may have thought again, *So this is how it will be now.* One long series of phone calls, agencies, doctors, social service workers, all the tending, caring, waiting, worrying, helping Dad make decisions, not trusting time, one foot in front of another for who knew how long? Where I may have laughed at the nurse Jill's pronouncement to Dad, "You know what's the best insurance policy, Joe? Have a daughter."

And past the central nurses' station from where they'd phoned to tell me about Mom's shingles diagnosis, to report the innumerable skin tears while using the hoist to get her out of bed, her skin the merest membrane that no longer protected, had become just another place where she could so easily be wounded. And where, last month, I asked the nurse practitioner a question about my mother's medications and she said, "Let me look at her charts," and heaved onto her desk a binder as thick as an old Sears catalog, with clipped and notated pages, many of them as frayed as a much-thumbed sacred text. A book not of answers, but mysteries.

My father and I walked out, away from the place I'd always felt so guilty leaving as I passed the residents, their wheelchairs parked in the hall or near the entrance, none of them able to leave.

The little lady clutching a doll, "My baby, my baby," she cried, waving it in the air on the occasions she wheeled herself into Mom's room as though she'd been invited to join us, circled around my mother's bed. The man no more than sixty with a bulging canvas bag of books strapped to his complicated, partly reclining wheelchair. The little, white-haired lady in a jaunty sailor top embroidered with anchors, a crocheted Afghan tucked around her legs, who never failed to ask, "Honey, can you tell me where I am?"

If they were there as we left, I did not see them. After saying a final goodbye to my mother—to my mother's body—I was too heartbroken at having the absolute freedom to walk out the door into the sunlight, able to choose whatever direction I wanted to go.

V

GONE

Next Time

As she spoke, it was hard to keep my eyes off the overly plucked eyebrows of the young woman who'd introduced herself as Amber. As though animate and with a will of their own, they rose, they darted, as if seeking to reclaim some sweet spot on her broad, high forehead or take cover in her thin, upswept hair. But her voice, as if she'd been born to this job, was meant to soothe. And she was exceptionally kind.

Kindness, a necessary virtue, along with exquisite timing. Of knowing what to ask, and when. Knowing how to hold back, wait, then gently probe, and where to strategically place boxes of Kleenex. All necessary for someone working in a funeral home. Though, actually, we were in a crematory—a first for me. Where bodies were reduced to ash, but this one with a chapel, a viewing room, and for lack of a better word, a "showroom." Here, my father and I, like shoppers at a mall, browsed the shelves of urns, as though we were merely picking out a china pattern or a pot in which to plop a plant.

Most everything we needed to do here had already been set forth in the burial plans my parents, to my surprise, had purchased. Two documents in slim folders my father kept in his "strongbox" that specified no funeral service, no casket. Instead, a cremation and to hold the body, only the type of sturdy cardboard container required for a cremation chamber.

"I want you to have some of the ashes, Deb," my father had told me earlier in the day. "It would be nice if you took them to Maine. Your mother would've liked it, too."

I understood his wish for me to have some of my mother's remains but failed to see the connection between her and Maine. She'd not flown east in almost seventeen years, in spite of my pre- and post-stroke invitations, all of which hit some unmovable bulwark.

Now, pointing to a blue-and-white, cloisonné-lidded urn with a thin brass lip and a dark wooden base, my father said, "I want that one. I think your mother would like it."

Flanking us were the seemingly countless ways to memorialize. The checklist on Amber's desk, like a sticker on a new car in a dealer's showroom, invited us to consider the options available for "remembrance ceremonies." All of it proof of how much others did and how little we were about to do. I felt an almost overwhelming need to apologize to this attentive stranger for seeming not to honor or love enough this newly dead wife and mother.

As my father sat at Amber's desk, signing more papers, I continued to roam the room. At the back were several closed doors. Suddenly I wondered, *Where is my mother now?* Not meant as an existential question, but where, actually, was she? Or what was left of her, her body, what had once been my mother and by whatever process would be—had already been?—reduced to clay, dust, and ash?

In the time I'd sat with her after her death, her face had become cold, her mouth more slack. Her familiar face transforming into a type of death mask like those of the famous and notorious I'd seen in Rome museums, but which, in a small, bland, and stuffy room in Prescott, Arizona, was just that of someone's mother, daughter, wife. An ordinary woman of, as many people might measure it, an unremarkable life. I returned to the desk where my father's selected urn now rested, like a reliquary holding fragments of the past.

"Well, then, I think we're all set," Amber said. "I can email the obituary over right away. Hopefully, the local paper can still get it in for tomorrow. That is, if you've made up your minds and still want no mention of any service or memorial in it." She waited, seeking final confirmation, maybe even hoping we'd changed our minds. Nearby and so handy were printed cards and notices meant for such purposes.

But I'd already checked with my father again. "Are you sure? You don't want a gathering of any sort? Not even just a few friends, neighbors, maybe some folks from work? Chris will be here in a couple of days. And what about Carol, the kids, her family? You know, we can keep it simple."

"No," he'd said, "not now. Maybe next time. Next time you come." He added, "I think your mother would rather have people remember her the way she was, you know, before."

Yes, that was precisely a memorial's purpose. That was the aim.

Every person, my mother included, is marked by the life they led, the imprint they leave, regardless of the spiffy option and extras the grievers choose or burial plans provide. Regardless of what I may have wanted as a means of remembrance, my father remained adamant, suggesting that this was something the two of them had discussed at some point.

I hated it, though. It was almost as if neither of them expected to be remembered.

We continued to make the necessary rounds. At the nursing home, we gave and got tearful hugs from the staff. In my mother's room, we discovered that someone had already emptied the drawers and closets. Her few items of clothing, toiletries, the photos from her wall had been neatly assembled, including the folded blue hospice quilt. I wanted to interpret this as a kind gesture, not an eagerness to fill this room, especially with its coveted proximity to the window. I half-expected to see some of the current residents hungrily queuing up in the hall.

As I put her few things into a bag, Jill came in. Earlier, at the crowded nurses' station, she clearly had something to tell me. Now, alone, she said, "I know how much you wanted to be here before your mother died. But I think you should know . . ." She paused. "You should know that the day before her death, when I was about to go off duty, I sat with her. I told her that you were coming the next morning. At that point, your mother was no longer speaking and was only minimally responsive. But I know she heard me."

I set the bag down on the bed, though it was my body that suddenly felt heavy.

"When I said you were coming, she closed her lips and very clearly shook her head 'no.'"

I wasn't sure what to do with such information. Was it meant to comfort, perhaps obviate some of my guilt at being late, something that with other families she'd seen happen before?

"What I'm trying to tell you," Jill said, reaching out, putting her hand on my arm, "is that I don't think your mother wanted you to see her, remember her this way at the end."

Or was it that she didn't want to see me? Hadn't wanted me bedside. Or didn't want to hear me encourage her once again to get better, get stronger, trying to pluck her back from whatever threshold she was ready—possibly had long been ready—to cross. If my mother had only known nothing could've been further from my intentions.

"That's so like your father," my mother might've said had she been sitting with me, watching Dad, who'd now stopped at the hostess stand as he made his way back to our table.

For a late lunch after leaving the nursing home, he'd suggested the local Red Lobster. "Your mother liked to come here for the scampi and the coconut shrimp." We'd ordered both though we barely touched them.

"Everything okay?" our waitress, Joyce, who'd obviously waited on Dad before, had asked as she cleared our plates.

"Not really," my father had been quick to say.

Poor Joyce, who clearly hadn't known what to say when my father told her his wife had died, while, and perhaps more important to her at the moment, she had orders up in the kitchen and several hungry, empty-plated customers looking her way. And now Dad had stopped to talk to the hostess. Clearly, he was confiding in her, too. She reached out to pat my father on the shoulder.

"He's never been good with boundaries," my mother had once said, sounding so uncharacteristically comfortable with such a term.

My father of few boundaries who I'd seen many times over the years drink too much, talk too loud, tell the same off-color jokes, sometimes using language and terms that belied his open-mindedness and general acceptance of almost anyone, one of his traits I'd loved best. In our family, by way of his political incorrectness, he'd earned what was meant as an endearing moniker: Archie Bunker. A "lovable Archie Bunker," one of my friends declared. My father who, at family weddings decades ago, as though he'd been appointed the master of ceremonies, his thick, dark hair slicked back, his collar undone, pulled me onto the dance floor to jitterbug or polka to

"You're Too Fat for Me," satisfied only when the whole floor cleared and his aunt Millie exclaimed, "Oh, that Sonny, he sure can dance."

But what now were the boundaries? Was it so inappropriate so soon after his wife's death to reach out as he had to the manager at Safeway's customer service desk who kindly offered, "Oh, Joe, I'm so sorry. I know your wife's been ill for a long time"? Was it within bounds to seek the comfort in a quick hug or kind word, even from near strangers, as though he were "Oh, Sonny," the young boy needing a warm lap to curl onto?

I'd watched my father in my mother's hospital rooms these past many months and he never looked totally comfortable or sure of what he was to do. He was more himself joking with the nurses and aides out in the halls. I wondered how it had been with my brother. It was hard to imagine him sitting quietly beside Joe's bed, simply holding his son's hand. Had anyone ever done that for him? Some of what I knew of his boyhood was that his father—Pa-Da—was often absent, and for as long as I knew her, my grandmother lavished her affection on her daughter, Doris, almost, it often seemed, to the exclusion of her son.

How much tenderness had my father known? How many times had he heard, "I love you, Son"? More than once he'd told me about his phone calls with Joey over the last few years. How, at some point, just before hanging up, my brother began to routinely say, "I love you, Pops," to which my father replied, "I love you, too." As if that was the most extraordinary thing in the world.

My father was clearly able to be much more forthcoming about the death of his wife of sixty years than the son he'd found dead who'd just turned forty-five. What language had yet to be invented for a parent to talk about the death of a child, for what's been called the most unspeakable of losses? With my mother, it was different.

Over the past year, he'd had time, a long run-up. Not that it meant he'd had time to adequately prepare. And it surely didn't blunt the loss. But maybe it made her death a little easier to accept, if only that the death of a very sick seventy-eight-year-old woman made more sense and was, perhaps, a less complicated story to tell.

Regardless of what the rest of us might need or want, he'd rejected a memorial service, some final sending off that, even if pared down, might've made him feel more hollowed out. He wasn't ready. Perhaps all he could picture was Joe's service, that first shock of seeing a small urn that bore no resemblance to his son. Perhaps he was thinking of his grandchildren—whether to expose them to another urn and all the disturbing images that likely sprang to mind as they tried to comprehend the means by which an entire body, this time their grandmother's, was made to fit within it. He'd barely begun to scratch the surface in learning how to live alone with the urn on the mantel and privately mourn. Perhaps his voluntary admissions to near strangers was an early signal that after I left and, later, when Chris had come and gone, he'd have to find ways to ward off impending loneliness. For nearly a year, his days had been structured around his daily trips to wherever it was my mother, in her debilitation, her options narrowing, resided. With what or whom would he put structure back into his life?

And what about my adjustments? Often, I still found myself measuring time by Joe's death. Just three months ago, he'd have turned forty-six. In just two months, he'd be dead a year. I was still reimagining again and again his final hours, still assessing the might-have-beens, attempting to separate the possible from the wishful fantastical, still sifting through, expanding on the pittance of details I possessed, most of them obtained secondhand.

And now my mother. What new timeline would I keep? Cruelly:

Where in my already heavy heart was I to make room for her? Selfishly: What shifts would I need to make in my thinking, my worrying? The calls to Arizona would now not be to Dad but about Dad. Checking in, coaxing out of him how he was feeling, and though still being rejected, trying again to suggest to him grief counseling, even though I was equally uneasy about such terrain.

After Joe's death, I'd rejected nearly all bereavement literature and recovery blogs proliferating on the Internet, the strategies and tools of grief and all the buzz phrases: coping, recovery, healing. One afternoon, out of curiosity, I'd searched and found a plethora of how-to handbooks and "practical guides" complete with checklists. About surviving a parent, surviving the loss of a child. A surprising number offered instruction on how to cope with the death of a beloved pet. In a genre that I'd read was the literature of widowhood, Amazon offered an abundance of titles, many of them, such as *From Grief to Gladness*, seemed unabashedly upbeat. One book's subtitle declared it offered to widows a thoughtful, practical guide to rebuilding their lives. An "indispensable guide," one reader-reviewer claimed, while another wrote that she'd added it to her "wish list."

Earlier in the day, after talking to his sister on the phone, my father said she'd not be flying out from Chicago. Not that my father had expected she would. Just as, I was beginning to suspect, he may not have counted on being with my mother when she took her last breaths. Years ago, after his ninety-year-old mother was taken to the hospital and he got the call she was dying, for whatever the reasons, none of them financial and still inexplicable to me, he got in his car and drove seventeen hundred miles to Chicago rather than take a three-and-a-half-hour flight. And of course, he missed it, my grandmother dying in her hospital room. Which he may or may not have regretted. It was as if such a thing was customary and to be expected, like the way new dads once didn't question being shut out of delivery rooms. Or as though the reluctance to witness, be present, was an inherited family trait. For all the novenas, holy cards, wakes, High Masses, and Catholic-sanctioned funeral practices, his family, it seemed, wasn't very good at witnessing death. More simply, for my father to be present with his wife at the end, perhaps he simply couldn't. But then who was I to judge, the daughter, "the best insurance policy," who hadn't gotten her butt onto a plane a day earlier?

At my parents' house, I discovered my father had become pretty proficient at doing his own laundry. One of his short-sleeved knit shirts hung on a hanger from the same cabinet knob my mother had used for such purpose. The same brand of detergent sat on the shelf and, were I to check, the hot water line to the washing machine was most likely turned off until the next load.

"There's no point in inviting problems," my mother once said when I asked her if she'd ever had a leak or burst pipe. Like her, Dad wasn't using the dishwasher much, but given that he was a considerably less skilled manual washer, I wished that he did. He had, however, reclaimed a large swath of the kitchen counter and hauled in the large microwave my mother, because of its size, had banished to the pantry.

I already knew he hadn't been sleeping much in their bedroom, opting instead for the small sofa in his TV room but more frequently falling asleep in his recliner. On those first nights we spent together after my mother's death, each of us curled around our grief, he retreated to the TV room at one end of the house while I took over the living room corner, sitting in Mom's wingback chair, my journal or a book in hand, but also succumbing to the lure of the remote and mindless clicking through what was available on their limited cable package, much of it personal shopping networks, sporting events, and reruns of movies and old TV series I had no wish to see. There was also an alarming amount of reality TV programs. Watching them, I gained a better understanding of why some people might not think it unusual to watch shows or read books with titles like *Funny Funeral Home Stories* or *Hilarious Headstone Epitaphs.*

I was still plagued by the sense that something more should be happening, more I should be doing in the wake of my mother's death. In Francine du Plessix Gray's essay "The Work of Mourning," she evokes *The Iliad* and the "clamorous terrain of Homeric battle," that brutal mayhem of lances driven through eye sockets, brains pouring out of mouths, bowels gushing through clenched hands, of limbless torsos being spun like marbles above the black-blooded earth. But both sides shared the commitment to an occasional truce when all fighting stopped to allow for the proper burial of the dead, when survivors could lament, wash, and anoint treasured corpses, adorn pyres with flowers. When the living could address a principal terror: the disgrace of "being insufficiently mourned and inadequately buried."

Dad and I had covered the bases regarding my mother's cremation, but without an organized remembrance did she remain "insufficiently mourned"? Without an organized remembrance in which I'd play a part, I'd have to settle, be grateful instead for my efforts that came before. Like those made during my last visit. It had become irrefutable that my mother would never again go anywhere outside the nursing home walls without serious assist—a couple of CNAs using the Hoyer hoist to lift her out of bed, lower her into her wheelchair, and once properly propped, wheel her to a van equipped with a lift. The nursing home van was only available for medical purposes or a few, select "off campus" activities she was too weak to participate in.

In April, I booked a private company to take my mother out for a drive. Maybe, if all went well, I'd contract the van service on a regular basis, just to get her out for a drive when I was back East, take her someplace farther than the small park adjacent to the nursing home I'd wheel her to when the weather was good or the protected place beneath the entrance canopy where we sometimes sat, watching the birds.

The day of our van drive was cool but clear. I'd bought her a blue fleece bed jacket. She wore her pink hat. I was told that the first CNA to enter her room in the morning was greeted with, "Today I'm going out in the van." But by the time my father and I arrived, any earlier excitement seemed to have diminished. She grew increasingly quiet. Even after we'd gotten her wheelchair into the van and locked into place, my mother comfortably propped, and I took the narrow seat closest to it, my father up front with the driver, she wasn't saying much. She'd never asked where we were going, nor stated a preference. She'd seemed happy enough just to be going somewhere.

As we drove onto Route 89, she looked around, taking everything in, a hungry look in her eyes, or so I thought. She said little, as though her engagement with the world, even here, farther out into it, was maintained mostly in silence, in unshared thoughts and recollections. As we drove past the strip malls and fast-food restaurants, my father occasionally twisted around in his seat, smiled, and asked, "Are you comfortable? Can you see okay?" He'd point and comment on some new restaurant going in, the expansion of a local shopping center, the new parking lot at the Goodwill store my mother and Chris, during previous years, had often scavenged.

Turning off at an increasingly pine-forested road, we wound our way up to Loon Lake, a destination my father had chosen. Unfamiliar with the terrain, I'd left it to him.

"It's pretty there," he'd said. "Your mother always liked it." It was also where they'd often gone with Joe, fishing from one of the piers.

The driver took the road around the lake, made a slow loop of the picnic and camping grounds, drove up to an elevated view of the entire lake, before parking in a shady spot near the boat ramp. It was a weekday morning in spring and there were few people around.

"So this is nice, isn't it?" my father asked.

But I'd been watching my mother, occasionally scooting over to her, pushing a pillow into place or tucking the blanket around her legs, taking her hand. What pictures were forming in her head? What upswelling of memory?

My father had determined that going by the house would be too painful, and I'd reluctantly agreed.

I'd said, "So, Mom, we're not going to get all the way down to Prescott Valley today, okay?" and she'd said, "Yes." But did she really want to see the neighborhood, the street, her house? The home she'd never return to? We didn't ask her.

And she didn't say. "Not this time," I told her.

And, nodding, she said, "Next time."

Simply to cruise by seemed too cruel. For her to go inside, take a look around, and then be driven back to her small room seemed even worse. And the house had no ramp, wasn't equipped. For months, she'd not been proactive in her treatment. After years of playing her own doctor, she'd left to others all diagnoses, treatments, and decisions about care and where she'd go next. As though she was no longer among us. If she ever felt angry about feeling a lack of control, of being under assault, having to sacrifice vanity and bear any indignity with a body she couldn't always move or adjust, she gave us little sign.

"Not this time," we concurred, choosing Loon Lake.

Was there any place we could've taken her that she needed most? There was no headstone, vault, or memorial bench where she might be tempted to openly weep, pound her fists, stroke a surface, rest her head. If only, sitting by the boat ramp, my mother could've reached for the door handle, gotten out of that van, walked through the pine trees down to the lake's edge, perhaps sat at the end of the pier where, presumably, her son had once plunked in his bait-weighted line, the two of them waiting for whatever would happen next.

Still(ed) Life

A life should leave
deep tracks.
—Kay Ryan

"Hey, I like your new still life," Bob once said as he entered the kitchen to help with dinner. He gestured toward three lemons on a blue plate and some red plums in a green wooden bowl I'd placed against a white wall. Above them hung a small pastel of a twilight sea and sky in muted tones of silvery violet.

I'd long appreciated his noticing my aesthetic efforts but was conflicted about his calling them "still lifes." Too pretentious, perhaps? As though I was dealing not with fruit but shape and form, and with my three lemons on a plate, had attempted a Cézanne-like variation on a sphere? Or that in some remote way, I'd tried to link myself with Chardin, who only needed a glass of water, a charred copper coffeepot, and three bulbs of garlic to achieve a masterpiece?

"Okay, then, so call it, I don't know, 'artful arranging'?" Bob offered, as he prepared chops for the grill.

Nearby, I tossed a salad. Later, I might pick up one of those plums and eat it or offer it to him. Here in our house where fruit was meant to be consumed but because it was "artfully arranged" and aesthetically pleasing, might feed the eye, too? And this was less pretentious?

Except for some high school art classes, I've never drawn or painted. If I did, I'd prefer still lifes. Portraits seemed too daunting, the attempted representation of the whole mind-clicking person in a tilt of the head, a particular cast of the eyes, a lock of hair coiled against forehead. And if faced with the open sea or a mountain range, where would I begin? Cézanne tackled Mont Sainte-Victoire again and again. My brush would hesitate over its smallest alpine daisy in a rocky crevice or the scabby trunk plates of a twisted, mistral-tossed cypress. Unlike Winslow Homer in his seascapes, I'd not get past one wave's fractured spray. Were I a painter, I'd likely focus on the intimate and familiar, on lemons and a wooden bowl. I'd try to capture onto canvas what the eye sees up close or what it misses, not for want of looking but for what can't easily be captured in paint—how the day's last light illuminating Bob's hand pointing to lemons on a blue plate fades with excruciating speed.

Regardless of what I'm comfortable calling it, I've long enjoyed and somehow need to move through my house, pausing to compose, choosing what, for a time, I'll see. It's a nurturing enterprise. Either on a gray, vacant winter afternoon or in July's full-blown sunlight, a simple arrangement invites my eye to relinquish its restless scanning, to focus attention, give full weight to something small, ordinary. To allow life to be stilled.

I've also come to see that my "arrangements" are a way my mother enters my house. She fed my eye early on. With paint samples and at her Singer with bolt-ends of discounted fabric, in endless reinventions of cafe curtains, slipcovers and complementing color schemes, she assembled what she could afford on a tight budget, attempting to make our house more than just comfortable. But also—and this took much longer to appreciate—after she and her pal Ruth made many trips "junking" at flea markets and yard sales, unlike Ruth, my mother cleared away clutter, grouped and gathered and arranged. She made of her finds small oases that, as far as I know, she never dreamed of calling still lifes. Without my knowing it, she began to shape what and how I see.

A still life painting is immutable, silent. As Mark Doty observes in *Still Life with Oysters and Lemon*, "No word will ever be spoken here." Objects are perennially poised "for a forward movement that will never occur." But can't they suggest a human presence might be just around the corner, about to reenter our field of vision and approach a fruit-laden table? Doesn't a still life suggest movement still to come? Of what might be whisked off the table or raised to the lips by an extended hand?

In any still life painting, even the unremarkable jugs, jars, and bottles in the seemingly stark arrangements of Giorgio Morandi, the human is not visible but implied. Suggested is the person who placed these items just so, who chose, in moments of attention, what has been offered, set apart. All these assembled objects, unlike the human lives they suggest, are fixed on canvas, but before being rendered in paint were as unfixed—as unfixable—as my plums in a bowl or lemons on a blue plate.

Or, in a gesture not dissimilar to mine, the fruit my mother gathered in her blue-and-white Willow Ware bowl the morning she was ambulanced to the hospital from the house to which it was presumed she'd return but didn't. I will never know what potential still life of hers resided in her kitchen that morning—solid, dependable apples, a few clementines, a ripening banana bright against blue? Not rendered in paint, there was no timelessness, nothing permanent caught in time.

But when I entered her bedroom for the first time after her death, her arrangement of a dinged-with-use pewter pitcher filled with dried grasses, a small, enameled dish holding a few polished pebbles, and a small, filigreed clock greeted me from a white wicker table. As did the carefully assembled clutch of miniature carved, lidded boxes on her dresser.

Ah, yes, *still* life, Doty reminds us, with "the deep pun hidden in the term: life with death in it." The darkness behind gathered things that is the not-here, the not-now. The big, dark unknown against which Chardin, who primed his canvases with deep-brown pigment, gathered objects joined "in a conspiracy of silence . . . a dialogue we cannot hear."

I was quite certain that my father, having camped out for months in the TV room on the other side of the house, had touched little in the bedroom he and my mother once shared, and that it was still pretty much as she'd left it. And it was here, among objects waiting to be picked up again when her life presumably resumed, that I'd been assigned a painful task.

"Before you leave, Deb," my father had said, "I want you to clean out her closets and drawers. You and Chris can take what you want, but the rest of it, her clothes and stuff, I want to donate. I can't do it. I really can't."

And so the agreement with my sister: I'd do the bedroom and she, when she soon arrived, would tackle Mom's sewing and crafts room.

I'd already decided I would not touch her still lifes. They were to be left as is, in a continued pretense of permanence and as a comfort to my father. Surely he'd grown accustomed to their presence. I also found comfort in recalling the narratives behind objects I recognized—the pewter pitcher she'd found at a flea market the same day she discovered a brass hall tree left out with the trash in an alley, finds she'd hauled with her from Chicago to Arizona decades before. Much harder was any attempt to invent stories for the objects I knew nothing about or to guess at whatever had merited my mother's attention and selection. Perhaps only later would I be able to admire her arrangements just for their composition, in the way she had surprised me on the last day of my visit the previous month.

I'd waited until then to share with her the album I'd put together to honor my parents' sixtieth wedding anniversary—photographs, some dating back decades, many of which, during my previous trips to Arizona the past several months, I'd scavenged from brimming shoeboxes where my mother had stored them. At a camera shop, I'd had several restored and resized. In a fat, compact, leather-bound album, I'd arranged them in chronological order. Pictures of my parents as young children—my mother in a dark pinafore sitting on a tricycle with pedals her feet can't reach, my father in a white shirt and belted, high-waisted trousers posing before a picket fence. My parents, high school sweethearts, at a dance, the beach, a football game—glimpses of who they were before they became my parents. And then as a couple marching forward into young parenthood, family gatherings, holiday celebrations, a bit of travel. Photos spanning more than seventy years.

Pulling the album from my canvas bag that last afternoon was, I knew, a potentially dangerous enterprise. Several photos included Joe, a progression of my brother from small boy to student to young father. I was potentially invoking more heartbreaking sorrow when my intention was to keep things celebratory and uplifting at a time when it was desperately needed.

As I perched on the side of my mother's bed, I watched her flip through the pages. She'd paused on an early photo, a black-and-white of her wearing a long tweed coat, a block-patterned scarf tied snugly over her head as she pushed a large stroller, presumably with me inside, along a sidewalk patchy with old, crusted snow.

"I think that was on Eggleston Avenue," she said.

"No, hon, pretty sure that was on Kensington," my father said, a map of Chicago's South Side still stamped within his head.

And then she said nothing until, nearly two-thirds of the way through, she stopped and said, "That's a nice picture."

Meaning, I'd thought, it brought back happy memories of what appeared to be a camping trip with my father, Joe, and Carol. Taken at night, my mother sat at a picnic table covered with an orange-and-yellow floral-printed oil cloth as she read by the light of a Coleman lantern. In the foreground, there's a campfire, its flickering flames suggesting it would soon burn out. Also on the table beside the lit lantern was a glass, a bowl, an open book. Clearly, though, the photo's subject was my mother reading, her upper torso and profiled face illumined.

As she continued looking at it, my father, standing on the other side of her hospital bed, leaned in, said something about what part of the state this was, naming whatever lake they'd camped beside. I was hoping for more from my mother. What did she remember?

Tapping the photo with her index finger, she said, "It's a nice composition."

Meaning what? That the composition, like those of the best still lifes, invites the eye, offers a path of entry, the nearby objects leading to others that recede into the background? The way an objective viewer's attention is drawn from glass and bowl and lantern to my mother, a single figure lit against darkness, that impenetrable black background unreachable by flash or flame?

She was looking at a photograph of herself at a particular point in time, but it was as if she were a stranger to the subject matter or assessing an ancient artifact only recently excavated, some fragment to which she was only being asked to critique perspective and foregrounding.

"Nice composition." A compliment to the eye of the photo-taker, Joe most likely, standing back in the dark on the other side of the fire, who, with a shutter's click and flash, had stilled, held the moment, pushed back the night. Joe, no longer with us, who had, across time, delivered this moment, though we could never know what prompted him to raise the camera.

When I look at this photograph now, I see my mother captured in a peaceful and presumably contented moment, the dark background presaging nothing and the soon-to-be-extinguished campfire mere foreground, not a foreshadowing.

But if I were to be asked to see it as something other, as a painting, perhaps, I'd say I see neither portrait nor landscape. Rather, a still life in which time had seemingly been stilled. The flames had not yet gone out. The lantern had not been doused. My mother had not yet turned the page.

Also, when I look at it now, I see my mother propped in her hospital bed on the last afternoon I saw her alive.

"Nice picture," she'd said.

My mother's still life arrangements in her bedroom were one thing. But, and though I was attempting to be an objective doer, I found a whole other, more painful terrain when I opened her closets. More clothes than I'd anticipated. All so clean and tidy—suddenly heartbreakingly—hung on matching plastic hangers. When had she worn them all?

Increasingly, in the years following her stroke, she and my father hadn't gone out much. According to Joe, in the months preceding her ambulance ride to the hospital, she'd often not changed out of her bathrobe or one of those loose, snap-front cotton dusters that, for as long as I could recall, she and my aunts called "housecoats." I hesitated reaching in, as though I'd been called in merely to survey the scope of the job.

True to his unspoken promise, my father had made himself scarce. Earlier in the morning, I'd heard him banging around in his work shed, tackling some new task he'd assigned himself. The day before it was a railing on the deck that to my eye already seemed secure, in need of no fix. I'd been reminded of the call from Mom when they still lived in Phoenix and my father was just getting accustomed to retirement but they were already flirting with the downsizing move that would take them to the Prescott foothills.

"You'll be happy to know that as of today we now have a new storage space with trapdoor access up in the eaves of the garage."

"For what?" I'd asked her.

"Now that's a good question."

I turned away from the closets and drawers and raised the window shades, pulled back the curtains. My mother had always liked to keep the bedroom dark, and increasingly, the rest of the house. My father, in another of his small taking-ownership moments, had already pulled back the blinds and drapes in the dining and living rooms. Now there were views of the hills, the yard, the bird feeders that in the past few days he'd worked even more diligently to keep filled.

For several moments, I watched a pair of kingbirds and what I was pretty sure was a mockingbird. The occasional flashes of bright orange I'd already identified as Bullock's orioles. A covey of bobbing quail pecked at the corn my father threw toward the back fence each morning. Doves perched on the lip of the bird bath. The night before, lying awake in the guest room, I'd heard coyotes in the hills. Creatures all hungrily feeding, indifferent, life going on.

It's said that when a person dies, a physical space the dead once inhabited retains life and does not die right away. What had I expected? To reach into my mother's closet and feel a remnant of some kind of body heat? Or a scent, perhaps? And what would that have been? Instead, an overwhelming absence. A nearly unbearable inertness.

All her neatly hung clothes mutely awaited a woman who would never return. Who'd never again wear whatever it was she'd worn that afternoon, during one of our visits when Bob and I took my parents to the Heard Museum. After, we planned to have lunch somewhere special. But we had no particular place in mind. The area was unfamiliar to us, my father was hungry, and at that in-between-lunch-and-dinner-hour when so many restaurants are closed, we wound up in a dark booth at a nearly empty, dismal Mexican restaurant. Perhaps the huge disappointment was only mine and didn't matter to my mother, who got out so seldom, but who'd clearly dressed that morning for something better. Sitting there, stabbing greasy corn chips into a bowl of soupy guacamole, I felt certain this place, this selection so not what I'd had in mind, reflected something about me. As though I'd declared my mother was undeserving of the kind of place I'd ordinarily go.

But hadn't my inclination always been to splurge a little? At, say, the Hermosa Inn the year before, where Bob and I arranged a springtime lunch on the patio with my parents and Joe and for which my mother had bypassed her usual embrace of pastels and chosen something I couldn't help but think she'd assumed would more align with my taste—a two-piece, black-knit pants outfit with a crisp white top.

She'd even broken out the thin gold chain necklace and earrings I'd bought her at Marshall Field's one long-ago Christmas. I imagined her on her walker before her closet and reaching into her drawers, making an effort to decide, as though trying to live up to expectations, trying, or perhaps feeling the need, to impress me, the daughter from away who could afford nice restaurants. The daughter who, following lunch, held a camera and, attempting a good composition, framed my parents flanking Joe. The last photograph, it turned out, of the three of them together.

Just a few months later, Joe would be dead and my mother would struggle on a ventilator in acute care. A photograph in which, since, I've had to look hard for signs of Joey's remaining jaundice but have found it easy to detect, in spite of my mother's loose-fitting top, her weight gain and the bloat of her face that should've been interpreted as warning signs.

I began to ease her clothes off hangers, fold and stack them on the bed, as though I'd only volunteered to get her ready for a long trip. By the time I moved on to her drawers, I felt like an intruder come to ransack and pillage, though her absence was so pervasive and undeniable, not once did I expect her to show up at the door and demand to know what I was doing pawing through her things.

Here were all the slippery polyester nightgowns she preferred after her stroke, because, she'd said, they made getting in and out of bed easier. Her sturdy cotton bras. Her thin white crew socks. Here, too, even among the humblest items, was evidence of my mother's conscious thought, her decisions of what to buy, what needed to be laundered, what she'd wear with what. So, too, whatever she'd thought of my myriad gifts over the years. Though I'd taken great care in selecting what I bought for her, I can't say I ever questioned that what I chose might be something she didn't like. As though just coming from me was enough. Items, often jewelry, from far-off places she'd never see. The cameo necklace from Sicily resembling the one her father had brought back from the war but over the years had gone missing. The small signet ring I bought in a jewelry stall on the Ponte Vecchio spanning the Arno River. Trophies from her daughter's successes. A daughter who too often failed to see that her experiences and accomplishments were not a substitute for her mother's aspirations and unrealized dreams.

"You and your sister should take some of your mother's things," Dad had said. But who was I to decide? I didn't know yet how to want what was hers. Or what to want. I hadn't known for a long time.

Her bathroom, I thought, would be easier. Although here, most emphatically, was the evidence: life stops. Where things have meaning only in the uses a life makes of them. Here the ruins: the clogged, dried-up, dusty, and nearly empty remnants. Of creams, makeup, nail polish. On the vanity, the small, mirrored makeup tray I couldn't remember her ever being without. In its little filigreed partitions, a couple of nearly used-up lipsticks, the stub of an eyebrow pencil.

One early morning in her kitchen long ago, both of us still in our pajamas, she'd asked me, "So what happened to your eyebrows? Did you pluck them all out?"

"No, I've never had eyebrows, Mom. I'm like you."

"Really? I never noticed."

The bathroom should've been easier. But here, too, were reminders of the day, post Dad's retirement, just after they moved to this smaller house. With both of them on the phone, my father had grumbled about how long it had taken my mother to decide on new ceramic tile. She'd even, "for crying out loud," hauled samples home. At that moment, I'd been very much my mother's daughter, near to where I was sitting, phone to my ear, a chair I wanted reupholstered had all but disappeared beneath a mound of fabric swatches.

But before I could defend her, she said, "Yes, but it's the tile I'm going to be looking at the rest of my life."

The bathroom should've been easier. And, at first, my choices there were clear. I dropped almost everything into the wastebasket. I didn't have to wonder, as I had in her bedroom, the stacks of discards from closet and drawers mounting: Was I being too hasty, too disrespectful? I still didn't know, though, what to want of what had been hers.

And then I did.

What I called a dopp kit, others might call a toiletries case or travel kit: my mother's black, nylon, soft-sided case nearly square in shape with a zip lid cover that lifted and almost resembled a small lunch box. Discovering it in her vanity cabinet, I assumed the contents would be tossed, the case added to the donation stacks. And then I opened it.

Inside, on top, were two small Ziploc bags, one containing a few packets of hand wipes and, in the other, a toothbrush and small tube of toothpaste. In one side pocket were some Band-Aids, a nail file, a black comb. And in another were a small plastic vial of aspirin and a round, paper-wrapped bar of soap swiped from some hotel, the kind she liked me to collect from my travels and send to her. Snugly tucked in the main compartment were deodorant, shampoo, moisturizer, and, long her favorite, a spray bottle of White Linen cologne, all in 3 oz. TSA-compliant sizes even though I couldn't remember when she'd last flown. A narrow fabric sack held some makeup, including a tube of lipstick in a shade compatible with mine, but which I knew I'd not consider using, wouldn't want to use up.

As though I'd come upon some important archaeological find,

I gingerly picked up each item. This artifact suffused with intimacy, with a silent, organized preparedness, a suggestion that she, like a pick-up-and-go pro, had been ready. Even if, in her lifetime, she'd traveled to so few places. Though organized and thoughtful, this arrangement of items in her dopp kit was not artful. There was no composition. But it had been assembled by my mother's hands and with her forethought. Something about it spoke more powerfully to me than just about anything else I'd thus far unearthed.

With some of her possessions and having been offered so few directives by my father, it had been hard to judge what to keep, take, discard, leave for my sister or Carol. I'd ask myself, *What might become important, even crucial, later?* As though I were provisioning for a long and possibly treacherous journey. But it was my mother who'd gone on a journey. Her final one. And she'd left empty-handed.

She no longer needed her dopp kit. But I did. Not to empty and use but preserve. For what purpose, I couldn't say, except that, like an archaeologist, I felt certain I'd stumbled upon an important relic.

We ran out of cardboard boxes. Rather than head out to find more, my father handed me a roll of large, black, plastic garbage bags. Garbage bags.

"Really, Dad?" His outstretched hand held the roll. As tears began to well up in his eyes, I looked away, down to his plaid shirt front. Beneath it, I knew he was wearing a thin chain with Mom's wedding ring and a crucifix that had belonged to Joe.

He set the bags down on the counter. In not much more than a whisper, he said, "Does it really matter now?"

I used the bags to finish packing my mother's clothes, shoes, and handbags that I would later drive to St. Vincent de Paul's charity thrift shop. I'd carefully folded her tops and jackets and pants, but now, transferring them into the bags, it was impossible to keep them neatly stacked. Again and again, I tried. It felt like such a violation to have everything so jumbled. What she'd tended so carefully, I was now mishandling, dishonoring. Here was the moment. The one I'd thought the task I'd been assigned would hold in abeyance. What had been like a trickling tide now rushed in, breaking through a seawall. I collapsed on her bed and wept.

A precursor as it turns out. For what could possibly have been worse than carrying those full bags to the car and then lifting them into the thrift store's bins, as though hauling junk to the dumpster? Was it only then I really understood my mother was dead?

Her clothes were gone, her bathroom cleaned out. But of course so many possessions remained. Her beloved blue-and-white Willow Ware and milk glass in the living room's maple hutch. And in the dining room's breakfront, some pieces of pewter, milk and depression glass, the collected objects that for years we'd called her "antiques," believing, as my father still did, that they were valuable. And maybe a few approached that threshold. But even if well-hidden, the nicks and cracks that had made her finds more affordable would likely make them less appealing to dealers and serious collectors. Their bottom line was monetary. Not the keen eye, not the search. Nor what, for me, was the real value—having lived with a way of looking, my mother's attempts at beauty.

Thankfully, my father wasn't talking about getting rid of any of these objects. I wouldn't have to put up a fight. They belonged in this house, helping to give its rooms meaning, to make it easier for us to remember. If taken from here, the Willow Ware's context in a much-loved maple hutch that my mother had moved from house to house would be stripped away. Its relationship to a particular place, those narratives and meanings, would vanish. Take out the charred coffeepot from Chardin's still life and you'd have what? A charred coffeepot. Or take my mother's dinged pewter pitcher from her wicker table, and what does it become? A dinged pewter pitcher that once belonged to a now dead woman. Or remove the lit Coleman lantern from the objects on the picnic table and the woman reading at the table might disappear.

"Do you want me to clean out some of this stuff?" I asked my father one afternoon, gesturing toward drawers and cabinets that brimmed with rubber-banded envelopes and receipts. "You really don't need a lot of it, you know."

"Just leave it. Wait until I croak," he replied, going back to his newspaper, a welter of sympathy cards stacked beside him on the counter. He'd become increasingly adept at monosyllabic responses and seemingly breezy one-liners. He'd punctuate the end of phone conversations with statements like, "But life goes on." What became an arsenal of similar, repeated catchphrases, as though he were trying to convince himself.

As I've discovered since, those drawers contained not stories behind old snapshots pressed and taped into albums and scrapbooks or distant voices within signed letters and cards spanning decades, but years' worth of canceled checks and paid invoices my mother insisted on keeping. Detritus, really. Nothing that merited keeping or artful arranging. Nor could they be counted as the familiar, everyday objects we unthinkingly gather around us daily, which require no special looking, ask for no concentrated attention. What seemingly lacks importance. My mother may have given little thought to the chipped Pyrex baking dish she always pulled out for a batch of brownies, or for a Sunday pot roast, the heavy Dutch oven pot with dented lid. But then who can say what thoughts they might have triggered in her? Not just by way of their imperfections, which she had long insisted made things more interesting, but that this dish and pot had once belonged to her mother. And now had once belonged to mine.

In her last months, my mother did not live among her still lifes or the ordinary objects of a familiar dailyness. So little of what helped define her house as her home had made it to the room where she died. Some things from there, however, now had a place here. I still found it nearly unbearable to look at the magnets decorated with heart-shaped construction paper cutouts affixed to the refrigerator door, the first thing my mother made after we'd coaxed her, in spite of her frailty and physical impediments, to be hoisted from her bed, propped up, and wheeled to the activity room for a crafts group. No less painful was the Easter card chick of glued yellow pom-poms and sequins, the crude work of a young child and not of a woman who'd once competently painted in oils, stitched fine crafts, sewed clothes for her daughters. And so much crueler than the watercolors she'd attempted after her stroke years before, when she'd been forced into learning to use her left hand. For more than a year, she diligently copied landscapes from calendars and postcards of faraway places, as though attempting to bring the world inside, as she, increasingly, seemed to find little reason to go out into it. Attempts she clearly found amateurish and unworthy until, finally, she shelved her sketchbooks, snapped shut the watercolors tin, washed her brushes, and returned them upright, like retired soldiers, to an empty Folgers coffee can, never to be enlisted again.

Had my mother, as death approached, been able to take some of her things with her, been permitted to pack a small suitcase—and likely someone's version of heaven might, if implausibly, entertain such a notion and for which I'd gladly give over her dopp kit—what would she have chosen to take with her? What, still within my arms' reach, was important to her? But how ridiculous. In death, we travel light.

A type of still life painting known as *vanitas* flourished in the early seventeenth century, primarily in the Netherlands. By way of largely symbolic objects, the intent of these paintings was to direct our focus toward the brevity of life, the certainty of death. With their somber *memento mori*, they aimed to remind viewers of life's transience and the meaninglessness of earthly pursuits.

Among the depicted, widely recognizable objects: rotting fruit, a decaying flower dropping its petals, an empty shell, an overturned goblet, an extinguished candle still emitting a curl of smoke, an hourglass, and, often, to punctuate the obvious, a human skull. Equally at home among the jumbled array were symbolic objects more specific to an individual's earthly vanities and transient pursuits of travel, wealth, music, the arts. Representing them: perhaps a globe, a piece of jewelry, a violin, an inkstand or palette.

Never mind that, ironically, the paintings were examples of such supposedly meaningless earthly pursuits as was the wealth it took to buy them, or that in seemingly pointing toward a kind of perfection mankind was to strive for, many of the paintings' objects, obviously used and enjoyed, refused perfection. Of what, as with Chardin's charred coffeepot, has been made more beautiful by use. In a vanitas, a violin is deployed to warn against the triviality of musical pursuits in our earthly time, but in the sheen of the fingerboard's wood, the evidence of hands capable of eliciting beautiful music, it seems intent on defying that message. As does the worn patina on a pocket watch case where, again and again, fingers pressed it open to check on the passage of time. Time that, only on canvas, seems arrested. All of it reminding me of lines by poet Kay Ryan: "Her things should / keep her marks. / The passage / of a life should show; / it should abrade."

Were I to attempt the arrangement of what might comprise a type of vanitas still life for my mother, what would it include? Rather than an hourglass, perhaps the glass-domed brass clock that mesmerized me as a young girl, its rotating pendulums whirling atop our redbrick ranch's mantel until its long-term home became the maple hutch. The bruised bananas in my mother's Willow Ware bowl. The mirrored makeup tray and small white hairbrush still holding a few last strands of her hair. Some stiff watercolor brushes, the chipped Pyrex dish, and as though to ward off any potential of it all possibly disappearing into the darkness of poorly chosen pigment, the Coleman lantern.

Merely arranging, being neither a master painter nor a woman learning to use her left hand after a stroke, I'd not have to contend with being judged on the quality of brushstrokes, the depth of shadows cast by whatever the light source, although wouldn't I still strive to elicit "nice composition"?

Most of my imagined vanitas selections were not the objects I'd already chosen to take back with me to Chicago. Along with her dopp kit and its intimacy-suffused contents secured within my suitcase, I'd set aside a small, long-out-of-date address book in her familiar pre-stroke handwriting; a squat blue glass bowl that fit in the palm of my hand and left, hopefully, only a slight, barely noticeable absence in her maple hutch; a funny, miniature sock monkey, the last, except for the one that swung from my father's rearview mirror, of a dozen or so she somewhat inexplicably stitched together years ago; and the blue rosary that had been left at her bedside and was not religiously symbolic to me but proof that someone had been with her near the end. Also packed into a box my father and I would be driving to UPS: the Pyrex dish and the lidded pot, both padded with—"No, you take it, Deb."—the blue hospice quilt. What kind of "artful arrangement" a continent away could I make with all this?

A still life distills. As if time has stopped, a still life attempts to preserve. And though it may suggest the hand that is about to reach in to pick up brush or lidded pot, the hard truth is no arrangement of objects with their histories, moments, associations, and gestures can return to us a human presence. Return to us a mother, a wife.

What Did I Know, What Did I Know

All through my high school years, my father rose in predawn darkness, even on those many Chicago winter days when cold temperatures forced whatever construction project he was working on to shut down. From the bedroom closest to the kitchen, I'd lie in my narrow twin bed and listen to him percolate the coffee, crack open the newspaper, his stockinged feet whispering across the linoleum floor. As traces of light began to fill the windowpanes, like the father in Robert Hayden's poem "Those Winter Sundays," who, with "cracked hands that ached / from labor in the weekday weather made / banked fires blaze," my father lightly tapped on my bedroom door and murmured my name.

For years, I didn't know how to be grateful. I was often clumsily quiet in the minutes we sat together in the kitchen. I wasn't sure what to do with my embarrassment when, out of love and possibly a diminishing sense of usefulness, he offered to drive me to the bus stop in his pickup with its front door's hand-painted sign proclaiming to the world his name, our phone number, his job as a cement mason. On mornings too cold to refuse his offer, he'd encourage me to wait in his idling truck until the bus arrived. But I almost always slipped out, hopefully unnoticed by classmates from another neighborhood. Doris with her science-teacher father. Becky, whose dad was a manager at a printing company. Never mind that I had no idea what such a manager did. It was enough that he wore a suit and tie and worked in an office. Climbing down from my father's truck, books hugged to my chest, my breath already escaping with white puffs into the brittle air, I barely waved goodbye.

I was still years away from my first reading of Hayden's poem, of being propelled to the dictionary by the surprising usage of its last word. How much easier now to recognize in my desire to escape my father's truck, "What did I know, what did I know / of love's austere and lonely offices?"

Now I was the first one up. In the house on Dapple Gray Trail, I rose before dawn. It was my stockinged feet that whispered over the vinyl floor as I crossed the kitchen to close the door to my parents' bedroom. Just a couple of nights before, my father had begun sleeping there again, although I had to wonder if, when I headed back east, he'd return to the TV room and drift off in his recliner.

The house where my parents lived in what had become their final years together would soon contain my father alone. Solo, he'd be held by it, and hopefully, by my mother's abiding presence even if her closets and drawers were now nearly empty, her side of the bathroom vanity swept clean, her walker donated. The house on Dapple Gray Trail: home now to the blue-and-white cloisonné urn, the vessel that contained my mother's ashes and bits of bone. And home to, presumably in a drawer where my father had stored them, the extra copies of her death certificate.

Trying to be helpful in ways that much practice had made familiar, Amber at the funeral home had said, "May I suggest you get multiple copies? I think you'll find that you need them." As if the world far beyond places my mother in life had traveled awaited official word. Strangers who needed unimpeachable black-and-white evidence that Leona Helen Bolda was no longer among the living. Cause of death: acute renal failure. Other contributing factors: dehydration, failure to thrive. Notably absent from the record: a broken heart, will-shattering grief, the labor of giving birth to her youngest child no match for the labor of battling the postpartum effects of his early death.

In the kitchen, I switched on the coffee maker, pulled a banana from the Willow Ware bowl, and plucked milk from the refrigerator. I let myself quietly out the door and walked down the driveway to retrieve the newspapers already delivered at the curb. In spite of the morning's chill, I paused to admire the rosy hues tinging the sky above the hills, the first light strafing tufts of grass in the dry, pebbly soil.

Among the many emails I'd recently received from friends back on the island came news from our neighbor that an abandoned week-old seal pup had been discovered on our shore and had to be rescued. Goldfinches, he wrote, were again mobbing our feeder, and migrant seabirds of species he couldn't identify had been touching down near the Mill Pond causeway. And yes, because he knew I'd especially want to know this, the ospreys of nearby Heart Island had returned, were again circling overhead.

I ached to be back. At this hour of the morning there, the rising sun would begin to torch the spruce tops with its golden maritime light, sky mirrored in the morning's calm sea. I yearned, too, for the way, in afternoon, the light's clarity this time of year could make every clapboard look like it just got a fresh coat of paint. At night, rather than to the yip of coyotes, I'd drift off to sleep to the insistent chorus of peepers in the swampy hollows at the end of our road. Here was where in the past few days I often returned in my head.

I turned to walk back to my parents' house. Correction. My father's house.

Once it had become clear my father would not change his mind and there'd be no immediate memorial service for Mom, my sister and I agreed that she'd postpone her trip west by a few days. Rather than be in Prescott together, she'd fly out and take my place, to finish cleaning out our mother's closets and to keep Dad company.

"Sounds like a plan," Dad had said of our decision.

Unlike me, he still seemed more willing to trust in plans. Unplanned was the routine that had developed over the eight days we'd spent together since my mother's death. Once awake, he poured himself coffee, using the same thermal mug each morning, the one I now knew to set by the coffee maker. He peeled his banana, bent over the newspaper, quietly turning the pages. I sat opposite him, at the table-height island counter, other newspaper sections or my laptop open before me. A tableau my parents had once inhabited, Dad going through the paper, Mom opposite him, shakily, her left hand still clumsy with scissors, clipping coupons. Now it was my father and I, at first saying as little as we had back on those winter mornings before heading to the bus.

Eventually, though, after our ration of caffeine and the day's news and announcements, and after we'd again absorbed the recognition of whom and what we'd now have to do without, we talked nuts and bolts.

"So, Dad, have you contacted Social Security yet?"

"I had better check back with the life insurance company about that beneficiary change." "Are you sure you want me as a signatory on your account?"

Dutifully I ticked items off my list. Often, though, just before that shift to the concrete and specific, to what I thought of as "necessary business" and was part of why I was here, those knowable, predictable bits of heavy lifting with which I could assist my father, before all that, I found myself slipping in an unanticipated question or was surprised by my father's giving voice to a sudden thought, as though, among the paper's headlines, he'd just discovered it there.

One morning, absent any context, he repeated his previously made claim. "I told your mother that last night before I said goodbye, I said, 'It's okay, hon. Joey is waiting for you.'" Repeated, as if he now felt he bore some responsibility for the timing of my mother's final exhalation. Or, worse, that his claim to her about Joey had been wrong.

More surprising, referring to the last time he was with her when, for a few minutes, she'd appeared to be struggling, he blurted to me, "You know, I asked her, 'What's wrong?' And she said, 'I don't know.' And then she said it again, 'I don't know.'" He was gazing out the window. "I keep thinking about it, and I'm sure of it. Those were the exact words. The last time I heard her speak."

In just a few days, sitting opposite my father, I'd watched him age. His body had become more weighted with an even heavier burden than had been heaped on it by his son's death alone. I knew he was holding things in. Was holding on and onto, in spite of his directions to me to cull and toss. In a house emptier now of more than just some of its contents, in a kitchen in the early morning hours, our roles, it seemed, had been reversed.

"Tending the sadness" . . . a phrase I'd come upon once but had not yet, until those quiet mornings with my father, been able to define.

Meanwhile, for all the time we were spending in the house, heads bent over the newspapers and our lists or while emptying closets or mindlessly watching TV, the month of May was rapidly advancing, trying to remind us that spring was not the time of year to stay inside.

It urged us out, forward, instructing us to turn our back on the dark season we'd just survived, even if, in Arizona, the signs were not as clear to me as the busting-with-bloom-forsythia fanfare and swamp-cabbage-and-peepers-in-the-hollows pronouncements back east.

True, my father had sometimes seemed ready to hurl himself onto the burning pyre, but now there were minute signs his gaze might be starting to shift toward the future, beyond illness, more specialized care, a diagnosis that could bring you to your knees, the whole world slipping off its axis.

The sad truth is people we love die and what was once theirs remains resolutely in place in the rooms they have left, while our lives resume their irrefutable forward motion, even if now there's a vacancy we cannot fill and we still possess questions that may never be answered.

"Dad, did Mom seem afraid?" I asked my father one morning. "Was she, I don't know, restless?"

"I don't remember," he said.

How was that possible? How could he have paid so little attention? But I had to concede he was probably telling the truth. And what did that signify? An unconscious blockage meant to protect? More evidence that argued against the notion we have a choice in what we remember and hold onto? Or that we can control what later might bubble up? Who can say what memories came to my mother wherever it was she retreated lying in her bed her final months? She'd locked all that in a vault, its key tossed, eased open only in her dreams.

But what about me? What were my answers? Was my mother happy?

"I don't know." Did she know joy? Yes, surely, but some days "I can't remember." It was harder to recall when. So many things I did not know with certainty. And never would.

Proving again there's so much we can't know. Our lives hit peaks we may not realize we've reached. We fail to recognize chances as they pass us by. One minute there's plenty of time. And then there isn't.

Since Joe's death, I, like my father, had spent much time dwelling in the past. We'd each planted our flag there, territory we weren't ready to abandon. Still a lot of terrain to cover, much digging yet to be done. Pieces to be discovered and uncovered, brought into the light, though there'd always be some pieces missing, fragments of a mosaic we could only plug or grout around.

"It'll never be like I remembered," I'd heard a woman exclaim in Assisi, Italy, the previous spring as she craned her head back to peer up at the once earthquake-ravaged basilica of St. Francis in spite of its meticulous restoration.

We had a long way to go, especially my father, and the way ahead was uncertain. But now we actually began to make plans. I went online and booked his airline tickets to Maine in August. We talked about what we might do in October when I flew back to Arizona for his birthday, although I held off sharing my sister's and my idea that maybe, for Christmas, he'd entertain the notion of his getting a dog to keep him company. As we sat and hatched and dared to plan, he and I were giving each other permission to feel some relief. Because, of course, there was that. Relief: the unspoken truth.

Yes, my father's "at last, her suffering is over," but also the release from our worry and dread. The freedom in knowing there will not be any middle of the night phone call, in being untethered to another rush to the hospital. Before us lay the opportunity to begin to peel away the scrim of sorrow and, possibly, be ambushed by joy. Relief: the unspoken truth.

Sitting in the kitchen, my father and I were decades beyond a time when we'd each recognized that life is, surely, a thing riddled with holes, perforated with a multitude of absences and losses.

As are we, pricked open in places where leakage occurs, seepages that can, perhaps, be so expertly masked that only the most discerning eye might notice. But each of us is also a reliquary holding fragments of our past, what we're surprised to dig up, turn over with a spade. Down in that deep place where grief resides, where light cannot reach.

The vessel I was before the deaths of my brother and mother will never be the same. It may not have shattered, but it possesses cracks, missing chips, some of which may be irreparable. And all, as I wrote in my journal at the time, a part of who I am, will become.

As we sat at the kitchen table reading a new day's news, completing a task, or contemplating future plans, I began to recognize that my mother's death was not solely about loss. It had also given me something: A new version of my father. And of what now our relationship might become. Which meant, didn't it, that I would have to change some version of myself in order to recognize, love him better? My mother's death, what I had now instead of her, was extending out in directions and ways I did not know about yet.

Threshold

Once again, I was on a plane heading east. I was again looking down on the world from a great height, though not trying this time to be a detached, invulnerable viewer. I wasn't as angry as when I'd flown to Arizona after Joe died. If anger was the stage I was supposed to be in now, it was as if I'd told myself, *To hell with it. I won't be angry. I can't. At least not like before.*

Now I knew that some of my fellow passengers—the young man in glasses who'd spent several minutes trying to shove his overstuffed backpack into the overhead, the middle-aged woman with clenched jaw, her lips pressed into a thin, grim line that parted only when she'd heaved a great sigh and plunked down in the wrong seat—might well be rushing to a hospital bed before it was too late. To do so, perhaps the grim-lipped woman, looking bewildered and lost as she began to search for her correct assigned seat, had no choice but to charge her credit card to the max and soon would be confronted with bewildering medical details, with painful choices dictated by hostile insurance requirements. Here, possibly, were fellow passengers who had to negotiate terrain and geographic obstacles similar to mine. Including, perhaps, the man sitting next to me, crisply dressed in a sports jacket and bold-patterned tie and smelling vaguely of something citrusy, who, blessedly, had no wish to converse and with earbuds in, plunked away at a spreadsheet on his laptop.

They, too, went on living. They, too, may have already recognized that, especially when it comes to a parent, we must bury a lot of what we couldn't confront or fix. And that a time comes, whenever it is, when we may realize we have to let go.

On the way to the airport from my father's house, I'd felt a great and simple sadness. My mother was dead. My father was now alone.

Turning off the main route, Dad had taken Fein Road, a two-lane highway alternate I'd not known about before this trip. Less trafficked, absent the otherwise ubiquitous fast-food joints and strip malls, it cut through open grazing land, now a straw gold expanse. Gusts of wind buffeted the car. Overhead, ballooning, big-bellied clouds scudded fast across the sky, casting their deep, fleeting shadows on the distant foothills. I had to admit it was beautiful. Still, the terrain remained more scenery than landscape, as did the words *wash*, *arroyo*, *gulch* that likely described it. None of its contours were mapped in my body, not like the narrow, winding rural roads of the island or the gridded, right-angled streets of the Chicago suburban neighborhood I grew up in. I could not imagine living here, especially now that the rope tenuously connecting me to it had become frayed, the remaining knot likely to come undone in the not-too-distant future.

I'd been surprised, though, before our turnoff, by how many landmarks, none of them tourist attractions, I could now identify in what had previously been an alien land. Mountain Valley Rehab Center where my mother had gone after her stroke and where I was forced into a crash course acquisition of insurance coverage lingo. The internist's office on Robert Road where I'd driven my mother for her appointment as my father, a few years before Joe's death, lay in a distant Flagstaff hospital bed, recovering from a serious spinal staph infection. The doughnut shop my sister and I had discovered the previous autumn, the first time we'd all thought Mom might die. Leff-T's Steakhouse & Grill, Dad's favorite, where he and I often dined during my past year's visits, sitting long with a second glass of wine, talking and sometimes surprising ourselves with laughter over the smallest things, our first-ever dinners out together without Mom's filter. The UPS store where I'd boxed and shipped home the hospice quilt and Dutch oven pot with dinged lid. St. Vincent's donation center where we'd hauled my mother's clothes in black plastic garbage bags. The parking lot where my father had waited for the airport shuttle to drop me off the morning I had to break the news he'd just missed the call from hospice telling him Mom had died, and for several minutes, we sat in stunned silence as heat waves shimmered up from the asphalt.

I was leaving a place I hadn't anticipated it becoming, a place shaped by events I'd never before experienced. Finally, it had come to mean something to me. More than mere backdrop, it was integral to what were now layers of experience and memory. And for the first time, some of its people who were not family, who had once been strangers, had remapped it, too.

Anna and Jill at the nursing home. Ron and Suzi at Elder Care who helped chart our course when we floundered in new waters. Lisa at Granite Mountain Hospice. Folks who shared for a brief time one of my life's major landmarks: my mother's death. People who understood how grief over Joe had cast such a deep shadow. Who now would help with my father's care, and with how and where we were to go from here.

Leaving: another in a long series.

But I was also returning. To Bob, the kids and grandkids, to family and friends. Returning home to my commitments, my book-in-progress, the new plans that would help make it possible to consider living full-time in Maine. I yearned to flee to the island, my place of healing, but first, I needed to pause in Chicago, pack up for the months away and make the long drive, mindlessly crossing the borders a map told me was the next state, crossings I had no idea I'd made until a sign proclaimed: WELCOME TO OHIO, PENNSYLVANIA, NEW YORK. The one mattering most: WELCOME TO MAINE. And then the series of bridges, the dip and sway of crowned rural roads, the gravel-pinging drive down our lane, and finally, the arrival at the door to our house. A familiar threshold.

On the plane, my fellow passengers and I had been at a threshold as we taxied and lifted into the sky. Perhaps the uncomfortable fliers among us gripped their seats, shut their eyes, while others went on talking, thumbing their magazines. It's long been my custom on takeoff to stop whatever I'm doing, and whatever the landscape, look at the land rushing past before the plane rises from the good stable earth into the unbuttressed sky. I prefer to be present in crossing from one element into another.

In flying parlance, the threshold is a physical place. It's marked by skinny white lines that run parallel to a runway's length just below its number—threshold markings that inform the pilot where a runway begins. At the other end, a displaced threshold is identified by a white perpendicular line and is used to increase obstacle clearance or a landing's roll-off when things don't go exactly as planned. Sometimes it's introduced when the beginning section of a runway is no longer able to sustain the continuous impact of landing aircraft. When a weight is no longer bearable.

From a passenger's perspective, none of this is visible. Just another of the many thresholds we're often on the verge of crossing and don't know it. On an airport shuttle bus to meet your father. On the July day the phone rings with the news your forty-five-year-old brother has died and you cross a threshold before you even put the phone down. What may have just hours before seemed so important is gone. Whatever had kept you from catching an earlier flight when your mother was taking her last breaths suddenly loses meaning.

Somewhere approaching the middle of the country, we hit turbulence. At first it was the usual bumps and lurches. But then the plane heaved several times. An empty coffee cup flew from my tray. The seat belt dug into my abdomen as I was lifted from my seat. Somewhere behind me a baby began to howl. Even the guy next to me stopped plunking on his laptop and looked past me out the window. Turning back, he caught my eye and squeezed out a small, nervous smile. Over the intercom, an attendant instructed us to be sure our seat belts were tightly fastened.

Shortly after, the pilot announced, "Attendants, take your seats."

I felt the thrust of the plane's engines as the plane accelerated. More bumps, more heaves, some almost violent. The overhead bins rattled and thumped. I was near the front of the plane and could hear glasses and plates banging in the galley. Something metallic crashed to the floor. The aging MD-80, an aircraft model the airlines were forever promising to phase out, had never felt so old, as though at any moment it might crack open, come apart at its aged, bolted seams.

In all my picturing this trip home, no accident, no plane going down had figured in. I'd been so customarily casual in my assumption I'd be delivered safely to my destination. But what was a plane, really, but a small metal cylinder traveling through space thirty-seven thousand feet above the earth?

No attendant was declaring we'd have to make an emergency landing. No one was instructing us on how to brace, something—Would I have to take off my glasses?—I'd only ever seen in the movies. And even though I'd flown in turbulence before, thinking of it only as a "rough patch," suddenly, somewhat irrationally, as though a fiery plummet was all but certain, I thought, *I so desperately do not want to die*. And just as quickly, *How could my father possibly handle this, too?*

Even as we continued to bump and buck, the pilot came back on the intercom, his voice confident and reassuring. Thunderstorms, he explained, were erupting in the area. "We're not going to be able to ride this one out comfortably, folks," he said in his amiable Southern accent. "I've begun our ascent to a higher altitude where things should smooth out. There will be some bumps along the way, but we'll climb above them."

We'd reached a threshold. And we were going over, rather than through it.

Behind me, the baby continued to cry and my seatmate, his hands now motionless in his lap, stared at his laptop screen. We were still lurching, being pummeled, and nothing outside my window suggested anything had changed, even though we'd been promised the ride would begin to get smoother. Suddenly I recalled my mother's voice, how it had instructed so frequently, back when I lived under my parents' roof and, years later, when I lost a job and divorced my first husband.

"You'll deal with it. You'll get over it." Or had she said, "You'll get through it"?

Though more painful and uncomfortable, wasn't there more to

learn by going through something rather than over or around it? But the chief aim for pilots in a patch of turbulence wasn't to test its possible severity or the skills necessary to keep the altitude readings steady. It was to keep us safe, and while doing it, calm nervous passengers, allow them to sip their juice without spills down a shirt front. Pilots went over, above, not through.

"Getting through it." One of those numerous expressions I'd grown to detest in the months since my brother died. Even before that, "One door opens, another closes," was another one I'd long thought cringeworthy. Usually it meant making the best of whatever scared, angered, or challenged us. But truth was, some doors, like a lid of a coffin, just stay shut.

"Death," wrote John Webster, "hath ten thousand several doors for men to take their exits."

Dropping from the sky in the company of strangers was not an exit I'd ever pictured for myself. If the plane crashed, I'd have no one within arm's reach to say goodbye to, just my seatmate, a guy whose balding spot at the back of his head suddenly seemed endearing, whose wedding band suggested there was at least one person who'd hugged and waved him off or was waiting at the arrivals curb, and to whom, upon a safe landing, he'd call or text. If the plane crashed, my last acts, hugging my father when he dropped me off and promising to let him know when I arrived home or my calling Bob just before boarding, neither of which hinted at a threshold, would be the moments they dwelled upon, sifted through, replayed, remembered. Last acts that in a string of acts comprised a life.

For those we leave behind, there would be questions that, in the parlance I detested, can never be laid to rest. Whether, for example, terror was present in our final minutes. A kind of terror that, over and over again, I'd imagined and imagine still, Joe may have felt in those last minutes in the shower where he'd only gone to clean himself off, expecting to return to a fresh and comfortable bed on the eve of a doctor's appointment that promised to provide him some relief, some hope of a future no matter how difficult its hurdles. Instead, he had collapsed on the tile floor, and, my worse fear, rather than passing out immediately, was that he'd struggled, resisted, was consciously aware that this was it. The one of ten thousand doors Death had reserved for him.

What of my last minutes would those who love me replay? Dad waiting by the phone, Bob, always early, already at the airport? How would they first find out about the smoldering remains of this airplane littering a field? The radio? The television? And long before the confirmation came that, yes, this was my flight, there'd be silence in a call or text that doesn't come.

Death, the cruelest reminder: Sometimes, we do not get to understand everything. We can only know so much.

Eventually, as the pilot promised, the ride did smooth out and, after a textbook perfect landing, a ripple of applause erupted somewhere in the back of the plane.

Snapping shut his laptop, my seatmate even allowed, "Wow, that was some ride."

Outside the window, as we'd descended and the airport came into view, I couldn't see the runway or its threshold, but I knew that, up in the cockpit, the pilot could.

If a threshold is, as one of its definitions maintains, a line that separates two territories, we'd crossed it. And if what's important is how you cross over, then perhaps we—I—had crossed to new ground, the as-yet-unseeable ahead where old patterns aren't repeated, where something else—new, better?—might emerge. Touching down, possibly a new door opened.

As we taxied, an attendant announced our gate, the farthest one out and thus the longest walk to arrivals, but I didn't mind. I needed the time to feel the good solid earth beneath my feet. Outside my window, a ground worker wearing a neon green vest and big earphones was waving a bright orange wand, instructing the pilot. Hand signals, their exact meanings mysterious to me, even after seeing them so many times before. But this time, the man, the vest, his arms' waving gestures seemed oddly familiar.

And then I remembered: It was the dream I'd had just two nights before. My mother and I were driving somewhere in my car and we'd gotten stuck in a long line of traffic, a big backup due to a highway construction project or possibly an accident, but it was too far ahead to tell which. We'd been inching slowly forward but had come to a complete stop. I don't recall the specific landscape outside the window, where we were or on what highway, only that none of it seemed familiar. We'd been making small talk but I'd started fussing with my phone. Focused on some messages, I didn't notice the traffic had begun to proceed again.

"Deb," my mother said. "He's waving you through."

I looked up to see a man in a green neon jacket sweeping the air with a bright orange flag.

"See?" she said. "It's safe now. You can go."

"Thanks, Mom."

Taking the wheel, I shifted back into Drive and turned toward her. The passenger seat was empty. She was gone.

Credits

"Prayer" from *Seasonal Woman* by Luci Tapahonso (Tooth of Time Books, 1982), is used by permission of Luci Tapahonso.

"Musée des Beaux Arts" and "September 1, 1939" by W. H. Auden Copyright © 1939, 1940 by The Estate of W. H. Auden. Reprinted by permission of Curtis Brown, Ltd. All rights reserved.

"Musée des Beaux Arts," copyright 1939, 1940 and © renewed 1968 by W. H. Auden; and "September 1, 1939," copyright 1940 and © renewed 1968 by W. H. Auden; from COLLECTED POEMS by W. H. Auden, edited by Edward Mendelson. Used by permission of Random House, an imprint and division of Penguin Random House LLC. All rights reserved.

Excerpt from "Aubade" from THE COMPLETE POEMS OF PHILIP LARKIN by Philip Larkin, edited by Archie Burnett. Copyright © 2012 by The Estate of Philip Larkin. Introduction copyright © 2012 by Archie Burnett. Reprinted by permission of Farrar, Straus and Giroux. All Rights Reserved.

References

Tapahonso, Luci. *Seasonal Woman*. Tooth of Time Books, 1982.

Auden, W. H. "Musée des Beaux Arts." In *Another Time*. Faber and Faber, 1940.

Keats, John "When I Have Fears I May Cease to Be." In *Life, Letters, and Literary Remains, of John Keats*, edited by Richard Monckton Milnes. Edward Moxon, 1848.

Whitman, Walt. "Song of Myself." In *Leaves of Grass*. Brooklyn, 1855. Printed by author.

Tennyson, Lord Alfred. "Crossing the Bar." In *Demeter and Other Poems*. Macmillan & Co., 1889.

Poe, Edgar Allen. "The Colosseum." In *The Works of Edgar Allan Poe in Five Volumes, Volume 5 (The Raven Edition)*. P. F. Collier & Son, 1904.

Wordsworth, William. "Surprised by Joy." In *The Complete Poetical Works of William Wordsworth*. James Monroe & Co., 1839.

Stevens, Wallace. "Sunday Morning." In *Harmonium*. Knopf, 1923.

Poetry Foundation. "Change's Purchase." Published April 14, 2014. https://www.poetryfoundation.org/articles/70113/changes-purchase

Shapiro, Alan. "Joy." In *Song and Dance*. Houghton Mifflin Harcourt, 2002.

Larkin, Philip. "Aubade." In *Collected Poems*. Faber & Faber, 2003.

Auden, W. H. "September 1, 1939." In *Another Time*. Faber and Faber, 1940.

Woodward, Christopher. "Ephesus without an Umbrella." *In Ruins*. Pantheon Books, 2001.

Ammons, A. R., "Tombstones." In *Sumerian Vistas: Poems*. W. W. Norton and Company, 1987.

Ryan, Kay. "Things Shouldn't Be So Hard." In *The Niagra River: Poems*. Grove Press Poetry, 2005.

Hayden, Robert. "Those Winter Sundays." In *Collected Poems*, edited by Frederick Glaysher. Liveright Publishing Corporation, 1985.

About the Author

Photo courtesy of the author

Deborah Cummins authored three poetry collections and a collection of linked essays, one of which was listed as Notable in Best American Essays 2013. She received her MFA in creative writing, and her work has appeared in eight anthologies and more than 60 journals, including *Yale Review, Gettysburg Review, Orion, Fourth Genre,* and *New England Review.*

From 2001 to 2005, she was the Board Chair of the Poetry Foundation in Chicago, and more recently, from 2016 to 2023, she served as Board President of the Maine Writers & Publishers Alliance.

In 2014, Deborah and her husband, Bob, relocated from Chicago to Maine, dividing their time between Portland and Deer Isle.

She passed away in the summer of 2023.